A Luminous Life

A Luminous Life

A JOURNEY INTO
CLASSIC CHRISTIAN SPIRITUALITY

Brock Bingaman

CASCADE Books • Eugene, Oregon

A LUMINOUS LIFE
A Journey Into Classic Christian Spirituality

Copyright © 2021 Brock Bingaman. All rights reserved. Except for brief quotations in critical publications or reviews, no part of this book may be reproduced in any manner without prior written permission from the publisher. Write: Permissions, Wipf and Stock Publishers, 199 W. 8th Ave., Suite 3, Eugene, OR 97401.

Cascade Books
An Imprint of Wipf and Stock Publishers
199 W. 8th Ave., Suite 3
Eugene, OR 97401

www.wipfandstock.com

PAPERBACK ISBN: 978-1-4982-7927-7
HARDCOVER ISBN: 978-1-4982-7929-1
EBOOK ISBN: 978-1-4982-7928-4

Cataloguing-in-Publication data:

Names: Bingaman, Brock, author.
Title: A luminous life : a journey into classic Christian spirituality / Brock Bingaman.
Description: Eugene, OR: Cascade Books, 2021 | Includes bibliographical references.
Identifiers: ISBN 978-1-4982-7927-7 (paperback) | ISBN 978-1-4982-7929-1 (hardcover) | ISBN 978-1-4982-7928-4 (ebook)
Subjects: LCSH: Spiritual life—Christianity. | Mysticism. | Christian literature.
Classification: BV4501.3 .B4945 2021 (print) | BV4501.3 (ebook)

For my beloved children, Mia and Jake:
May God's light shine in your hearts,
so you can know the glory of God
that is seen in the face of Jesus Christ.

2 Cor 4:6

Table of Contents

Chapter 1. Invitation to a Luminous Life 1

Chapter 2. Biblical Images of the Spiritual Life 20

Chapter 3. Historical Models of Spiritual Development 35

Chapter 4. Theologically Grounded Spirituality 49

Chapter 5. Prayer: The Mother of Spiritual Virtues 66

Chapter 6. Fasting: Self-Denial for a Greater Good 84

Chapter 7. Solitude and Community: Retreat to Re-Engage 103

Chapter 8. Cataphatic and Apophatic Spirituality: The Positive and Negative Ways 121

Chapter 9. The Cross: Suffering and the Crucified Life 137

Chapter 10. The Desert: Seasons of Dryness, Death, and New Life 150

Chapter 11. Spiritual Mothers and Fathers: Spiritual Guides, Spiritual Direction 167

Chapter 12. Service: Contemplatives in Action 178

Conclusion: Go in the Strength of God's Love 193

Appendix. Fasting: Practical Suggestions 197

Acknowledgments 201

Bibliography 203

Index 213

Chapter 1.

Invitation to a Luminous Life

> "The LORD make his face to shine upon you,
> and be gracious to you."
> —Num 6:25

> "... The light of the knowledge of the glory of God
> in the face of Jesus Christ."
> —2 Cor 4:6

> "Shining upon those that are cleansed from every spot, the Holy Spirit makes them spiritual by fellowship with Himself."
> —Basil of Caesarea, *On the Spirit*

> "The servants and disciples of Christ are light and truth and life ... He is called light, Who transcends all light, because He illumines us ..."
> —Symeon the New Theologian, *On the Mystical Life: On Virtue and Christian Life*

DESERT. DARKNESS. DECONSTRUCTION. THESE are definitely words that, according to conventional wisdom, should not begin a book. But here they are, and they pointedly describe the difficult season in which this book was born. Seven years of spiritual desert, a dark night of the soul, and inner deconstruction. I am not alone, though. Many of you can relate to these words, to this kind of season.

These words also describe aspects of the current cultural context of the Western world. It is indeed a challenging time on many fronts. However, this book does not attempt to analyze our contemporary context.

Others have done a fine job of that.[1] What can be noted is that the current situation is one of massive tectonic shifts: socially, politically, economically, technologically, and spiritually. Some allege that these are dark days, the twilight of peace and prosperity, at least in the American milieu. This may be the case. There are various views on the situation. And we should read, stay informed, remain vigilant, and be prepared to follow Christ in these or any other times of great change.

Inner and Outer World

While there are different views on these changes and the current situation in the West, what Christians can agree on is that the God of the universe is at work, no matter how bleak any circumstance or context looks. "For God, who said, 'Light shall shine out of darkness,' is the One who has shone in our hearts to give the Light of the knowledge of the glory of God in the face of Christ" (2 Cor 4:6, NASB). The following pages stem from this reality: that God causes light to shine out of darkness, in our hearts, our church communities, and the nations of the world. No matter how the current situation plays out, in the West or anywhere on the planet, the light shines in the darkness, and the darkness will not overcome it (John 1:5).

I also think that we can agree that no matter how challenging our external circumstances or contexts might become, we can tend to our inner life with great vigor. The world around us may quake and fracture, but we can build and strengthen our inner world in the love and grace of God. As Maximus the Confessor (580–662), the esteemed Orthodox theologian, says, by grace our inner life becomes a splendid and vast spiritual world, filled with the glory and knowledge of God.[2] Though human kingdoms decline and fall, the kingdom of God, established in the hearts of God's people, endures forever (Dan 2:44; Luke 17:21).[3]

---

1. For example, see Taylor, *A Secular Age*; and Hauerwas and Willimon, *Resident Aliens*. Another interesting perspective, though too alarmist and provocative according to some, is Dreher, *The Benedict Option*.

2. *Philokalia* 2:85.

3. Cf. Dan 4:34; 6:26; 7:27.

An Invitation

In view of these things, this book is an invitation to seek the kingdom within, to cultivate your inner life, to grow as a magnificent world of God where the Holy Trinity can dwell and bring love and life. This invitation, more specifically, is to deepen your relationship with Jesus and his people by learning from Christian classics on the spiritual life. These classics, rooted and formed in the matrix of meditation on Scripture, are like road maps that provide invaluable wisdom and guidance for the spiritual journey.

Spiritual life

What exactly do I mean by the "spiritual life" or "spirituality"? In short, these words suggest *life in the Holy Spirit*.[4] Romans 8 speaks at length about this kind of life. Life in the Spirit includes, among other things: freedom from condemnation, sin, and death; life and peace of mind; being indwelt by the Spirit who raised Jesus from the dead; being led by the Spirit as beloved children of God who call God "Abba" as Jesus did; spiritual adoption into the family of God; redemption of our bodies, hope, and salvation; the help of the Spirit in our weakness and intercessory prayer; justification, glorification, and transformation into the image of Jesus; knowing that God is for us and graciously gives us all things; living as more than conquerors through divine love; and never being separated from the love of God in Christ Jesus.

Furthermore, Sandra Schneiders, a Catholic theologian, says that Christian spirituality

> is that particular actualization of the capacity for self-transcendence that is constituted by the substantial gift of the Holy Spirit establishing a life-giving relationship with God in Christ within the believing community. Thus, Christian spirituality is trinitarian, christological, and ecclesial religious experience.[5]

Christian spirituality is life in the Holy Spirit, with all the transformative effects the Spirit brings. Through an ongoing, vital relationship with the Father, Son, and Holy Spirit, we become all that God created us to be as

---

4. Regarding the biblical background of the Holy Spirit in the Old Testament (*ruach* in Hebrew) and the New Testament (*pneuma* in Greek), see Kärkkäinen, *Pneumatology*, 23–36.

5. Schneiders, "Theology and Spirituality," 266.

individual members of the body of Christ. Christian spirituality, therefore, is rooted in the ground of the Holy Trinity, the life, death, and resurrection of Jesus, and our life together as the people of God.

Classic Christian spirituality

What do I mean by "classic Christian spirituality" or "Christian spiritual classics"? A spiritual classic is a text characterized by its quality, influence, and ongoing appeal. Arthur Holder, an Episcopal priest and historian of Christian spirituality, says that classics of Christian spirituality are not only important as historical-cultural artifacts and as literary texts, but they are documents of living wisdom that invite contemplative reflection and existential response. A spiritual classic is a text "claiming a religious truth that has made a profound difference in the lives of generations of readers across time and space." A common feature of Christian spiritual classics "is a deep conviction that the God revealed in Jesus Christ has spoken (and continues to speak) words of loving wisdom and truth to a world that needs to listen and respond."[6] Christian spiritual classics, therefore, invite us to reflect on the love of God in Christ, to open ourselves to the work of the Holy Spirit, and to cooperate with Jesus in his mission to the world.

Thomas Oden, a Methodist theologian known for his work with classic Christian sources, writes: "Classic writers have one distinct advantage over modern sources: they have been thoroughly tested, questioned, interpreted, probed, analyzed, reinterpreted, preached, taught, and utilized in different historical situations." Thus, "Modern interpretation does well to build upon that extensive examination."[7] In the following pages, we will listen to the seasoned words of wisdom and truth that emanate from the Christian spiritual classics. Through these classics, the Lord will continue to speak to us, draw us deeper into communion with the Word of God, and lead us in our spiritual journey.

---

6. Holder, in the edited volume *Christian Spiritual Classics*, xiv–xv. See the reflections on the Christian classics by Tracy, in *The Analogical Imagination*.

7. Oden, *Classic Christianity*, vol. 1, 343.

A Contemporary Renaissance

Amidst these times of tectonic shifts and various challenges, many Christians are discovering and rediscovering lifegiving streams that flow through classic spirituality. In fact, theologians, pastors, and leaders from numerous traditions suggest that in recent decades we have been undergoing a renaissance of Christian spirituality.

One of the clarion calls of the Renaissance during the fourteenth to sixteenth centuries was *ad fontes*, Latin for "to the fountains" or "[back] to the sources." Likewise, the current renaissance of Christian spirituality is calling believers back to the ancient fountains and classic sources. Signs of this rebirth and renewed interest have been clearly traced by Catholic, Orthodox, and Protestant theologians. Though these days are challenging, it is also an exciting time, especially for those of us who are longing to learn more from our ancient Christian heritage.[8] As in the days of Jeremiah, the Lord says: "Stand at the crossroads, and look, and ask for the ancient paths, where the good way lies; and walk in it, and find rest for your souls . . ." (Jer 6:16).

Perhaps this revival of Christian spirituality should not be that surprising. Jesus spoke of how certain spiritual leaders are like owners of houses that bring out of their storerooms new treasures as well as old (Matt 13:52).[9] Even as Jesus taught new things about the kingdom of God and life in the Spirit, current leaders are retrieving fresh insights on the spiritual life from classic sources. They are entering the ancient storerooms, uncovering neglected or forgotten spiritual wisdom, and presenting it to those who are hungry for deeper life in God.

Further, two leading twentieth-century theologians, Karl Rahner (a Catholic, 1904–84) and Dietrich Bonhoeffer (a Protestant, 1906–45) asserted that the future health and vitality of Christianity lie in the rediscovery of its mystical and spiritual roots. *A Luminous Life*, therefore, seeks to help readers get in touch with some of these roots, so that we might survive, thrive, and fulfill the church's mission in the coming years.[10]

---

8. For examples of the renaissance in Christian spirituality, see the seven-volume series by McGinn, *The Presence of God*; Ware, *The Orthodox Way*; Foster, *Celebration of Discipline*; and the ecumenical collection, Holder, ed., *The Blackwell Companion to Christian Spirituality*.

9. Jesus, using the preference for vintage wine as a picture of spiritual things, said, "The old is good" (Luke 5:39).

10. Rahner claims: "The Christian of the future will be a mystic or will not exist at

Purpose of This Book

Fuel passion to explore

In view of this growing renaissance of Christian spirituality, the driving purpose of this book is threefold. First, I hope *to fuel your passion for exploring the riches of classic Christian spirituality*. As scholars and lay people alike are saying these days, there are forgotten mines of wisdom, containing veins of spiritual gold, waiting to be unearthed. Over the past twenty years, I have been digging and discovering some of these riches. I am grateful to those leaders, mentors, and friends who have suggested certain sources that have led to discovering spiritual riches in Christ Jesus (Col 2:2–3). In many ways, this book is motivated by a desire to share some of these rich discoveries and to encourage you to do some of your own digging and mining in the coming days.[11]

Seek the presence

However, mining the riches of Christian spiritual classics is actually a means to a greater end. Therefore, the second purpose of this book is the real driving force: *to invite you to seek and experience the transformative presence of God*. As you will see, this was typically the reason the authors of the Christian classics wrote what they did, to illuminate and encourage readers in their spiritual journey, to offer a road map into the heart of God.[12] They recorded their hard-earned knowledge and practical wisdom for others, like you and me, to discover, absorb, and practice. It is amazing to think that we can study and learn from great women and men who devoted their entire lives to seeking God, growing in Christlikeness, and preserving their insights for future readers. As we meditate on the God-intoxicated

---

all" (*Concern for the Church*, 149). See Lovat, "Bonhoeffer." Thomas Merton also suggests that the most important need in the Christian world today is to recover the ancient "spirit of contemplation . . . Without contemplation and interior prayer the Church cannot fulfill her mission to transform and save [humankind]." *Contemplative Prayer*, 115–16.

11. Unearthing and rediscovering spiritual riches are recurring themes in church history. See the interesting stories of younger spiritual pilgrims who sought these treasures and someone to spiritually direct them: Ware, "St. Nikodimos and the *Philokalia*"; McGuckin, "The Making of the *Philokalia*."

12. See the bracing description of theology and spirituality, as well as commentary on the different approaches in the Eastern and Western traditions, provided by Lossky, *The Mystical Theology of the Eastern Church*, 7–22.

teachings of people like Augustine, Gregory of Nyssa, the Desert Fathers and Mothers, and Teresa of Avila, we will sense the call of God, the wooing of the Holy Spirit, to offer ourselves more fully to the One who made us for intimate friendship with the Lord Jesus.[13]

Encourage a way of being

A third purpose behind this book is *to encourage you to develop a particular way of being in the world*. The various voices, texts, and lives you encounter in this book provide vivid examples of women and men who devoted themselves to God through particular practices. The point, as we will hear from them many times, is not the spiritual practice or exercise, or to exhibit how "spiritual" or "holy" we might be, but to posture ourselves before God in specific ways. The various spiritual exercises or disciplines, simply put, are constructive ways to position ourselves under the waterfall of God's love, grace, mercy, and passion for us. These spiritual masters teach us how to open our hearts to and cooperate with the power of God's transformative grace. The journey of the spiritual life is indeed a grace infused endeavor.[14]

By studying examples within these Christian classics, and gleaning wisdom from them, we will learn to develop a way of being in the world: more fruitful ways of relating to God, to one another, and to the broader community of creation. As we learn from their practical ways of living in communion with God, our lives will be infused with new meaning, purpose, and direction.

In accord with the views of Jesus, Rahner, Bonhoeffer, and many other believers over the centuries, this book claims that one primary way we experience God is through rediscovering our ancient roots, through prayerful reflection on Christian spiritual classics, and the Scriptures on which they are established. With the Holy Spirit as our guide, we will search for those treasures of the kingdom, old and new, that will lead us deeper into

---

13. The common of goal of these classic teachers is *union with God*. All their various insights and methods lead to Jesus himself, an experiential knowledge of the Holy Trinity, or beatific vision. For example, see: Teresa of Avila, *The Interior Castle*, 263ff.; Guyon, *Experiencing the Depths of Jesus Christ*; and Gregory of Nyssa, *The Life of Moses*.

14. See Nassif, "Concerning Those Who Think That They Are Justified by Works." Nassif demonstrates that the good news, the gospel of God's grace, is the heart of Christian spirituality, whether Orthodox, Protestant, or Catholic. See also the volume on spirituality by Orthodox, Catholic, mainline Protestant, and evangelical theologians, Gundry and Demarest, eds., *Four Views on Christian Spirituality*.

transformative relationship with God, the body of Christ, and the world in which we live.

Method and Features

A Luminous Life is an invitation to experience the transformative presence of God through the study and practice of classic Christian spirituality. It is a call to learn from others about how to contemplate the glory of God in the face of Christ, to be transformed into his image from one degree of glory to another (2 Cor 3:17–18; 4:6). This, put simply, is the essence of a "luminous life." Empowered by the Holy Spirit, we learn to inwardly gaze upon the glory and beauty of God, then carry and reflect this spiritual radiance in our daily lives.[15] This is a journey into divine love and grace. It is the glory of the Lord, not ours. "Grace alone illuminates human nature with supernatural light," says Maximus.[16] What do we have that we have not received (1 Cor 4:7)?

Deeply Ecumenical

In the academic world, many books bog down (and bore readers) with too many details about methodology and other features. However, I want to provide some information that I think will be helpful before we proceed. First, the approach in *A Luminous Life* is deeply ecumenical.[17] It is born out of a love for the whole church.

---

15. A common image used in ancient Christian spirituality, stemming from the Apostle Paul's teaching, is that of a mirror. The image of God (*imago Dei*) in each of us is like a mirror that reflects the glory of God. By cooperating with the gracious work of the Holy Spirit, we keep the mirror clean through prayer and other spiritual exercises, so that we display the image and likeness of God in our thoughts, words, and actions. See *Philokalia* 1:177 and 3:25; and Colless, "Syriac Mysticism," 181.

16. Maximus the Confessor, *Questions to Thalassius* 22, in McGinn, ed., *The Essential Writings of Christian Mysticism*, 411.

17. "Ecumenical" and "ecumenism" come from the Greek word οἰκουμένη (*oikoumene*). The word is used in the Bible to speak of the Roman Empire (as "all the world") (Luke 2:1), the world or inhabited earth (Matt 24:14), and the universe or world subject to Christ after his return (Heb 2:5, 8). "Ecumenical" has been used in the history of Christianity to describe the one, unified, universal church before the schism between the East and West in 1054. It has also been used to describe the seven "Ecumenical Councils" (325–787). Ecumenical and ecumenism are often used today to speak of activities that foster dialogue, cooperation, understanding, or unity between various churches and

Sometimes, when asked about my denominational background, I say that I am a "mutt." Let me explain. My family has Methodist roots. I grew up in evangelical churches and earned my Master of Divinity at Trinity Evangelical Divinity School. In Chicago, I served on the pastoral team of a Vineyard Church. During this time, I was deeply impacted by the lives of great Catholic spiritual leaders like Ignatius of Loyola, Teresa of Avila, and John of the Cross, as well as Anthony the Great and many of the Eastern Desert Fathers and Mothers. I went on to earn a PhD in constructive theology at Loyola University Chicago, where Orthodox theology and spirituality opened up new vistas of the spiritual life. Working with Mark McIntosh, a leading scholar on Christian spirituality, studies in the *Philokalia*, and a dissertation on Maximus the Confessor (c. 580–662) and Jürgen Moltmann (1926–), further stoked my love for the theology and spirituality of the whole church. These experiences in various traditions inform this book.[18]

As the Moravian bishop Nicolaus Zinzendorf (1700–60) taught, each tradition or denomination, metaphorically speaking, preserves a particular jewel regarding the revelation of God that they highlight and preserve.[19] Therefore, different facets of the splendor, grace, and wisdom of God, as experienced and recorded by many believers, can be seen in the various churches. Variety of thought and practice is something beautiful, according to Zinzendorf. *A Luminous Life* illustrates this, drawing from the riches of the many beautiful traditions of the Christian churches.[20]

Being rooted in a particular tradition, however, is a good thing. In an age of "church hopping" and "church shopping," staying put in our home tradition is admirable and rewarding. Jürgen Moltmann, one of my theological mentors, says, his origins are Reformed, but his future is ecumenical.[21] We can be at home in our tradition *and* respect the traditions of our Christian sisters and brothers. This love and appreciation for the many streams of spiritual theology found in the churches has inspired *A Luminous Life*. I encourage you to stay rooted in your particular tradition, while

---

denominations.

18. Particularly important books in my journey, that I recommend, are: McIntosh, *Mystical Theology*; Balthasar, *Cosmic Liturgy*; Ware, *The Orthodox Way*.

19. Snyder, *Yes in Christ*, 228. See also the helpful description of the best aspects of six traditions in various churches: contemplative, holiness, charismatic, social justice, evangelical, and incarnational, in Foster and Griffin, eds., *Spiritual Classics*, xii–xiii.

20. Also instructive is the comparative ecclesiology, which considers seven traditions, by Kärkkäinen, *An Introduction to Ecclesiology*.

21. Moltmann, *Experiences in Theology*, xxiii.

at the same time opening your mind and heart to the diverse ways that God has worked and continues to work in traditions other than your own.

This openness to other traditions has been a hallmark of other books that encourage Christians to critically appropriate teachings and practices from ancient traditions, including some you might be familiar with, like *Celebration of Discipline* (1978) by Richard Foster. This well-known treatment of Christian spirituality impacted me deeply and paved the way for many others to explore and write on the spiritual classics. However, all too often books like *Celebration of Discipline* tended to focus mostly on the Western Christian traditions, while neglecting the equally important and valuable traditions of the Christian East. Because the spiritual traditions of the Christian East have enriched my life so significantly, and because a truly ecumenical perspective includes Western and Eastern sources, *A Luminous Life* draws equally from both.[22]

Bridge Academy and Church

A second characteristic of the perspective in *A Luminous Life* is that it attempts to bridge the academic and the ecclesial (or pastoral). Informed by twenty-five years of teaching and conversation in the academy and church, this book seeks to establish links between these two communities, and to demonstrate the mutually enhancing relationship between the scholarly and the popular.

Sometimes we hear complaints from both sides. Some academics argue, "Churches, in Sunday school or other contexts, tend to water down the richness of these traditions, offering oversimplified presentations of what can and should be an intellectually rigorous experience." While some church leaders and parishioners counter, "The academy tends to be too intellectual, focusing on confusing or less important details at the expense of what is practical." Are there ways to create bridges between academic and

---

22. Foster's influential *Celebration of Discipline* scarcely references Eastern spiritual theology. Reviewing the index reveals two: the *Apophthegmata* ("Sayings of the Fathers") and Theophan the Recluse. While *Celebration of Discipline* opened up a new perspective on the spiritual life, especially among Protestants, it is a limited view that needs to be broadened. Foster has written subsequent books that engage the Orthodox tradition (and numerous others), including the outstanding *Streams of Living Water*. There is a growing interest in Eastern Christian spirituality among Protestants. *A Luminous Life*, along with many others, seeks to address this desire to learn more about Orthodox spirituality.

church circles, to encourage constructive conversation instead of antagonism? There need not be enmity between these two communities.

Informed by leading scholarship *and* committed to the practice of Christian spirituality, *A Luminous Life* aims to be intellectually stimulating *and* practical. As we will see, this is exactly what the writers of the Christian spiritual classics intended: rigorous thought and vigorous practice. They reach the heart through the mind and move readers to action. They look to engage the whole person, to empower them to love God with all their heart, soul, mind, and strength. Their approach has influenced mine. We do live in a different ecclesial and cultural context than they did, but there is much to learn from their understanding of the connections between the life of the mind and life in the Spirit.[23]

Another facet of bridging the academic and pastoral involves making some of these ideas and practices more accessible to a broader readership. The great Orthodox saint, Symeon the New Theologian (949–1022), was known as a missionary of the spiritual life. Referring to the experience of contemplative union with God, he claimed that "the best is for all."[24] The invitations extended through the pages of *A Luminous Life* are not for some spiritual elite, but for *everyone*.

As Jürgen Moltmann and other scholars sought to develop a "theology for the people" over the past forty years, *A Luminous Life* joins others in developing a "spirituality for the people."[25] God's invitation to drink from the lifegiving streams of the Spirit is extended to everyone, to anyone willing to come and drink (Isa 55:1). As Nicodemus of the Holy Mountain (1749–1809) said in his preface to the *Philokalia* (published in 1782), the writings of these spiritual masters are not solely for cloistered Orthodox monks, but for all Christians. Union with God is the ultimate purpose for which all of us have been created, therefore, writings that assist us in this process should be available to all.[26] While there might be potential problems and pitfalls for

---

23. On the relationship between the life of the mind and life in the Spirit, see: Sertillanges, *The Intellectual Life*, and Balthasar, "Theology and Sanctity."

24. In the *Philokalia*, the preface to the writings of Symeon explains: "Convinced that contemplative union with God is possible for all alike, [Symeon] believed that it was his duty to share with others his experiences of divine grace. When he spoke in this way about his visions, it was not from pride but from a radical humility. 'If God has show such mercy to me a sinner,' he was saying in effect, 'then certainly he can and will do as much and more for you. The best is for all—if only you will accept it.'" *Philokalia* 4:6.

25. Moltmann, *A Broad Place*, 59.

26. And if the *Philokalia* is a work of the Spirit, it has universal appeal, even though

inexperienced Christians who encounter these writings, Nicodemus stated, they still should have equal access to the work of the Holy Spirit that is engendered by reading them.[27]

Rooted and Relevant

A third feature of *A Luminous Life* is the goal to be both rooted and relevant. The road to a fruitful future runs through the past. The Christian spiritual classics root us in the rich soil of the past so that we might thrive in our (post)modern present. In our explorations, we will draw from classics established on Scripture, tradition, reason, and experience, what scholars of John Wesley call the "Wesleyan Quadrilateral," a topic we consider in chapter 4.[28] Attuned to our contemporary milieu, we will look for ways to creatively and constructively appropriate knowledge and practices from our rich Christian heritage. Immersing ourselves in the spiritual teachings of these great classical writers will equip us to deepen our relationship with God and live healthier spiritual lives in the coming days.[29]

Egalitarian Vision

A fourth characteristic of *A Luminous Life* is the commitment to an egalitarian vision of the Christian spiritual life. One example of the egalitarian nature of this book is the gender inclusive language used when speaking

---

it was intended for an Orthodox readership. In fact, the title of Ware's essay makes this assertion, "The *Philokalia*: A Book for All Christians."

27. Ware writes: "In his introduction Nikodimos maintains that St. Paul's injunction, 'Pray without ceasing' (1 Thess 5:17), is addressed not merely to hermits in caves and on mountain tops but to married Christians with responsibilities for a family, to farmers, merchants, and lawyers, 'even to kings and courtiers living in palaces.' Unceasing prayer of the heart is a universal vocation. The best is for everyone." In Bingaman and Nassif, eds., The *Philokalia*, 12 (cf. 25–27).

28. On the sources of Christian spirituality, including Scripture, tradition, reason, and experience, see the helpful essays in the sections Scripture and Christian Spirituality, Interdisciplinary Dialogue Partners for the Study of Christian Spirituality, and Special Topics in Contemporary Christian Spirituality, in Holder, ed., *The Blackwell Companion to Christian Spirituality*.

29. For helpful reflections on theological and spiritual *ressourcement* (a "return to the sources"), particularly among evangelicals, see Webber, *Ancient-Future Faith*; and Williams, *Evangelicals and Tradition*. A more in-depth historical analysis is Flynn and Murray, eds., *Ressourcement*.

of God. In line with biblical teaching (Num 23:19; John 4) and the classical Christian writers, God is not human, though many of us have been conditioned to think and speak of God in exclusively male terms. God, the mysterious and ineffable Creator of the universe, transcends all creaturely existence, language, and symbols.[30]

We will consider this in greater detail in chapter 8, as we reflect on the mystery of the Holy Trinity, but for now it is important to note why this book addresses God in more inclusive language, and how it is committed to the biblical vision of women and men created equally in the image of God (Gen 1:26–27), and living in community where "all are one in Christ Jesus" (Gal 3:28), regardless of race, gender, social class, or other distinctions.[31] This vision of equality and unity in Christ, as we know from Scripture and the spiritual classics, does not mean the loss of individual characteristics. As the Apostle Paul says, there are many individual parts, but one body (1 Cor 12:20). Christian equality is not homogeneity. We will discuss this further in chapter 7.

Ecologically Attuned

A fifth feature of *A Luminous Life* is that it seeks to be ecologically attuned. As we know, one hallmark of our postmodern context is the problem of a threatened environment. This is a topic of debate among some Christians, one that is politically charged, particularly in the United States. Our goal is not to debate this, but to notice ways that these ancient voices address this problem, presenting a vision of spiritual life that is holistic, balanced, and corrective to modern tendencies toward anthropocentrism and exploitation of nature. Their understanding of the goodness and sacredness of creation, the human body, and our relation to the broader community of creation, will suggest alternatives and even solutions to environmental problems. Indeed, Christian spirituality has much to contribute to the conversations around religion and ecology, and other related themes.[32] Regardless of what

---

30. See Johnson, *She Who Is*, 3–16.

31. For compelling arguments for equality in Christian community, based on the work of Maximus the Confessor, see McIntosh, *Discernment and Truth*, 251–54; and Carter, *Race*, 343–69.

32. See Moltmann, *God in Creation*, xi–40; Chryssavgis and Foltz, eds., *Toward an Ecology of Transfiguration*; Burton-Christie, *The Blue Sapphire of the Mind*, ix–31; and Bingaman, "Orthodox Spirituality and Contemporary Ecology," 98–124.

we think about the current debate over climate change (and related issues), as Christians we are to love and respect the Creator and the creation.

Autobiographical

Sixth, *A Luminous Life* is autobiographical or personal. As we know, books are influenced by the background, story, and environment of the author. While speaking previously of the ecumenical commitment of this book, I mentioned the traditions I have had the privilege of studying as well as the influence of various communities on my spiritual life. Many seeds from Catholic, Orthodox, and Protestant spirituality have been planted in my heart and mind over the decades.

My Methodist family heritage has inspired a passion for biblical justice, holiness, and faith working through love.[33] Education and service in evangelical churches and schools have fueled a love for the Scriptures and the importance of experiencing the Christian faith. The Vineyard movement and the teaching of John Wimber instilled a love for the whole church, a commitment to doing the works of Jesus in the power of the Holy Spirit, to making disciples and training leaders, and to serving in AIDS hospice ministry in the 1990s. Involvement in missions and international ministry propelled me into Christian-Muslim dialogue and relations.[34] Studying the lives of Christian mystics and spiritual writers over the years, along with earning a PhD at a Jesuit university, deepened my appreciation for the work of the Holy Spirit in Catholic, Orthodox, and Protestant communities, education that leads to serving the common good, and both ecumenical and interfaith dialogue.[35]

---

33. The work of Thomas C. Oden influenced my early thinking on theology and spirituality, particularly his three-volume masterwork of "paleo-orthodoxy," *Classic Christianity*.

34. Studying with Wayne Grudem, Scot McKnight, and D. A. Carson at Trinity Evangelical Divinity School fueled a love for Scripture, New Testament Greek, church history, and systematic theology. Serving on the pastoral team at the Vineyard Church in Evanston, Illinois, being mentored by the senior pastor, Steve Nicholson, and studying the teachings of John Wimber and Jack Deere, instilled a passion for mentoring young leaders, doing the works of Jesus in the power of the Holy Spirit, ecumenical theology, missions, and developing friendships with Muslims.

35. Doctoral work at Loyola University provided the opportunity to build on earlier interests, particularly Christian mysticism and spirituality, Orthodox-Protestant dialogue, comparative theology, and interfaith dialogue. My dissertation led to the recently published volume, *All Things New*.

Scholarship and teaching have provided opportunities for ongoing conversation and debate on key issues in the study of Christian theology and spirituality. Involvement in the American Academy of Religion, particularly groups focusing on Christian spirituality and ecology, Orthodox-Protestant dialogue, comparative theology, and contemplative studies, have led to fruitful conversations and opportunities to publish research.[36] These opportunities to learn, teach, and interact with students and colleagues, have enriched my life beyond measure. *A Luminous Life*, in many ways, is a bringing together of many things learned from fellow spiritual pilgrims, as well as an opportunity to give to others what has been given to me (Matt 10:8).

Limited Scope and Perspective

Finally, as with all publications on Christian spiritual life, *A Luminous Life* is limited in scope and perspective. Contemporary theologians speak of the contextual nature of all theologies. That is, each work on theology or spirituality emerges from a particular context and is therefore limited and deficient.[37] The notion of a universal or perennial theology of the spiritual life is misleading. This is not surprising, especially when we consider the

---

36. While *A Luminous Life* focuses on Christian spirituality, some of my other work engenders dialogue between different spiritual traditions, including Christian and Muslim spirituality. What is exciting about this kind of dialogue these days is that it values *particularity* without homogenizing the distinct traditions. In the past, there were tendencies to highlight commonalities between traditions and ignore the irreducible differences. Today, in the American Academy of Religion and other forums, Christians and Muslims (among many others) discuss common theological and spiritual themes, concerns, and practices, while remaining deeply rooted in their particular traditions. Many Christians involved in these endeavors explain that such deep dialogue makes them "a better Christian, a more faithful disciple of Jesus." By interacting with someone from another tradition, someone who believes and practices differently, new questions and perspectives emerge, and we return to study our own Scriptures, traditions, and histories with new vigor and insight. This is illustrated in my article, "A Common Vision."

37. See Moltmann, *Experiences in Theology*, xvii. James Cone, the founder of Black Theology, explains the contextual and limited nature of theology. His comments, I think, also apply to spirituality: "[Theology] is a finite image, limited by the temporality and particularity of our existence. Theology is not universal language; it is *interested* language and thus is always a reflection of the goals and aspirations of a particular people in a definite social setting . . . Although the revelation of God may be universal and eternal, theological talk about that revelation is filtered through human experience, which is limited by social realities." *Theology of the Oppressed*, 36, 39.

topic here: life in the Holy Spirit, the third person of the Holy Trinity who brings us into the very depths of the mystery of God.

Each of us is on a particular, unique journey, as were the authors of the classics we will explore. While there are common themes, experiences, and responses to the work of God in the lives of Christians (each being measured by Scripture and the teaching of the church), they are all limited. When we encounter the uncreated God of the universe (a universe that is itself expanding by the millisecond!), we are aware that we see and know only in part (1 Cor 13:12). Our spiritual theologies and experiences are equivalent to viewing our solar system with a small telescope or taking a thimbleful of water from the vast ocean of the boundless nature of the infinite God. Therefore, *A Luminous Life* is a commentary on the view from the small telescope and the tiny thimble; a limited, encouraging word among many others, a humble attempt to catalyze our lives in the Holy Spirit through the study of classic Christian spirituality.[38]

A Few More Thoughts

Now that you have a clearer picture of what this book is about, as well as the journey it invites you to join, I want to make a few brief suggestions and comments before we embark.

Prayer

I encourage you to pray as you read *A Luminous Life*. It is meant to be both an informative and transformative experience. Along with other spiritual exercises, we will consider *Lectio Divina* (Latin for "divine reading"). This Benedictine exercise, rooted in Jewish and early Christian practice, involves reading, meditating, praying, and contemplating Scripture, as well as other spiritual writings. The goal is to encounter Christ, the Living Word, in the text, to deepen one's relationship with him, and to be transformed into his likeness through the power of the Holy Spirit.[39]

---

38. In chapter 8, we consider a story about Thomas Aquinas that illustrates the limited nature of all theology and spirituality in light of the transcendent mystery of God.

39. Regarding *Lectio Divina* and other important approaches to the prayerful reading of Scripture, see Schneiders, "Scripture and Spirituality." On biblical meditation in the Eastern Christian tradition, see Burton-Christie, *The Word in the Desert*; Špidlík, "Meditative Reading"; and part II, "The Bible in Use among the Greek Church Fathers,"

As you are struck by passages in the Bible, the spiritual classics, or other stories in the following pages, ask for the grace of the Lord Jesus, the love of the Father, and the fellowship of the Holy Spirit (2 Cor 13:14) to be with you, for Christ to be formed in you (Gal 4:19). Take time to pray, ponder, listen, and journal as you read.

Relationships

A Luminous Life can be read by anyone, anywhere, at any station in life. However, as the Scriptures and spiritual classics teach, personal transformation occurs in relationships with other people. There are times for solitude, retreat, and other individual practices, but these bring us back to other people, to our communities, where we know and are known by those we love.[40]

Further, what God works in us, as individuals and communities, propels us into the world. When we venture into the loving heart of God, we are catapulted back into the broken heart of the world.[41] Often times, we are most aware of God's presence and love as we fellowship with spiritual sisters and brothers or as we serve others in ways that put their needs and interests before ours. Therefore, consider ways to share this spiritual journey with others. Read this book with someone else, a small group, a mentor, or someone you can mentor.

Love and Grace

Keep the love and grace of God at the center of your mind as you make your way through the book. Sometimes we are inclined to shift the focus to our own efforts. How much am I praying, fasting, reading, meditating, or giving? Are my efforts pleasing to God? How do I measure up to the examples I am reading about or to other Christians around me? It is natural to think and feel such things, but remind yourself of several truths. First, God loves

---

in Blowers, ed., *The Bible in Greek Christian Antiquity*.

40. See the stirring chapter by Williams, "Life, Death, and Neighbours."

41. Ware, commenting on the model of St. Antony of the Desert (c. 251–356), explains: "Antony has had many successors, and in most of them the same outward pattern of events is found—*a withdrawal in order to return* . . ." *The Orthodox Church*, 40. In the following pages, we will see that solitude, community, and mission are intrinsically connected.

you. Let me rephrase that: God absolutely adores you. God does not love you more or less based on your knowledge of Scripture and the spiritual classics, your engagement in spiritual exercises, or your spiritual growth. As a good parent looks at his or her child, overflowing with love and pride, so God looks at us, saying, "You are mine. You are beautiful. I am thrilled as I watch you become all that you are created to be."[42] When we operate from a starting point like this, knowing how much God loves us and is pleased with our desire to become more Christ like, we are more motivated, encouraged, and relentless in our pursuit of God.

Celebrate Small Victories

Second, learn to celebrate small victories and savor each stage in your journey. It is easy to grow frustrated, to be overcome with negative thoughts and feelings. Why can't I be at a more advanced place in my spiritual journey? Why do I stay stuck in the same place, ruled by the same unhealthy habits? Why can't I pray and meditate like others? Scripture urges us to not despise small beginnings (Zech 4:10). Jesus taught that the kingdom of God, the dynamic presence and reign of God that operates in our lives, is like a tiny seed planted within us (Luke 17:21; Matt 13:31–32). It may be difficult to discern that the seed of the kingdom is growing, but it most certainly is. Planted and hidden in the soil of our hearts is the life of God. As we place ourselves, through spiritual practices, and in community with others, under the sun of God's grace, watered by the showers of divine mercy, we grow and become the people we were created to be. In fact, God is more committed to us, our spiritual life, and spiritual progress than we could ever be. God longs to be gracious to you (Isa 30:18). Ask God to help you cooperate with this grace, to recognize its transformative effects, and to be thankful for every victory and step of progress.[43]

---

42. God is actually described as one who finds great joy in us, delights in us, renews us in love, and sings over us: "The LORD, your God, is in your midst, a warrior who gives victory; he will rejoice over you with gladness, he will renew you in his love; he will exult over you with loud singing" (Zeph 3:17).

43. I am reminded of the 1991 film, *What About Bob?* Learning to celebrate, as Bob did, all the "baby steps" in our spiritual journeys can change everything. The spiritual life is a marathon, not a sprint. As Teresa of Avila teaches, the spiritual life is like cultivating a garden. Consistency, endurance, and reliance on God's grace are crucial. See her description of how we cooperate with God in this process in *The Book of Her Life*.

Spiritual Athletes

Celebrating small victories and incremental progress is what athletes do. As we will see, some of the texts in *A Luminous Life* portray Christians as "spiritual athletes." Interestingly, the Greek word *ascetic* (*áskēsis*) signifies someone who engages in spiritual exercises or training in order to reach certain goals. Athletes forego certain good or natural things (e.g., more sleep, certain foods, leisure) in order to get in better shape, run farther, swim faster, climb higher, or lift more. Celebrating their accomplishments and improvements, as small as they might be, is a key to success. Likewise, spiritual athletes are willing to give up certain things to attain spiritual goals. Scheduling regular time for prayer, meditating on Scripture, fasting, or serving others requires discipline. As you practice some of these things, try not to be so hard on yourself. Value moderation. Approach this endeavor with a sense of humor and learn to laugh at yourself.

If you want to be a great spiritual athlete, take the long view. If you want to develop into a person of prayer and meditation who communes with God throughout the day, set small goals. Learning to pray a minute or two develops into half an hour. After doing this for several weeks, months, and years, you grow into someone who communes with God throughout the day. Prayer is no longer a segmented activity during the day. You actually "become prayer," finding God amidst the mundane routines of everyday life. Look for and celebrate those small steps of growth. Give thanks to God, our Guide and Goal, who is more committed to our success than we are! As we exert ourselves in the pursuit of God, the grace of God works mightily in us, accomplishing all that God has intended for us. Be encouraged, sisters and brothers: the Lord is in the journey. Let's get started.

CHAPTER 2.

Biblical Images of the Spiritual Life

"As you, Father, are in me and I am in you, may they also be in us, so that the world may believe that you have sent me."
—John 17:21

"My little children, for whom I am again in the pain of childbirth until Christ is formed in you . . ."
—Gal 4:19

"The soul is moved by heavenly love and longing when, having clearly beheld the beauty and the fairness of the Word of God, it falls deeply in love with His loveliness . . ."
—Origen of Alexandria, *Commentary on the Song*

"You have formed us for Yourself, and our hearts are restless until they find rest in You."
—Augustine of Hippo, *Confessions*, Book 1

"The passion of love . . . when rightly directed unites it with the divine."
—Maximus the Confessor, *Philokalia* 2:94

Some say a picture is worth a thousand words. While this is open to debate and different opinions, there are times when pictures do help us. When assisting my son recently with his math homework, words helped to some extent. But when I sketched an image to illustrate the fraction and algebra exercises we were working on, the lights came on for him. The image along with the words helped explain the concepts.

In a similar way, pictures can clarify concepts related to the spiritual life. For example, detailed descriptions of spiritual hunger, satisfaction, and celebration come into focus when the Scriptures speak of a spiritual feast. When Teresa of Avila describes growth in prayer and union with Jesus as moving deeper into the interior castle of our heart, we understand more clearly. The following two chapters exemplify how authors have used words and pictures, or word pictures, to convey their insights into life with God. This chapter explores biblical images of the spiritual life. The next chapter considers historical models of spiritual development. These images and models are symbols, not fixed patterns. They are heuristic devices that enable us to discover more about God, ourselves, our progress in the spiritual life, and our growth in Christlikeness. As we reflect on particular images in Scripture and models developed later in the Christian spiritual classics, we recognize common elements.

Common Elements

While there are key differences between the images and models—from biblical, early Christian, medieval, and modern eras—they share some common elements.

1. They provide a map of sorts, a picture that helps lay out what spiritual growth might look like. From the journey of Abraham and Sarah to a new land, the formation of Christ within the soul, to traversing the desert of modern criticism, each image or paradigm offers practical wisdom for the spiritual life. In some sense, these images and models actually draw us in to participate in the spiritual reality they describe.

2. The models illustrate the necessity of diligent work in cooperation with divine grace. We do not wish our way to spiritual maturity. But, like physical training, spiritual training requires time, effort, sacrifice, energy, and self-discipline.

3. A thread that runs through these various models is the important role of Scripture in the life of a Christian. Consistent meditation on the Bible, as we will discuss in further chapters, is one of the primary sources of nourishment for the believer.

4. These paradigms describe and share parallel goals: contemplating God through Scripture, encountering the Holy Trinity, experiencing

union with God, and being transformed into the image of the Lord Jesus. Each image or model is a descriptive means to these ends.

With these common elements in mind, we turn now to a number of biblical images.

Biblical Images and Models

In his book *Christian Spirituality*, Anglican theologian Alister McGrath, discusses the use of biblical images as models of the spiritual life. He notes that meditation upon the biblical text has been of central importance to Christians through the ages. "It should therefore be no surprise that many biblical images have exercised a controlling influence over Christian spirituality. It is much easier to reflect upon an image than an idea."[1] McGrath proceeds to reflect on a number of key biblical images that serve as models of the spiritual life and spiritual growth. We will consider some of these images.

The feast

Jesus taught that the kingdom of God was like a great feast. As with a lavish banquet to celebrate a marriage, Jesus invites those on the margins to enter into the great feast of the kingdom (Luke 14:15–24). The story of the lost son and loving father describes the feast the father threw when the son returned (Luke 15:11–24). The image of the feast suggests several things regarding the spiritual life. First, the image implies that the abundance of food and drink provided by God satisfy spiritual hunger and thirst. Without these provisions, human beings remain spiritually hungry and thirsty. Augustine of Hippo (354–430) expresses this point in his well-known prayer to God: "You have made us for Yourself, and our hearts are restless until they find rest in You." Second, the image of the feast conveys the idea of invitation. We can only participate in a feast when invited. Jesus was known for inviting and fellowshipping with those on the margins of Jewish society (Matt 11:19; Luke 15:2). As "the friend of sinners," Jesus continues to invite those on the margins into the feast of the kingdom, where he rules as king and bestows honor on those who accept the invitation. Third, the feast is about celebration and rejoicing. Feasts signify important occasions,

---

1. McGrath, *Christian Spirituality*, 88. McGrath's reflections provide a framework for the discussion here.

like a wedding, bringing together loved ones who celebrate and rejoice in those who are getting married.

These aspects of the image of the feast are developed within Christian spirituality, particularly in relation to the Lord's Supper. The bread and wine are reminders that human need and desire can only be satisfied by divine provision. Drawing from the story of the miraculous provision of manna for Israel in the desert, Jesus said, "I am the bread of life. Whoever comes to me will never be hungry, and whoever believes in me will never be thirsty" (John 6:35). Richard Foster comments on our spiritual hunger and divine provision: The "Holy Spirit continually feeds us by enacting the death and resurrection of Christ in the Communion service, or Eucharist."[2]

In Christian spirituality, the Lord's Supper also brings together the actions of looking backward and forward. Paul, based on the tradition he received from the Lord, reflects on both of these dimensions in his instructions to the church at Corinth:

> For I received from the Lord what I also handed on to you, that the Lord Jesus on the night when he was betrayed took a loaf of bread, and when he had given thanks, he broke it and said, "This is my body that is for you. Do this in remembrance of me." In the same way he took the cup also, after supper, saying, "This cup is the new covenant in my blood. Do this, as often as you drink it, in remembrance of me." For as often as you eat this bread and drink the cup, you proclaim the Lord's death until he comes (1 Cor 11:23–26).

With the Eucharist, we remember the death and resurrection of Jesus and look forward to his return. At the institution of the Lord's Supper, Jesus explains, "I tell you, I will never again drink of this fruit of the vine until that day when I drink it new with you in my Father's kingdom" (Matt 26:29). Therefore, the Lord's Supper offers a foretaste of the heavenly banquet, "the marriage supper of the Lamb," when the Bridegroom and bride are united forever (Rev 19:9).

The journey

Another image is that of a journey. The Bible is filled with stories of journeys, beginning with the Old Testament. Abraham and Sarah's journey to Canaan. Israel's forty years of wandering in the wilderness before entering

---

2. Foster, *Streams of Living Water*, 263.

the promised land. The return of the Jews to Jerusalem after seventy years of exile in Babylon. The biblical images of these journeys have significantly informed Christian spirituality.

In the New Testament, the image of a spiritual journey is seen when the early Christians called themselves followers of "the way" (Acts 9:2; 24:14). As God led the Israelites out of captivity in Egypt to the promised land through Moses, the early Christians understood that through Jesus God leads his people from spiritual bondage to salvation in the heavenly city (Rev 21).

The Apostle Paul employs the image of a spiritual journey. He says the Christian life is like a long race, a strenuous journey that involves great pressure and culminates with a reward for those who complete it (Gal 2:2; 2 Tim 4:7). The Letter to the Hebrews also uses the image of a race, encouraging readers to run with perseverance, keeping their eyes focused on Jesus who has gone before them (Heb 12:1–2).

In light of the image of a race or journey, Paul speaks of spiritual training that enables Christians to run to win, to grow in godly character, and to fight the good fight of faith (1 Cor 9:24–27; 1 Tim 4:7–8; 6:2). We will explore this spiritual training further in chapter 6.

The struggle

A further image is that of a struggle. Scripture speaks of various spiritual struggles or conflicts. A struggle between God and the world, good and evil, light and darkness (Col 1:13). This does not mean, however, that Christians view the world itself as something evil. In fact, from the beginning, God looks upon all of creation and says that it was "very good" (Gen 1:31). The problem arises when humans look to the created world for satisfaction, fulfillment, or salvation. Maximus the Confessor explains that the created world is meant to point to and draw humans to the Creator. There are desires within human beings that can only be satisfied through relationship with God.[3] Struggle or conflict arises when humans look to created things for fulfillment instead of their Creator. This is indicated in biblical passages like 1 John 2:15–17, which contrasts love for the Father with love for the world, as well as worldly desires versus desire to do the will of God.

Paul elaborates on the image of struggle in the Christian life. He speaks of the need for Christians to put on "the whole armor of God"

3. Maximus the Confessor, *Philokalia* 2:260–61.

(Eph 6:10-18) as protection in spiritual warfare. Elsewhere, Paul says that Christians are to serve as "good soldiers of Christ Jesus," who share in his suffering, persevere, and seek to please him (2 Tim 2:3-4). The spiritual life of Christians involves the struggle of spiritual warfare and the mind-set of a warrior in battle.

The biblical image of struggle is developed in three different realms within Christian spirituality. One is the *external struggle against that which is hostile against Christians and the Christian faith*. The New Testament presents hostility against Christians as something to be expected. Jesus suffered; so will his followers (1 Pet 2:21). The Roman authorities put Jesus to death on a cross. For generations after the crucifixion, Rome continued to persecute Christians. Church history details other groups of Christians who struggled against opposition and hostility, including seventeenth-century Puritans who felt victimized by the Anglican authorities in England, Russian Orthodox believers persecuted under Stalin, and contemporary Christians in the Middle East opposed by certain Muslim authorities.

Second is the *internal struggle against temptation*. Various authors of the spiritual classics describe the struggle against temptation and sin. One example is the Desert Father, John Cassian (c. 360-435), whose writings expound on how Christians can identify the allures of "the eight deadly sins," overcome them through grace, spiritual exercises like fasting and prayer, and experience union with God.[4] Another example, one considered in detail in the next chapter, is provided by Teresa of Avila (1515-1582), in *The Interior Castle*. This classic urges Christians to seek Christ in the depths of their heart, to grow in their knowledge of God and self, and to fight against sin as they realize mystical union with Jesus. An additional work that addresses the theme of struggling against temptation is Lorenzo Scupoli's *Combattimento Spirituale* ("Spiritual Combat"), first published in 1589.[5]

Third is *the struggle with God*. Christian spirituality portrays external struggle against persecution, internal struggle against temptation, and, what may surprise some, a struggle with God. The biblical image often referenced in this respect is the mysterious struggle during the night between Jacob and an unidentified man by the River Jabbok (Gen 32:22-32). It is often interpreted as an image of human struggle to apprehend or comprehend God more fully, or to prevail with God in prayer. Ancient Jewish

---

4. Cassian, *The Conferences*, 183-96.
5. This was followed by 250 editions through 1750.

exegetes of this passage, including Philo of Alexandria (c. 20 BCE–30 CE), held that the change of Jacob's name to "Israel" ("one who sees God") suggested that he was granted spiritual vision of God. This interpretation influenced subsequent Christian writers. The editors of the *Ancient Christian Commentary on Scripture* explain that this scene of struggle signifies the point in the spiritual life where one is granted the gift of contemplation, inner tranquility, and "seeing God";[6] but only after wrestling with God.

McGrath elucidates other biblical images that informed Christian spirituality, including *exile, purification, the internalization of faith, the desert, ascent, darkness and light,* and *silence.* For the sake of concision, and because we cover some of these themes later in the book, we proceed to a further biblical image, one not covered by McGrath, yet equally important: the growth of love.

Marriage: Divine-Human Love

Another biblical image that informs Christian spirituality is the symbolic marriage relationship between God and the people of God. This metaphor of the divine-human love relationship is found in the Old and New Testaments. In the Old Testament, particularly the prophets, the covenant relationship between God and Israel is likened to a husband and wife. For example, Isaiah exclaims, "For your Maker is your husband, the Lord of hosts is his name"(Isa 54:5). Other Hebrew prophets elaborate on this image. They remind Israel of the Lord's love, urge them to be faithful to the Lord and the covenant, and call them to return to the Lord when they stray after other gods. Ezekiel says, "I passed by you again and looked on you; you were at the age for love. I spread the edge of my cloak over you, and covered your nakedness: I pledged myself to you and entered into a covenant with you, says the Lord God, and you became mine" (Ezek 16:8). The prophet Hosea explains that his own broken relationship with his wife, who has relations with other men, is a prophetic picture of the fractured relationship between God and Israel (Hos 1:2; 3:1). This image conveys the faithful love of God, the tender call of God to return, and the willingness of God to take back wayward people, time and again (Hos 6:1–3; 13:4). The persistent love and tender mercy of God prevail, according to this prophetic picture.

In the New Testament, this image is developed further. John the Baptist refers to Jesus as the bridegroom and himself as his friend: "He who has

---

6. Oden, ed., *Ancient Christian Commentary on Scripture,* Genesis, 218.

the bride is the bridegroom. The friend of the bridegroom, who stands and hears him, rejoices greatly at the bridegroom's voice. For this reason my joy has been fulfilled" (John 3:29). Continuing this theme, Jesus says that his disciples, "the friends of the bridegroom," do not fast while with him, but will fast when he is gone (Mark 2:19–20). Jesus also uses bride, groom, and wedding imagery in some of his parables, often to convey a sense of eschatological urgency and watchfulness as the end of the age approaches (Matt 22:2; 25:1–13).

The Apostle Paul reflects on the love relationship between the Lord Jesus and his people. While addressing husbands and wives in Ephesians 5:21–33, Paul explains that the conjugal relationship points beyond itself to a deep mystery. The love relationship between man and woman is a powerful symbol of the love between Jesus and his church.

The book of Revelation also utilizes the image of the bride and groom to signify the divine-human love relationship. Written to encourage Christians during times of persecution, Revelation describes Jesus as a warrior-king and bridegroom who is returning for his church, the bride. Their reunion is like a great marriage feast, and the bride has made herself ready to meet Jesus (Rev 19:7). As an apocalyptic culmination to the entire canon of Scripture, Revelation concludes with the image of spiritual union between the Lord and his church, when the reign of God is finally established on the earth (Rev 21:2–3).

Appropriating these biblical images, Patristic theologians and authors of the spiritual classics expand on the relationship between Jesus and his church. An early example is Origen of Alexandria (c. 185–254). Like other Jewish and Christian commentators before him, Origen interprets the Song of Solomon as a spiritual allegory that describes the union of the soul with God. The Song provides an image of ever increasing intimacy between individual Christians, as well as the collective church, and Jesus. Origen writes: "It seems to me that this little book is . . . a marriage-song, which Solomon wrote in the form of a drama and sang under the figure of the bride, about to wed and burning with heavenly love towards her Bridegroom, who is the Word of God." He adds: "And deeply indeed did she love him, whether we take her as the soul made in his image, or as the church."[7]

---

7. Origen, *Commentary on the Song of Songs*, in McGinn, ed., *The Essential Writings of Christian Mysticism*, 7.

Theosis or Deification

Another image of spiritual life that springs from the Scriptures is that of *theosis* or deification. Unfortunately this doctrine and image of spiritual growth is lesser known or often misunderstood, especially in Protestant circles or churches in the West that are less familiar with Eastern Christian theology. For those who are particularly interested in learning more about deification, the bracing study by Normal Russell, *The Doctrine of Deification in the Greek Patristic Tradition*, is highly recommended. Russell's comprehensive treatment has informed the following reflections on deification. In order to clarify what *theosis* is (and is not), I propose the following:

1. The doctrine of *theosis* is rooted in Scripture.

One of the clearest passages that informs the doctrine of deification is 2 Peter 1:4, which reads: "Thus [God] has given us, through these things, his precious and very great promises, so that through them you may escape from the corruption that is in the world because of lust, and may become *participants of the divine nature*."[8] Through the invaluable and astounding promises of God, Peter says, we not only break free from the clutches and corrosive powers of lust, but we are actually drawn into the very life of God. By meditating upon, treasuring, and living into the promises about the love and grace of God, we partake of the very nature of God.

To some Christians, this idea may sound (borderline) blasphemous, like something outside the bounds of Scripture. But upon reviewing other biblical passages that speak of things similar to participating or partaking of the divine nature as 2 Peter 1:4 states, we find some astonishing things. For example:

The incarnation of the Word enables us to receive from the very fullness of God:

> And the Word became flesh and lived among us, and we have seen his glory, the glory as of a father's only son, full of grace and truth. . . . *From his fullness we have all received*, grace upon grace (John 1:14, 16).

---

8. The Greek word for "participants of" or "partakers in" (κοινωνοί, *koinōnoi*) is used six times in the New Testament: Matt 23:30; Luke 5:10; 1 Cor 10:18; 2 Cor 1:7; Heb 10:33; and 2 Pet 1:4.

Biblical Images of the Spiritual Life

The glory that God gave to Jesus has been given to us, we are indwelt by the presence of the Holy Trinity, and are being unified to reveal the love and saving activity of God in Jesus:

> The glory that you have given me I have given them, so that they may be one, as we are one, *I in them and you in me*, that they may become completely one, so that the world may know that you have sent me and have loved them even as you have loved me (John 17:22–23).

The great mystery now revealed by God through the church is that the glorious Christ indwells human beings. Paul explains that

> the mystery that has been hidden throughout the ages and generations but has now been revealed to his saints. To them God chose to make known how great among the Gentiles are the riches of the glory of this mystery, *which is Christ in you*, the hope of glory (Col 1:27–28).

God has chosen to recreate human beings, reshaping us to correspond to the image of his Son, so that he might be the archetype or ideal pattern for the other children within this new family:

> For those whom he foreknew he also predestined *to be conformed to the image of his Son*, in order that he might be the firstborn within a large family (Rom 8:29).

Through the new covenant established by God in Christ, we are transformed by the Spirit into the image of the Lord in increasing glory:

> Now the Lord is the Spirit, and where the Spirit of the Lord is, there is freedom. And all of us, with unveiled faces, seeing the glory of the Lord as though reflected in a mirror, *are being transformed into the same image* from one degree of glory to another; for this comes from the Lord, the Spirit (2 Cor 3:17–18).

Along with 2 Peter 1:4, it is these kinds of biblical passages that inform the doctrine of deification. In some ways deification parallels doctrines that Protestants are more familiar with, like sanctification, growth in holiness, or becoming perfect as God is perfect.[9] In fact, Maximus the Confessor links justification and deification in his teaching on the church. He says

---

9. Randy Maddox (of Duke Divinity School) has elucidated some of the intriguing parallels between Protestant teaching on holiness and the Orthodox doctrine of deification, "John Wesley and Eastern Orthodoxy."

that through faith and divine grace, God justifies sinful human beings, transforming them into the likeness of Jesus through the power of the Holy Spirit.[10]

Scripture teaches some radical ideas about these things. For example, Christians are called to be holy because God is holy (1 Pet 1:16). Jesus tells his followers to be perfect as God is perfect (Matt 5:48). Is it really possible for Christians to be as perfect as God is, to be holy as God is holy, to participate in the divine nature?[11] Understanding the meaning of these passages requires some thoughtful work, prayer, conversation within our communities, and engagement of the rich exegetical heritage within various Christian traditions.

The same is true for understanding the meaning of the doctrine of deification. Yes, the notion of partaking of the divine nature might be difficult to grasp, but so is the call to holiness or perfection. Just because it is difficult to understand deification or because some have misunderstood or distorted its true meaning, does not mean that Christians should avoid it. Instead, we should seek the wisdom of God, the mind of Christ, and the illumination of the Spirit as we grapple with the doctrine. It is found in Scripture, as the passages above illustrate. If we are going to be faithful to the teachings of Scripture and the broader Christian tradition, we cannot ignore the doctrine. Perhaps if we delve into this biblical concept—that Christians are called, graced, and empowered to participate in the very life of the Holy Trinity—we may find ourselves surprised by renewed discoveries in ancient sources, fresh insights into God's glorious work within us and our communities.

---

10. Maximus, "The Church's Mystagogy," 211; cf. Chia, "Salvation as Justification and Deification."

11. C. S. Lewis asserts: "The command 'Be ye perfect' is not idealistic gas. Nor is it a command to do the impossible. He is going to make us into creatures that can obey that command. He said (in the Bible) that we were 'gods' and He is going to make good His words. If we let Him—for we can prevent Him, if we choose—He will make the feeblest and filthiest of us into a god or goddess, dazzling, radiant, immortal creatures, pulsating all through with such energy and joy and wisdom and love as we cannot now imagine, a bright stainless mirror which reflects back to Him perfectly (though, of course, on a smaller scale) His own boundless power and delight and goodness. The process will be long and in parts very painful; but that is what we are in for. Nothing less. He meant what he said." *Mere Christianity*, 205–6.

2. *Theosis* does not mean that a human being, saved by divine grace, ever becomes God.

Maximus the Confessor explains, in a key text on *theosis*, that human nature is transformed by Christ through his incarnation, but never changed into the divine nature:

> A sure warrant for looking forward with hope to the deification of human nature is provided by the incarnation of God, which makes man god to the same degree as God Himself became man. For it is clear that He who became man without sin (cf. Heb. 4:15) will *divinize human nature without changing it into the divine nature*, and will raise it up for His own sake to the same degree as He lowered Himself for man's sake. This is what St. Paul teaches mystically when he says, "...that in the ages to come He might display the overflowing richness of His grace" (Eph 2:7).[12]

The incarnation of the Word guarantees the deification of human beings. It also sets the guidelines. Maximus reiterates the teaching of Hebrews 4:15, that Jesus is a high priest who can sympathize with our weaknesses and has been tested as we are. Preceding Maximus, Irenaeus (c. 130–200), explains that "the Word of God, our Lord Jesus Christ, who did, through his transcendent love, become what we are, that He might bring us to be even what He is Himself."[13] In other words, the *kenosis* of Christ assures the *theosis* of human beings. Jesus emptied and lowered himself (Phil 2:6–8) in order to raise us up. But human nature is never deified or transformed into the divine nature.[14] The transformation of human nature based on the incarnation displays throughout eternity the superabundance of God's grace, love, and power.

Maximus and other theologians have suggested metaphors to illustrate that human nature is deified without being changed into the divine nature. For example, when an iron sword is plunged into fire, the iron takes

---

12. Maximus, *First Century of Various Texts* 62, in *Philokalia* 2:177.

13. Irenaeus, *Against Heresies*, Book 3, 19:1; in *The Ante-Nicene Fathers*, Volume 1, 448.

14. See Moltmann's comments on the famous axiom of Athanasius ("God became human so that human beings might be deified"), *The Coming of God*, 272. Moltmann turns to Dimitru Staniloae's remarks concerning *theosis*, where the Romanian theologian explains that the maximal union with God [of which deification speaks], "in which the person is interpenetrated by God's fullness without being absorbed into it, means at the same time the deification of the human being," 376n35, from Staniloae, *Orthodox Dogmatik* I, 359.

on characteristics of the fire as it glows red and emits heat. The iron is penetrated by the fire, becoming like the fire, though remaining iron by nature. At no point does the sword cease to be iron and become fire. Likewise, as human beings are enabled by grace to participate in the divine nature, they are penetrated by the Spirit of God, and transformed into the likeness of Christ.[15] Because of the incarnation of the Word, we are drawn into and filled with the presence of God, who is a consuming fire. We glow with the fire and heat of God's love, but are never transformed into God. Iron remains iron; fire remains fire. Creature remains creature; God remains God.

To reinforce the point that deification means being transformed into Christlikeness or godliness, while not being changed into God, theologians claim that human nature is transfigured by participating in the *energies* of God, not the *essence* of God. Kallistos Ware explains: "The idea of deification must always be understood in the light of the distinction between God's essence and His energies." Therefore, "Union with God means union with the divine energies, not the divine essence: the Orthodox Church, while speaking of deification and union, rejects all forms of pantheism [the idea that God is all and all is God]."[16] In the same way, little "o" orthodox Catholic and Protestant churches agree with this teaching: that union with God does not mean union with the divine essence.[17] The creature is never absorbed into the Creator, as pantheism suggests.

3. *Theosis* is God's design for all Christians, not for a select few.

Deification, like sanctification, regeneration, and other doctrines that describe transformation in Christ, is God's purpose for *all* Christians. All who are baptized into Christ are clothed with Christ; all divisions are washed away in the baptismal waters; there is unity and equality among those in Christ (Gal 3:28). In Christ, there are no insiders and outsiders, haves and have nots, or spiritual elite and the rest of us. All Christians are joined to Christ, filled with the Spirit of God, and destined to be transformed into the

---

15. Lossky, *The Mystical Theology of the Eastern Church*, 146.
16. Ware, *The Orthodox Church*, 232.
17. The "big O" Orthodox Church is simply a way of referring to the Eastern Orthodox Church. The "little o" orthodox churches are those that worship and live in a manner that aligns with the biblical, historic, creedal Christian faith. "Orthodox" simply means "right worship or opinion." The first is a proper name and is therefore capitalized. The second is an adjective that describes those who worship and live in a manner that lines up with the teachings of the Bible.

likeness of Christ. All Christians, by grace, through faith, become partakers of the divine nature (2 Pet 1:4). Deification is the destiny of all Christians. Kallistos Ware explains that *theosis* is a universal, present, and future calling for all Christians:

> Deification is not something reserved for a few select initiates, but something intended for all alike.... [I]t is the normal goal for *every* Christian without exception. Certainly, we shall only be fully deified at the Last Day; but for each of us the process of divinization must begin here and now in this present life.[18]

Therefore, *theosis* is rooted in Scripture, effected by divine grace, safeguards the distinction between Creator and creature, and is the destiny of all Christians. Deification, moreover, is a social process. Christians are deified as individual members of the wider body of Christ. Deification is not accomplished alone or in isolation. For deification is intrinsically connected to love: for God and neighbor. And if no one is around to love, then how is one to grow in love, and experience the deifying grace of the Spirit?

Essence of the Spiritual Life

Before looking at the biblical images of the spiritual life, we should remind ourselves of the most important teaching on the spiritual life ever given. As a rabbi well versed in the Torah, Jesus highlighted two texts, indicating they were the essence and foundation of the law and prophets. Bringing together Deuteronomy 6:4 (known as the *Shema* in the Jewish tradition) and Leviticus 19:18, Jesus says:

> The first is, "Hear [*Shema*], O Israel: the Lord our God, the Lord is one; you shall love the Lord your God with all your heart, and with all your soul, and with all your mind, and with all your strength." The second is this, "You shall love your neighbor as yourself." There is no other commandment greater than these (Mark 12:29–31).

All-encompassing love for God and altruistic love for neighbor, these are *the* foci of the Christian spiritual life. Whatever models of the spiritual life we might utilize to help us grow in our relationship with God, these twin

---

18. Ware, *The Orthodox Church*, 236. Evangelical theologian Clark Pinnock agrees that the aim of Christian life is union with God: "The Spirit summons us to a transforming friendship with God that leads to sharing in the triune life... The purpose of life is a transforming friendship and union with God." Pinnock, *Flame of Love*, 150, 152.

commandments should remain at the forefront of our minds and the center of our practice.

For Augustine, these interconnected commandments serve as the primary hermeneutic or method of interpreting the Scriptures.[19] They also serve as the hermeneutic of the spiritual life: the goal, measurement, and litmus test for spiritual growth. In what ways are we cultivating love for God and neighbor? What practical steps are we taking, on a daily basis, to nurture love for God and others? Is our approach to the spiritual life founded on what is primary—love for God and neighbor —or some other secondary idea?

In his *Centuries on Love*, Maximus writes extensively about the radical love of God for human beings. Love is the reason God became human. Love is the way we share in the divine life, as we are transformed into the image of Christ. And the fruit of love, for God and others, is engendered in us by the work of the Holy Spirit. Maximus says, "The person who loves God cannot help but loving every man as himself..."[20] This is the essence of the spiritual life: receiving the love of God in Christ, responding to the love of God, and sharing that love with others. The next chapter continues this discussion as we explore historical models of spiritual growth.

---

19. Love "is the essential and supreme hermeneutical criterion in Augustinian exegesis," from the introduction to Augustine's *Teaching Christianity*, 21. Augustine writes: "So if it seems to you that you have understood the divine scriptures, or any part of them, in such a way that by this understanding you do not build up this twin love of God and neighbor, then you have not understood them." *Teaching Christianity*, 124.

20. Maximus the Confessor, *Philokalia* 2:54. Commenting on Maximus' teaching on love, Hans Urs von Balthasar writes: "Love for God and love for the world are not two different loves but two aspects of the one indivisible love." The one who loves "is the revelation in the world of God's hidden love." *Cosmic Liturgy*, 340.

CHAPTER 3.

Historical Models of Spiritual Development

"I write to you, children, because you know the Father. I write to you, fathers, because you know him who is from the beginning. I write to you, young people, because you are strong and the word of God abides in you, and you have overcome the evil one."
—1 John 2:14

"The Son of God cries out plainly that our union with him through communion is such as the unity and life which he has with the Father. Thus, just as he is united by nature to his own Father and God, so are we united by grace to him, and live in him, by eating his flesh and drinking his blood."
—Symeon the New Theologian, *The Third Ethical Discourse*

"Blessed is the man whose help is from you! . . . However many interior steps are set out, nothing will happen unless divine aid comes to our assistance."
—Bonaventure

"He who has repented travels towards the Lord. The way to God is an inner journey accomplished in the mind and heart."
—Theophan the Recluse, *The Art of Prayer*

THIS CHAPTER CONTINUES OUR reflection on biblical images and spiritual models that was started in the previous chapter. If you recall, we noted how pictures can help clarify concepts related to the spiritual life. This was illustrated through biblical images pertaining to spiritual life and other facets of our relationship with God, including the feast, journey, struggle, nuptial metaphor, and deification. Here we discuss three models of spiritual life development, from various times and traditions.

Three Models of Spiritual Growth

The first, often referred to as *the threefold way*, was popularized among the Desert Fathers and Mothers of the fourth and fifth centuries. It describes spiritual development in terms of a contemplative journey towards union with God. A second model is found in the book on prayer written by Teresa of Avila, *The Interior Castle* (1577). This model portrays spiritual progress as an inward odyssey of ever-increasing union with Jesus. A third was developed by Paul Ricoeur, a modern philosopher who described the spiritual journey in terms of entering into a *second naiveté*. This paradigm explains the way biblical texts are read and interpreted in three phases. Each phase reflects a stage of the spiritual life, from the childlike to the analytical and the mystical.

We could consider many other models, but I have chosen these three for a few reasons. For one, these paradigms represent understandings of spiritual development from three different historical periods: the ancient, medieval, and modern. Further, on a personal note, these models have deeply influenced and enriched my own spiritual life, especially as I struggled to make it through arid desert seasons, dark nights of the soul, and periods of doubt and disillusionment. Reading ways that others describe the spiritual journey, with all its ups and downs, can provide practical wisdom and encouragement.

While reflecting on these models, please keep in mind that our ultimate goal is deeper friendship with God. As we grow in this relationship, we grow in Christlikeness. We naturally become like those we spend time with. "We become what we love," as Clare of Assisi (1194–1253) said.[1] Sometimes it is easy to shift our focus onto things like spiritual paradigms, as we try to figure out "where we are" in the journey. Our aim is not progress according to a paradigm or model, but intimate friendship with the triune God: to grow in the grace of the Lord Jesus, the love of God, and the fellowship of the Holy Spirit (2 Cor 13:14). We are seeking to become more mature lovers of God and lovers of people. Keeping our eyes riveted on the Lord Jesus, the One who goes before us and beckons us to follow, we turn to the first model.

1. Plato said, "We become what we contemplate."

Historical Models of Spiritual Development

The Threefold Way: Evagrius and Maximus

Some early Christians portray the spiritual life in two basic stages. For example, two theologians from Alexandria, Clement (c. 150–215) and Origen (c. 185–254), view Martha and Mary (Luke 10:38–42) as symbols of the active life (*praxis* or *praktike*) and the contemplative life (*theoria*).[2] Origen builds further on this model, speaking of three stages of the contemplative life: *ethics*, *physics*, and *enoptics* or mystical theology. With his penchant for creative biblical interpretation, he links each stage with a book of the Bible: *ethics* with Proverbs, *physics* with Ecclesiastes, and *enoptics* or mystical theology with the Song of Songs. Meditation on each book, and implementing its wisdom, accordingly, leads to growth in a particular area of spiritual knowledge and practice.[3]

This threefold scheme is further developed by subsequent writers, particularly Evagrius of Pontus (346–399) and Maximus the Confessor.[4] Before considering them, two comments are in order. One is that within the historical contexts that Evagrius and Maximus were writing, contemplation was understood as a primary way of advancing in the spiritual journey towards union with God. Both Evagrius and Maximus were monks, fully devoted to the contemplative life. Secondly, according to Maximus, the threefold way occurs as one is involved in the sacramental life of the church. In fact, Maximus connects each of the three stages to the worship and practices of the church community.[5] Therefore, progress on the contemplative journey takes place in relationship to other Christians, not in isolation.

While this model speaks of three stages, it is more helpful to think of them as overlapping, interrelated spheres, rather than sequential steps. The first stage, *praktike*, involves the practice or active struggle to overcome negative spiritual forces and unruly passions. The mind (*nous*), as the chief contemplative organ, learns to conquer the temptations of sin and demons. Through prayer, repentance, fasting, and other ascetic exercises,

---

2. We reflect on the relationship between contemplation and action, as personified in Mary and Martha, in greater depth in chapter 12.

3. See the helpful exposition by Louth, *The Origins of the Christian Mystical Tradition*, 56ff.

4. On the threefold way, see: Ware, "Ways of Prayer and Contemplation"; Louth, *The Origins of the Christian Mystical Tradition*, 97–110; Konstantinovsky, *Evagrius Ponticus*, 47–52; and Thunberg, *Microcosm and Mediator*.

5. See Maximus the Confessor, "The Church's Mystagogy."

the passions are refined as they are redirected toward divine things rather than materialistic distractions, and the mind is purified. Through watchfulness over the inner movements of the heart, and prayer that draws from the grace and power of the indwelling Spirit, one is freed from the tyranny of the passions and ravished with love for God. A state of inner tranquility is attained. This purification of mind and heart, and the freedom and tranquility it brings, prepares the Christian for the next stage, though one must always continue the struggle of inner watchfulness.

The second stage, *physike*, is called natural contemplation. Natural contemplation involves the contemplation of God in the natural world. As the mind and heart are purified through meditation on the Scriptures and inner watchfulness, one is enabled to see God in and through all that God has made. The prayerful, contemplative eye is graced to see God in all things and all things in God (1 Cor 15:28). For the glory of the Lord fills the whole earth (Isa 6:3), the heavens declare the glory of God (Ps 19:1), and all of creation reveals the divine nature and power (Rom 1:20). Maximus says that the indwelling Spirit empowers Christians to discern the revelation of God in three realms: Scripture, the human person, and the cosmos. We will return to these three realms of revelation and contemplation in chapter 12.

Spiritual practices that purify the mind and heart enable a Christian to discern the beauty and power of God in creation. These steps, according to Evagrius and Maximus, lead to the third stage: *theologia*, a direct encounter with the living God. The contemplation of God in *creation* brings one face to face with the *Creator*. Here an *apophatic* (or negative) posture in theology and prayer is required.[6] Recognizing that God is beyond all language, concepts, and symbols, the Christian surrenders herself to the transcendent mystery of God. Evagrius explains:

> When you are praying, do not shape within yourself any image of the Deity, and do not let your mind be stamped with the impress of any form; but approach the Immaterial in an immaterial manner. . . . Prayer means the shedding of thoughts. . . . Blessed is the intellect that has acquired complete freedom from sensations during prayer.[7]

---

6. Regarding the apophatic approach (or negative way), see Ware, *The Orthodox Way*, 13–15, 121–22.

7. Evagrius, *On Prayer*, Philokalia 1:63, 64, 68.

As Kallistos Ware explains, "At the higher levels of contemplation, then, awareness of the subject-object differentiation recedes, and in its place there is only a sense of all-embracing unity." For "no verbal formula can contain the fullness of the transcendent mystery. In the realm of prayer it means that the mind is to be stripped of all images and concepts, so that our abstract concepts about God are replaced by the sense of God's immediate presence."[8]

This is what Gregory of Nyssa (c. 335–395) was getting at as he developed his own threefold model of the spiritual life. Based on the manifestations of God to Moses recorded in Exodus, Gregory speaks of three stages: the *light* of the burning bush (3:2), the *cloud* represented in the pillar of cloud and fire (13:21), and the *darkness* atop Mount Sinai (20:21). As one is brought higher into the contemplative experience of God, "Every concept grasped by the mind becomes an obstacle in their quest to those who search." The goal is to reach the summit of Sinai, to experience the Lord in ways beyond all words and symbols. As Gregory says, to attain "a certain sense of presence," for "the Bridegroom is present, but he is not seen."[9] Therefore, just as we noted at the beginning of the threefold way, the aim of this paradigm is purification, illumination, and union with God. We proceed now to another model of the spiritual life that speaks of a growing experience of union with the Bridegroom, *The Interior Castle*.

The Interior Castle: Teresa of Avila

Teresa of Avila, a Carmelite nun, was ordered by her confessor to write *The Interior Castle* (partly because he knew how helpful her spiritual insights were). At sixty-two years old, Teresa had learned much more about the mystical journey since completing her personal and spiritual reflections in her previous work, known as *Life* (or *The Life of Teresa*). Regarded by many as her most lucid and compelling work, *The Interior Castle* delineates "a cartography of the soul,"[10] which envisions the spiritual life as a passage through seven interior dwelling places. The first three dwelling places represent what can be attained through human effort with the ordinary help of divine grace. The remaining four dwelling places symbolize passive,

---

8. Ware, "Ways of Prayer and Contemplation," 399.

9. Gregory of Nyssa, *The Life of Moses*, in Ware, "Ways of Prayer and Contemplation," 399.

10. Hunt, *The Trinity*, 129.

mystical aspects of the spiritual life. In these four dwelling places, one experiences "supernatural prayer" or contemplation in all its various forms. "Perfect contemplation" speaks more specifically of a pure contemplation experienced in the final three dwelling places.[11] This will make more sense as you read Teresa's explanations.

Like the threefold model considered above, the point of the castle metaphor is to encourage readers to seek God more earnestly through prayer, not get lost in all the details, such as trying to discern which dwelling place they are in. The goal is to provide a model that illuminates the spiritual journey and offers practical advice on how to draw ever closer to the indwelling presence of Jesus. My aim is to introduce you to Teresa's illuminating model, to whet your appetite so that you might read her works for yourself. Of the three models we are considering, this is the lengthiest, so my overview and commentary may seem too detailed or extensive for some. If you find this segment too long, feel free to peruse it quickly or skip ahead to the next section on Ricoeur's second naiveté.

Teresa explains how she came up with the idea of using a castle to symbolize the inner life:

> Today while beseeching our Lord to speak for me because I wasn't able to think of anything to say, nor did I know how to begin to carry out this obedience [of writing this book], there came to my mind what I shall now speak about, that which will provide us with a basis to begin with. It is that *we consider our soul to be like a castle* made entirely out of a diamond or of very clear crystal, in which there are many rooms, just as in heaven there are many dwelling places.[12]

In her earlier work, the *Way of Perfection*, Teresa urges readers: "let us imagine that within us is an extremely rich palace, built entirely of gold and precious stones; in sum, built for a Lord such as this . . . Imagine, also, that *in this palace dwells this mighty King*."[13] For Teresa, the human soul is a dwelling place for the Lord Jesus, a temple of the Holy Spirit, where each of us is called into ever deepening communion.

---

11. The introduction to *The Interior Castle* by Kieran Kavanaugh is helpful and has informed my reflections, in *The Collected Works of Teresa of Avila*, Volume Two. The two volumes are excellent sources for the works of Teresa and insightful commentary.

12. Teresa, *The Interior Castle*, I, ch. 1, no. 1, p. 35.

13. Teresa, *The Way of Perfection*, ch. 28, no. 9, p. 268.

Historical Models of Spiritual Development

The First Dwelling Places

To embark on this inner journey, we must move beyond the outer wall of the castle, the body, into the castle of the soul, where each dwelling place opens into others, and leads ultimately to the inner chamber of the King. Teresa explains that "the door of entry to this castle is prayer and reflection" (I:1, 7). Entering the *first dwelling places* of the castle, a few glimmers of light from the king's royal chamber appear. Like rays from a distant light house, this beckons us, and begins to clarify the need to move beyond worldly things, and grow in self-knowledge, sin, and grace that beautifies the soul.

The Second Dwelling Places

Those who are responsive to the call to grow in prayer, self-knowledge, and humility, are enabled to move deeper inward, to the *second dwelling places*. The struggle with evil forces intensifies, so divine grace comes through various means to strengthen the soul. Teresa underscores the importance of learning from those experienced in prayer, not relying on "consolations" or spiritual delights, persisting in prayer, and embracing the cross of suffering as the will is conformed to God's will.

The Third Dwelling Places

In the *third dwelling places*, Teresa exhorts readers to regularly meditate on the Scripture, "Blessed is the one who fears the Lord" (Ps 112:1). Through the fear of the Lord, the goodness and mercy of God, and continual conversation with God through prayer, we move further through the dwelling places, towards the center, where the king's chamber resides. So that we more clearly understand our sin and need for divine mercy, "God withdraws His favor a little" (III.2). This creates deeper dependence on God. It also strips our reliance on reason, fears about health and material possessions, and cultivates humility. The notion of divine withdrawal sets the stage for the next dwelling places, where Teresa speaks of the difference between consolations and spiritual delights.

The Fourth Dwelling Places

The *fourth dwelling places* mark the transition to passive or infused contemplation, where one is drawn into ever-deepening stages of union with God by God's action alone.[14] Teresa explains that because "these dwelling places now are closer to where the King is, their beauty is great" (IV.2, 316). While it may seem that in order to get to these dwelling places, one may have to live in the others a long time, "there is no certain rule . . . For the Lord gives when He desires, as He desires, and to whom He desires. Since these blessings belong to Him, He does no injustice to anyone" (IV.2, 317).

In the transition to passive, infused, or mystical prayer, Teresa distinguishes between *consolations* and *spiritual delights*. Consolations are "those experiences we ourselves acquire through our own meditation and petitions to the Lord, those that proceed from our own nature—although God in the end does have a hand in them . . . without Him we can do nothing" (IV.4, 317). Spiritual delights are "supernatural" in that they "begin in God," are infused by God, and are not experienced as a result of efforts in prayer (IV.4, 318).

To clarify this distinction, Teresa uses an analogy of two founts with two water troughs. Consolations are like water that comes to us through aqueducts and the use of ingenuity. Spiritual delights are like an internal fountain that springs up within, overflowing the trough, and forming a large stream (IV.2, 323). The point Teresa makes is that, like the threefold model discussed earlier, certain practices help us clear the mind and heart, enable us to descend more deeply into the heart, and there encounter and experience union with the Lord who lives within us (see IV.3, 328: "God is within us . . . a gentle drawing inward"). Yet there are times in the spiritual life when torrents of God's love burst forth within our hearts. It is all the work of grace. We learn to surrender, to "leave the soul in God's hands," and "let Him do whatever He wants with it" (IV.3.6, 330).

The Fifth Dwelling Places

In the *fifth dwelling places*, Teresa reflects on the prayer of union. She explains that this "union is above all earthly joys, above all delights, above all consolations, and still more than that." At this stage, the experience of union with Jesus is felt "in the marrow of the bones," and the faculties

---

14. McGinn, ed., *The Essential Writings of Christian Mysticism*, 451ff.

become suspended or silent. The intellect is unable to fully understand this experience of union (V.1.6, 11 pp. 338, 340).

Employing another analogy, Teresa explains that the union of these dwelling places is like the metamorphosis of a silkworm. Beginning the size of a tiny seed, the silkworm spins and encloses itself in a cocoon. Undergoing something like death in the cocoon, in time the silkworm emerges as a beautiful butterfly. Therefore, through the help of God, diligent prayer, and embracing a life hidden in Christ, a mutual indwelling is realized. God dwells within the soul and the soul dwells in God. "How transformed the soul is when it comes out of this prayer after it has been placed within the greatness of God and so closely joined to Him for a little while—in my opinion the union never lasts for as much as a half hour" (V.2.7, p. 343).

Teresa explains, further, that entering these dwelling places is like the process of betrothal and marriage between a couple in love. In her day, before a couple got engaged, they met several times to interact and consider if there was any likeness between them and any chance for love. If they discovered these things were so, they met further to deepen their knowledge of each other. Likewise, in this spiritual betrothal and union, Christ and the Christlike soul commune with one another, and the soul longs to know him more, "enkindled in his love" (274; V.4.10, 358).

The Sixth Dwelling Places

The section on the *sixth dwelling places* is the longest in *The Interior Castle*. Again, we remember the point of her nuanced description: to encourage intimate communion with Jesus. Teresa begins by saying that, with the help of the Holy Spirit, she aims to discuss these dwelling places, "where the soul is now wounded with love for its Spouse and strives for more opportunities to be alone and, in conformity with its state, to rid itself of everything that can be an obstacle to this solitude" (VI.1.1, p. 359). In ardent pursuit of the spouse and king who dwells in the innermost places of the soul, Teresa urges readers to embrace the path and role of suffering. Not only is this an imitation of Christ, a walking in the steps of the Suffering Servant, but it is also an acknowledgment that suffering increases dependence on Jesus and a deeper desire to enjoy his presence (VI.4.1, p. 378), a theme we will consider in chapter 9.

Teresa proceeds to reflect on the mystical suffering of the "wounds of love." She explains that, like an arrow fired from the hand of God, divine love pierces the very depths of the soul. Pierced by God's ravishing love, God pulls out the arrow, "drawing these very depths after Him." Moreover, Teresa says that sparks of God's love leap forth and strike the soul, leaving it aflame with love for God. What is peculiar about this "pain" is that it is "delightful." As the soul is pierced and set aflame, it longs for deeper intimacy with God, and is prepared for encountering the king in subsequent dwelling places (VI.2.4, p. 368).[15]

The Seventh Dwelling Places

The *seventh dwelling places* describe the final stage in Teresa's vision of the inner life. As in all the dwelling places, it is *God* who reveals, gives grace, and brings about this union with Christ at the center of the soul. As Christ is exalted in the highest place in heaven, so he is found at the inmost part of the soul, in "a room where he dwells alone" (VII.1.3, p. 428). In the sixth dwelling places, the soul is made blind and deaf, like Paul in his mystical experience of Christ on the Road to Damascus (Acts 9:1–9). But in the seventh dwelling places, the faculties are no longer suspended. The scales are removed as one is brought into a most luminous place. Here we encounter the intellectual vision of the Trinity.

Further, "The Lord appears in this center of the soul . . . as He appeared to the apostles without entering through the door when He said to them *pax vobis* [peace to you]" (VII.2.3, p. 433). Teresa explains that this delightful vision of Christ and the Trinity in the extreme interior is overwhelming and ineffable. "What God communicates here to the soul in an instant is a secret so great and a favor so sublime—and the delight the soul experiences so extreme—that I don't know what to compare it to" (VII.2.3, p. 433).

---

15. Teresa also spends a good amount of time elucidating various mystical experiences that may occur in these dwelling places. She talks about raptures, ecstasy, locutions (or words spoken by God), and visions. One insight worth noting is the importance of discernment. Teresa explains that when God speaks to the soul or grants a mystical experience to a prayerful person, it must be "in close conformity with scripture." If it does not line up with the teachings of Scripture, then its source is not God, but the imagination or the devil (VI.3.4, p. 372). Another way to discern whether or not a mystical experience is from God is by evaluating the fruit it bears in one's life. Does the experience engender, among other Christlike characteristics, deep devotion to God, humility, peace of soul, or courage to serve God (VI.3-4, pp. 372–78)?

Yet, elaborating on the image she introduced in earlier dwelling places, Teresa says that what is experienced here is "spiritual marriage." The goal of this seven-stage journey is union with Christ. In the "spiritual betrothal" of previous dwelling places, union with Christ is like two wax candles joined together, sharing the wick, flame, and wax, yet may still be separated. In the spiritual marriage, union is like rain falling from the sky into a river, or like a little stream that enters the sea. There "is no means of separating the two" (VII.2.4, p. 434). However, these are metaphors. The distinction between Creator and creature always remains.

The Second Naiveté: Paul Ricoeur

Along with the threefold way developed by Origen, Evagrius, and Maximus, and *The Interior Castle* by Teresa, is a third model of spiritual development. Referred to as "the second naiveté" by scholars, it was devised by French philosopher Paul Ricoeur (1913–2005).[16] While the second naiveté is a post-critical[17] approach to the interpretation of biblical texts, it may also be understood as a working model of the spiritual life. In this approach, reading biblical texts is linked to "reading and practicing" the spiritual life. That is, the way one reads the Bible informs and indicates the way they live the Christian life. The three stages in this model are: the pre-critical, critical, and post-critical. Like the other models we considered, these three stages are interrelated, overlap each other, and are not to be understood as discrete steps. As with the other paradigms, the ultimate goal is deeper, experiential knowledge of God. This involves a shift from knowing about God to knowing God in more direct, personal ways.

The Pre-Critical Stage

The *pre-critical stage* is characterized by naive realism.[18] The focus is on the literal meaning of biblical texts. The stories are taken at face value, even those that pose serious ethical and logical questions. To illustrate, a child-like reader of the Bible may ask questions, when reading the story of Adam

---

16. On the second naiveté, see Ricoeur, "Conclusion."

17. In short, post-critical is a term that signifies responses to critical approaches to knowledge that emphasize suspicion and doubt that were popular with René Descartes and subsequent Enlightenment thinkers. See Poteat, *Polanyian Meditations*.

18. See the informative article by Jansons, "What is the Second Naiveté?"

and Eve: What do you think Adam and Eve looked like? Or when reading the story of Noah's ark: How did Noah fit all those animals on the boat, and do you think the ark may one day be found on Mount Ararat? At this stage, the poetic and metaphorical nature of the biblical text may be acknowledged, but the real focus is on its literal, factual, and historical aspects.

The pre-critical stage may also be characterized by the need of the reader to "defend" the text, perhaps motivated by the notion of biblical inerrancy and infallibility. However, pre-critical faith "is by no means fundamentalism, although it can become so. But it is better described as innocent or naïve realism. The word naïve, far from being pejorative, simply acknowledges that most of the time we live within the Christian faith without interrogating it."[19] This view of the Bible often translates into how God, the world, and the spiritual life are viewed. God is involved in every tiny detail of life.[20] And walking with God through life tends to be a rather black and white affair, rather than acknowledging situations that may be gray or ambiguous.

The Critical Stage

Moving to the *critical stage*, we transition from a childlike, naive realism to a more analytical perspective. When reading the Bible, new questions and concerns emerge. The critical stage is characterized by distance between the biblical world and the reader's contemporary world. This distance is often increased by exposure to critical or analytical scholarship on the Bible. Reading the Bible in an academic context or manner leads some to shift from a hermeneutic of certainty to a hermeneutic of suspicion. "In place of naïve acceptance, we now inquire about causes, processes, motivations, agendas, biases, hidden meanings, and the like."[21]

Dealing with the same two stories in Genesis referenced previously, new questions are asked: How do we interpret the Genesis accounts of

---

19. Jansons, "What is the Second Naiveté?," 2.

20. We are talking about something other than a balanced perspective on the sovereignty of God. God is involved in our lives, but at this stage, some may attribute God's involvement (or lack of it) in nonsensical ways. For example, I remember hearing someone tell a story about a Christian who "knew" they were supposed to be at the mall that day because a good parking spot opened up close to the door. It seems more likely that God would be involved in moving our hearts to give to the poor than to open parking spots at the mall.

21. Jansons, "What is the Second Naiveté?," 2.

Historical Models of Spiritual Development

creation or a flood in light of other ancient cosmogonies or flood stories like *Enuma Elish* or *The Epic of Gilgamesh*? In what ways have the biblical authors appropriated and adjusted elements of these ancient myths in order to convey their own theological messages? Further, how are we to understand difficult texts like the command for Joshua to utterly destroy the city of Jericho and all that is in it (or place it under the ban, *herem* in Hebrew, as in Joshua 6:17)? How can a God of love or a God who prohibits murder of human beings made in the image of God command such a thing? Taking these passages at face value may present challenging problems. A more nuanced or sophisticated method of interpretation is needed in order to answer difficult questions like these.

In the critical stage, the challenges of "reading" life (along with biblical texts), walking with God, and discerning God's activity in the world pose equally difficult questions. Unlike the tendency toward a black and white view of the world in the pre-critical stage, here one understands that some things exist in the ambiguous gray zone.[22]

The Post-Critical Stage

What follows is the *post-critical stage*. As you can imagine, there are various responses from those who are in the previous critical stage. Some never move beyond the critical stage. They are swallowed up by their doubts and questions. Their faith evaporates in the desert of criticism. Others manage to preserve their faith. Somehow they navigate the desert of criticism, working through the challenges of critical inquiry, drawing strength from a pre-critical oasis of personal faith. Still others, who have not fully maintained a pre-critical oasis of faith, traverse the desert of criticism, come to its edge, and long for something more. Feeling the effects of the sandy expanse, they "wish to be called again . . . beyond the desert of criticism," as Ricoeur says.

In the post-critical stage, the way we read the Bible has changed, along with our relationship with God. Mark I. Wallace, a scholar who studied with Ricoeur, says of the second naiveté: "After passing through, but never around the first innocence of original understanding and the desert trial of rigorously examining the text's parts, the reader is asked to risk reading the text critically and naively once more—to become adult critic and naïve

---

22. This does not suggest a shift into relativism, but a growing awareness of the complexities of certain biblical texts, life situations, and decisions.

child . . ."²³ Reading passages about Adam and Eve, Noah, and others, we no longer solely have the pre-critical or critical mind-set. We are now adult critics and naïve children, at the same time.

The residue or effects of the critical stage remain, but we enter into something different. Gone are the childlike, pre-critical questions and interpretations about Adam and Eve and Noah's ark. So are the all too often immobilizing questions and suspicions of the critical stage; at least their powerful grip has diminished. We now read the Bible with more mature eyes, faith that has been deeply challenged, and a fresh perspective. The world of the Bible beckons us once again. This time we understand that texts about Adam and Eve and Noah's ark are invitations to encounter God, to search out and be searched by God, and to ponder questions about our relationship to God, one another, and the community of creation.

As Ricoeur says, the rich symbols of the Bible serve as "hierophanies" or manifestations of the bond between human beings and the sacred.²⁴ The Bible, like an icon, is a symbol that points to a greater reality, to the mystery of God. It is a window through which the transcendent glory of God shines upon us, infusing our hearts with divine immanence and love. In short, the written Word becomes the means through which the living Word comes to us.²⁵

Thus, the hermeneutical and spiritual journeys are intrinsically connected. The way we read and interpret the Bible is often reflected in the way we read and live the spiritual life, and vice versa. As Ricoeur's model illustrates, the spiritual journey is often characterized by painful progression from the childlike realism of the pre-critical to (and hopefully through) the desert of criticism to the second naiveté of the post-critical. This insightful model offers much wisdom for our spiritual journeys. Knowing that we can indeed make it through desert seasons, even if at times we are crawling with our parched tongues hanging out, we take courage. The voice of the Lord can be heard, calling us beyond the desert. In the next chapter, we consider the importance of spirituality rooted in rich theological reflection. A theologically grounded spirituality, as we will see, helps sustain us through various seasons of life in God.

---

23. Wallace, *The Second Naiveté*, xiv–xv.
24. Ricoeur, *The Symbolism of Evil*, 356.
25. There are examples of this in the spiritual and theological classics, from Origen to Karl Barth. The Scriptures are understood as a sacrament, a means by which Christians encounter the living God.

CHAPTER 4.

Theologically Grounded Spirituality

"Let the word of Christ dwell in you richly..."
—Col 3:16

"The Bible is an entire universe, it is a mystical organism, and it is only partially that we attain to living in it... The Bible is a heavenly constellation, shining above us eternally while we move on the sea of human existence. We gaze at the constellation, and it remains fixed, but it is also constantly changing its place in relation to us."
—Sergius Bulgakov, *The Orthodox Church*

"Christ is not a text but a living person..."
—Georges Florovsky, *Collected Works*, vol. 1: *Bible, Church, Tradition*

"Tradition means the handing down of Christian teaching during the course of the history of the church, but it also means that which was handed down.... Tradition is the living faith of the dead; traditionalism is the dead faith of the living."
—Jaroslav Pelikan, *The Christian Tradition: Emergence of the Catholic Tradition (100–600)*

"I have found that it is not possible to read the church fathers without the Bible open before me. The words of the Scriptures crowd the pages of their books and essays, and their arguments often turn on specific terms or phrases from the Bible."
—Robert Louis Wilken, *The Spirit of Early Christian Thought*

> "Theology, as dialogue between bride and Bridegroom in the unity and communication of the Spirit, continually brings to light new modes of union and interpretation."
> —Hans Urs von Balthasar, *Theology and Sanctity*

A LUMINOUS LIFE, AS we saw in the two previous chapters, is informed by prayerfully studying various images and models of spiritual life and development found in the Scriptures and Christian classics. In this chapter, we will see that a luminous life entails a *theologically grounded spirituality*.

If theology is, simply put, reflection on God in the presence of God, then theology and spirituality are unified endeavors. As Hans Urs von Balthasar (1905–1988) says in the quote above, theology is a dialogue between the church and Jesus, an intimate conversation in the Spirit that deepens union, understanding, and insight into the things of God. A life illumined by this communion between the bride and Bridegroom is one that is consistently nourished on the spiritual theology of our rich Christian heritage. Unfortunately, for some Christians today, spirituality and theology are separated, rather than mutually enhancing one another in our life with God.

After briefly discussing how this separation occurred, particularly in the West, we will explore ways that we can rediscover the more unified spiritual theology of ancient Christians. Further, we will consider classic sources and guidelines of Christian theology and spirituality, including: Scripture, tradition, reason, and experience.

Theology and Spirituality: Divided or United?

Catholic scholars Sandra M. Schneiders and Hans Urs von Balthasar have studied the history of theology and spirituality that spans the past two thousand years and noted a troubling division in certain circles of Western Christianity between theology and spirituality.

Early Christians: unified endeavor

For early Christians, from Paul and other biblical writers to roughly the eleventh century, theology and spirituality were entwined, united, and essentially one endeavor. To engage in *theology*, reflection on God in the presence of God, entailed *spirituality*, life in the Holy Spirit. When Paul or Augustine or the Desert Fathers and Mothers engaged in reflection on the nature and ways of God, they naturally included how these ideas are integrated in the life of a disciple, one who is filled with and walks with the Holy Spirit. Doctrine and discipleship, dogma and doxology, teaching and practice, thinking and worship, theology and spirituality—these were inseparable. As Evagrius succinctly put it, "If you are a theologian, you will pray truly. And if you pray truly, you are a theologian."[1] According to Evagrius and the desert tradition, theology and prayer, prayer and theology, were interrelated activities.

So, according to Balthasar, Schneiders, and other Christian historians, what went wrong? When and why did this separation or drift between theology and spirituality begin to occur? These are complex questions that require detailed historical examination that would take us off our overall course. At the risk of oversimplifying their thorough observations and nuanced arguments, let me briefly summarize what I think are some key points.[2]

Unity maintained

For the early medieval theologians in the West, as with Augustine and others who preceded them, the unity of theology and spirituality was maintained. Anselm of Canterbury (c. 1033–1109), a leading figure in the scholastic theology of the Middle Ages, was a bishop and doctor of the church. His rigorous intellectual activity was part of his service to God and the church, and instructing others in the practices of the spiritual life. This was also the case with Bernard of Clairvaux (1090–1153), Peter Damian (1007–72), and Thomas Aquinas (1225–74), the most prominent figure of scholasticism, who played a critical role in the rediscovery of Aristotelian philosophy.

A shift

A shift, however, began with Thomas, as theology increasingly took on a scholastic form. Through the application of Aristotelian philosophy to theology (and other fields), the gains in clarity, insight, and mastery were

---

1. *Philokalia* 1:61, 63.

2. Balthasar describes this separation in his bracing essay, "Theology and Sanctity." His insights have informed my thoughts here.

significant. Augustine suggested that "the spoils of Egypt" belonged to the people of God.[3] Appropriating true knowledge and wisdom, no matter where they are found in the world, was the prerogative of Christian thinkers. Thomas was simply utilizing the "spoils or booty" of Aristotelian philosophy. Applying these philosophical tools and insights engendered significant changes for the discipline of theology.

New tensions

Further, philosophy emerged with great vigor as a special discipline alongside theology. Balthasar asserts, "[T]he Aristotelianism of the thirteenth century did not only enlarge the basis of theology, it was itself the start of the modern sciences of nature and mind as independent disciplines, and rightly so." It also "gave birth to modern 'secularism,' and thereby introduced new tensions and set new problems to the Christian."[4] Thus, there were benefits and drawbacks to the study and practice of theology, and its relationship to spirituality, as a result of scholasticism. For Thomas, the study of theology and the practice of spirituality were unified. There was no division. He would not have approved of formally separating the two. Theology and spirituality were inseparable.

Separate spheres

However, influenced by Thomas's proclivity for categorizing and systematizing, future theologians witnessed the separation of theology and spirituality into separate spheres. "Theology and spirituality have become, as it were, each a world of its own, with hardly any point of contact . . ."[5] Schneiders comments: "In the thirteenth century Thomas Aquinas divided his great theological synthesis, the *Summa Theologiae*, into three parts: Part I dealing with God as first principle; Part II dealing with God as last end of creation including humans; and Part III on the Incarnate Word as the way to the end." Therefore, Thomas "established the divisions of theology as they would be understood until Vatican II (1962-65): dogma, moral, and christology." He "put most of what he had to say about the Christian life

---

3. Augustine, *Teaching Christianity*, ch. 40, sections 60–61.
4. Balthasar, "Theology and Sanctity," 184.
5. Balthasar, "Theology and Sanctity," 191.

Theologically Grounded Spirituality

in Part II of the *Summa*, thus effectively establishing what would be later called spiritual theology or spirituality as a division of moral theology. And thus the situation has remained until very recent times."[6]

Eventual separation

The point here is to highlight the fact that this eventual separation of theology and spirituality occurred, not to blame any particular person or movement for it. Furthermore, our aim is to consider remedies to the problem. For many Christians are tired of "the bones without the flesh" or the "flesh without the bones." As we know, the study of theology without the practice of spirituality can become dry, while the study of spirituality without theological grounding can become like eating a kind of "porridge . . . that is indigestible through lack of substance."[7] In our day, there is a growing desire to amend the problem of "theology at prayer" that was superseded by "theology at the desk."[8] The spirituality of a luminous life seeks to combine the rigorous study of theology with the robust practice of the spiritual life. In the words of the Orthodox theologian Vladimir Lossky (1903–58), what we seek is "a spirituality which expresses a doctrinal attitude."[9] Revisiting some of the sources of classic spirituality will inform and inspire us in our pursuit.

The Quadrilateral

Old Testament example

Four main sources and guidelines for Christian theology and spirituality are Scripture, tradition, reason, and experience. These four sources also serve as guidelines for theology and spirituality. Biblical scholar F. F. Bruce (1910–1990) says that at an early stage in the transmission of the biblical text, during the time of Ezra (c. fifth or fourth century BCE), we can identify these sources: reading from the law of God, interpreting it, and giving the sense of it, so the people understood its reading (Neh 8:1–12). Bruce explains that here "we can recognize the threefold cord: Scripture;

---

6. Schneiders, "Theology and Spirituality."
7. Balthasar, "Theology and Sanctity," 193.
8. Balthasar, "Theology and Sanctity," 208.
9. Lossky, *The Mystical Theology of the Eastern Church*, 7.

interpretive tradition (incipient, but already necessary); reason (apart from which neither text nor interpretation could have been understood). The pattern then established retains its validity today."[10] I would add that *experience* is also present in the passage: the people are physically engaged, standing up, raising their hands, bowing in worship with their faces to the ground, and moved in their affections, weeping and rejoicing at the reading of the law. It is a holistic experience of the revelation of God through Scripture, one that illumines the mind, engages the body, and stirs the affections.

Further development

Among Anglicans and Methodists, these four sources are known as the quadrilateral, which literally means "four sides." Based on the image of the four "fortress cities" of Lombardy (in Northern Italy), the quadrilateral suggests that Christian teaching and practice are to be constructed within a fourfold fortress. Methodist theologians explain: "Wesley believed that the living core of the Christian faith was revealed in Scripture, illumined by tradition, vivified in personal experience, and confirmed by reason."[11] Thomas Oden (1931–2016), the aforementioned Methodist scholar well known for promoting reflection on classic Christian sources, adds that divine revelation "empowers and requires a written word (Scripture), a remembering community (tradition), an appropriation process (experience), and internal consistency (reason)."[12] The quadrilateral underscores the unity and symbiotic relationship between these four sources. Each of these is a means to deepen our knowledge of the triune God, to cultivate Christlike character in community, to grow in our love for God and neighbor, and to cooperate with the Holy Spirit in the *missio Dei* or mission of God. The four sources elucidate the person and work of Christ, who is the revealed Word. The following helps picture this.[13]

---

10. Bruce, "Scripture in Relation to Tradition and Reason," 64.

11. *The Book of Discipline of The United Methodist Church, 1996*, ¶68, p. 74, in Oden, *Systematic Theology*, I:333.

12. Oden, *Systematic Theology*, I:333.

13. This grid is found in Oden, *Systematic Theology*, I:331.

CHRIST	SCRIPTURE	TRADITION	EXPERIENCE	REASON
The Revealed Word	Written Word	Remembered Word	Personally Experienced Word	Word Made Intelligible

Each of the sources helps to explain the saving work of God in Christ, implement it within the life of the church, and serve as a guideline for theological reflection and practice.

Scripture

Theo-drama

The Bible is a record of divine revelation, and is regarded as holy Scripture by Christians of various traditions and denominations. The word *Bible* (*biblia* in Greek) literally means "books." It is a library or collection of books that narrate the story of God's creative and salvific activity in history. Some theologians refer to the overall story of the Bible as a "theo-drama," an account of the actions of God and the human responses, from creation to the making of "all things new."[14] Christian spirituality is deeply rooted in the divine-human drama of Scripture, and draws us into it. Christian spirituality is a Logo-centric endeavor. Its focus is on the saving work of God in Christ, the living Word who comes to us through the pages of the written Word.[15]

Norming norm

In the Christian spiritual classics, the Word of God is central. In the quadrilateral, it is first for a reason. The Word is primary and uniquely authoritative. It is the "norming norm," as some theologians say. It is the inspired record of how the people of God have struggled to keep covenant with the God of Abraham, Isaac, Jacob, and Jesus. As we see in the New Testament, Jesus and the apostles were "people of the book." Their lives were

---

14. For example, see Balthasar, *Theo-Drama I*; and Vanhoozer, *The Drama of Doctrine*.
15. Burton-Christie, "The Luminous Word," 75.

suffused with Scripture. This set the example for followers of Jesus in every generation.

Source and foundation

Robert Wilken, a specialist in early Christianity, says that authors of the Christian classics "turn always to the Bible as the source of their ideas." No matter how rigorous, abstruse, or complex their thinking is—as when discussing the nuances of trinitarian doctrine in the second and third centuries—"Christian thinkers always begin with specific biblical texts." Wilken adds: "I have found that it is not possible to read the church fathers without the Bible open before me. The words of the Scriptures crowd the pages of their books and essays, and their arguments often turn on specific terms or phrases from the Bible."[16] Our approach to Christian spirituality, guided by the classic Christian authors, is established on the foundational teachings of the Bible. The ancient wisdom of the Bible shows us how to live in our modern world as disciples of Jesus who are guided by the Holy Spirit.

Written Word, living Word

Yet the luminous life, a life centered on the Word of God, is not ultimately about a relationship with a book. John 1 explains that Jesus himself is the Word (*logos* in Greek). Through his incarnation, he embodies the revelation of divine truth and love.[17] As the classical writers suggest, the *written* Word is intended to bring us into vital contact with the *living* Word. "For Christ is not a text but a Living Person . . ."[18] Maximus the Confessor actually warns against a subtle danger when reading the Bible. One can read the Bible and "unwittingly receive not God but things appertaining to God." One can "feel a dangerous affection for the words of Scripture instead of for the Logos [Christ himself]."[19] With a bit of wit, Maximus says the Logos will elude those who think they have "grasped the incorporeal Logos by means of His outer garments, like the Egyptian woman who seized hold of

---

16. Wilken, *The Spirit of Early Christian Thought*, 26.

17. John 1:18 says that as the Word, Jesus has explained (*exēgesato*) the Father to us. He is the "exegesis" of the Father, relating, declaring, and explaining (in his own person) who the Father is.

18. Georges Florovsky cited in McGuckin, *The Orthodox Church*, 93.

19. *Philokalia* 2:155.

Joseph's garments instead of Joseph himself" (cf. Gen 39:7–13).[20] Readers of Scripture are encouraged to focus on the Logos within and beyond the text; otherwise, they will find that the Logos himself has slipped away.

Aim of Scripture

Karl Barth (1886–1968) shared a similar idea when he confronted his fellow Protestant theologians for their "biblicism" and "bibliolatry."[21] Barth said that many Protestants failed to discern the difference between the Logos and the logos, or the Word as the revelation of God and the Bible as the record of that revelation. This failure to distinguish between the two elevated the Bible onto the same plane as God, creating a "Fourth Person" of the Trinity. The aim of Scripture is to reveal the glory of God in Christ through the power of the Holy Spirit. To simply read, study, or be enamored with the biblical text, without engaging God, is to miss the point. It is like obsessing over a biography when the person about whom it is written is standing outside the door, ready to come in and have a conversation.[22]

Avenue to intimacy

Jesus said that the expert interpreters of Scripture in his day were misguided. They searched the Scriptures thinking that in them they had eternal life. It was not the writings that give life, but Jesus, to whom the Scriptures pointed (John 5:39–40). As Kallistos Ware explains:

> The real purpose of Bible study is much more than [analyzing and gathering information]—to feed our love for Christ, to kindle our hearts into prayer, and to provide us with guidance in our personal life. The study of the words should give place to an immediate dialogue with the living Word himself. "Whenever you read the Gospel," says St. Tikhon of Zadonsk, "Christ himself is speaking to you. And while you read, you are praying and talking with him."[23]

---

20. *Philokalia* 2:155.

21. See also Karl Rahner's caution against biblicism, *Foundations of Christian Faith*, 14.

22. See my "Scripture as Divine Mystery," 109–10.

23. Ware, *The Orthodox Way*, 111.

If we seek to go deep in God and become more like Jesus, we know that this means prayerfully reading, studying, meditating upon, and practicing Scripture. It is a life-giving source of spiritual wisdom and power, a vital means of conversing with God. The Bible is an avenue to intimacy with God. Reading Scripture is both informational and formational. We will talk more about this in the coming chapters.

Tradition

Remembered Word

A second source and guideline for Christian theology and spirituality is *tradition*. While Scripture is the *written* Word, tradition is the *remembered* Word. For some Christians, especially Protestants suspicious of Catholic or Orthodox teaching, tradition is an ambiguous or misunderstood concept.[24] They think of tradition as something stale, dead, potentially misleading, or something altogether separate from Scripture. But this is a misunderstanding. For Scripture itself is tradition: the faith and practice which Jesus Christ taught the Apostles, and which has been "handed down" (Latin, *traditio*) from generation to generation in the church.[25] Oden explains that Scripture is a result of oral tradition, the teaching of the early church before it was written down:

> It is difficult to distinguish between Scripture and tradition since Scripture itself is a product of oral tradition, taken, like a still photo of a moving picture, and frozen at one crucial point, so that the heretofore oral witness could be transmitted to subsequent generations. The unwritten oral tradition was a preached word, a teaching of the living church prior to the writing down of New Testament Scripture. As such it is surely not less valid than the

---

24. See Lane, "Scripture, Tradition, and Church."

25. F. F. Bruce discusses the unfortunate tendency among some Western Christians to think of Scripture and tradition as two distinct entities. He says that for Eastern Christians, "tradition has a more comprehensive sense, approximating to its New Testament usage: it embraces practically everything that goes to make up Christian life and thought, and is indistinguishable from the abiding witness of the Spirit. In this indivisible tradition Scripture occupies a leading place. This tradition is not simply that which has been handed down from the past: it retains its vitality in the present, as the Spirit continues to give substance to the gospel and pours the love of God into the hearts of believers." In "Scripture in Relation to Tradition and Reason," 37; cf. Ware, *The Orthodox Church*, 196, 215.

written word, although it remains less accessible to us precisely because it is not written down.[26]

Transmitting apostolic teaching

Further, it was critical that the oral tradition be recorded in written form. Since the accounts of Jesus' life and teaching were written years after his death, the oral traditions preserved and kept them alive until they were written down. The "written tradition emerged only when the oral tradition was in danger of losing some of its immediacy and authority through the impending deaths of the eyewitnesses." It was the written tradition that "made the revelation more exact and transmissible to subsequent generations through a continuous succession of ministries of preaching and teaching."[27] This clarifies why the New Testament itself underscores the importance of carefully transmitting the apostolic teaching. Jesus told the disciples that the Spirit would guide them into all the truth (John 16:13), and that they were to teach other disciples to obey all that he had taught them (Matt 28:19–20). Paul handed down the tradition that had been imparted to him: that Christ died for our sins, in accordance with the Scriptures (1 Cor 15:3). Paul exhorts Timothy and other leaders to steward, preserve, and pass along what had been entrusted to them (1 Tim 6:20–21; 1 Cor 4:1–2).

Scripture: preeminent tradition

Therefore, Scripture forms a part of tradition and exists within tradition. All too often, in Protestant and other circles, the two are separated and contrasted. One reason for this separation is the issue of authority, but venturing into that debate would take us off course.[28] Yet there is, as Christians from various churches agree, something unique and authoritative about Scripture. As Ware explains: "Among the various elements of Tradition, a unique pre-eminence belongs to the Bible . . ."[29] Ware, representative of

---

26. Oden, *Systematic Theology*, I:345.

27. Oden, *Systematic Theology*, I:345.

28. For those interested in reading more about the relationship between Scripture and tradition, and the debate over authority, see the various chapters in Bauckham and Drewery, eds., *Scripture, Tradition, and Reason*, as well as the brief reflection by Webber, *Ancient-Future Faith*, 180–82.

29. Ware, *The Orthodox Church*, 197.

the Orthodox Church, along with Catholics, Anglicans, and others, would also view the Nicene-Constantinopolitan Creed and seven Ecumenical Councils as crucial parts of tradition. But the foundation of these sources is Scripture, so it is understood as pre-eminent.[30] Scripture is "one of the purest manifestations of tradition" and is greater in importance and richness than other writings of the saints. However, we must remember that "the church existed before it actually had a recognized New Testament, and the evangelical writings themselves were the first outflowings of the Holy Tradition presided over by the Spirit of God."[31]

Tradition: living and creative

Tradition, therefore, includes the Scriptures, but in the broader sense, it entails the apostolic teaching faithfully handed down through creeds, councils, and the church's liturgical worship. As the remembered Word, tradition continually reminds the church of who the triune God is and all that God the Father, Son, and Holy Spirit have done and continue to do in human history. Tradition, accordingly, is not dead but living. It is not like a fossil to observe behind glass at a museum, but an organic and dynamic way of life, rooted in the teachings of Jesus and the apostles. "Tradition is living and creative: it is the new in the old, and the old in the new."[32] Tradition "is not static but dynamic, not defensive but exploratory, not closed and backward-facing but open to the future."[33] The ancient wisdom of Scripture, preserved and handed down over the centuries, is always fresh: "Tradition is Scripture applied to human life, Scripture made contemporary."[34] As McGuckin asserts: Christian tradition is not hanging on to the "customs of men," but passion for the word of the Lord. Tradition is not past-looking only. Tradition

> bases its claims to authenticity on the fact that it speaks the words of Christ in the here and now, faithful to his own Spirit; but as

---

30. Cf. Augustine, *City of God*, cited in Bauckham and Drewery, eds., *Scripture, Tradition, and Reason*, 211.

31. McGuckin, *The Orthodox Church*, 101.

32. Bulgakov, cited in McGuckin, *The Orthodox Church*, 97.

33. Ware, *The Inner Kingdom*, 9. He adds: Tradition "is not merely a formal repetition of what was stated in the past, but is an active reexperiencing of the Christian message in the present."

34. Ware, foreword to Staniloae, *Orthodox Dogmatic Theology*, xvii.

much as it looks to the past and stands in unbroken continuity with it, thus "passing on" the Gospel of life (which is the root meaning of the word "tradition"), it also looks to the future. The Tradition is the Spirit's energy of proclaiming the Gospel and energizing the church's worship and knowledge of God in the present generation, and for future generations to come. [Tradition is] essentially charismatic, and alive, and full of the power and freshness of the Spirit of God, concerned with bringing new generations to Christ until the end of time . . .[35]

As the remembered Word, tradition is "the process of the church's advancement into the Life of Christ." It is "the record of a whole people's long pilgrimage towards God across the desert horizons of a long history, as well as a compass for keeping the right course for the future."[36] The Christian tradition then, including the entire canon of Scripture, recounts and preserves the story of the people of God.

Experience

Personally experienced Word

Christ is the revealed Word. Scripture is the written Word. Tradition is the remembered Word. This brings us to the third source and guideline of Christian spirituality: *experience* or the personally experienced Word. Scripture and tradition are passed on to remind us of who God is, who we are, and who God has called us to become in Christ. A theologically grounded spirituality views Scripture and tradition as an invitation to *experience* firsthand the grace of the Lord Jesus, the love of God, and the fellowship of the Holy Spirit (2 Cor 13:14).

Scripture, tradition, and experience coincide and complement one another. "It is misleading to pit tradition against experience, for tradition is simply the memory of this vast arena of social and historical experiencing." For there "is a profound affinity and synchronicity between corporate tradition and personal experience . . ." Christian tradition suggests that what "was once someone else's experience can become part of my own experience. Christian teaching seeks to enable this corporate experiencing to become personally validated and authenticated as 'one's own.'"[37]

---

35. McGuckin, *The Orthodox Church*, 90–91.
36. Florovsky, *Collected Works*, vol. 1, 14; McGuckin, *The Orthodox Church*, 102.
37. Oden, *Systematic Theology*, I:338.

Further, Scripture and tradition invite us into a corporately remembered experience. This remembering as a community is to be personally appropriated, to inform and form our thoughts and feelings. "The integration of the tradition into one's own feeling process most powerfully occurs in worship." This is the aim of corporate celebration. "Christian teaching does not simply reflect on corporate memory as an abstract or distant datum, but, rather seeks to integrate social memory congruently within one's own feelings."[38] When we worship, we are connected with worshippers who have gone before us: Abraham and Sarah, David, Anna, Mary, believers under the tongues of fire at Pentecost. We enter into this rich history of worship. Their worship inspires ours. Their experiences of the presence, love, and power of God become ours.

Validation and evaluation

This "does not imply, however, that personal experience may unilaterally judge and dismiss Scripture and tradition. Scripture and tradition are received, understood, and validated through personal experience, but not judged or arbitrated or censored by it." On the contrary, "Scripture and tradition amid the living, worshiping community are the means by which and context in which one's personal experiences are evaluated as 'of God's family.'"[39] Thus, Scripture and tradition invite us into communion with God and one another. This communion is both personal and experiential. As the temple of the Holy Spirit, collectively and individually, we experience an ongoing Pentecost. At the same time, the indwelling Holy Spirit guides and teaches us, so that we worship in Spirit and truth. In line with the teachings of Jesus, the apostles, and the early church, Christian spirituality is, therefore, biblical, traditional, and experiential.

Reason

Word made intelligible

Scripture, tradition, and experience evince the written, remembered, and experienced Word. A fourth essential source and guideline for Christian

---

38. Oden, *Systematic Theology*, I:338.
39. Oden, *Systematic Theology*, I:339.

spirituality is *reason*: the Word made intelligible.[40] Robust Christian spirituality is fueled by rigorous theological reflection. Theology and spirituality, as we are seeing, are unified not separate activities. Theology is reflection on God in the presence of God. Spirituality is life in, with, and by the Holy Spirit. Some misunderstand these things, thinking that reason or critical analysis is somehow bracketed out or perhaps suppressed in the spiritual quest. To be sure, we encounter profound mysteries in our spiritual journeys. The triune God is the supreme mystery of the Christian faith. "God cannot be grasped by the mind. If he could be grasped, he would not be God."[41]

However, as the fourth wall of the quadrilateral fortress, reason urges "the critical analysis of all that has been asserted in order to avoid self-contradiction, to take appropriate account of scientific and historical knowledge." As Tertullian (c. 155–c. 240), the Latin father who lived in Carthage, the Roman province of Africa, says, "God is rational, and Reason was first in him . . ."[42] Therefore, employing reason is an integral part of our quest for God. Reason enables us "to credit appropriately new information and empirical data, and to try to see the truth as a whole and not as disparate parts or incongruently separable insights."[43] The pursuit of God, which involves the diligent study of God, "is a cohesive, rational task of thinking out of revelation, yet in thinking it does not cease being active faith." Believers "need not disavow the gifts of intellect in giving thought to their Giver."[44] In fact, Justin Martyr (100–165), the early Christian apologist, asserts that Christians honor Jesus Christ "in accordance with reason." Augustine of Hippo (354–430), explains that a "good will" involves a will to live rightly and honorably and to reach the highest wisdom. Bonaventure (1221–1274), the Italian Franciscan theologian and philosopher, speaks of the importance of intellective power and reason in the pursuit of truth.[45]

---

40. Rebekah L. Miles suggests that reason is more properly understood as a *tool*, not a source. She provides two helpful word pictures: reason as a highly sophisticated computer processing program, and reason as pickaxe. Her essay is helpful: "The Instrumental Role of Reason."

41. Evagrius of Pontus, cited in Ware, *The Orthodox Way*, 11.

42. Tertullian, *Against Praxeas* 5, in *The Ante-Nicene Fathers* III, p. 600; cf. Cassian, NPNF 2 XI, 295–318.

43. Oden, *Systematic Theology*, I:339.

44. Oden, *Systematic Theology*, I:339.

45. Justin Martyr, in Cross, ed., *The Early Christian Fathers*, 249; Augustine, in *Augustine: Earlier Writings*, 127; cf. Bonaventure, in *Breviloquium*, 96.

Theologically grounded spirituality involves faith that seeks to understand itself, "a faith that is in search of its own intrinsic intelligibility, yet that respects mystery and knows of its own limits." Christian spirituality "lives out of a community of faith that does not hesitate to ask serious questions about itself."[46] Among communities of faith, deep questioning and even doubt are to be welcomed, not resisted. Kallistos Ware explains: "It is by no means impossible for faith to coexist with doubt. The two are not mutually exclusive." There may be some "who by God's grace retain throughout their life the faith of a little child, enabling them to accept without question all that they have been taught." But for many of us, "such an attitude is simply not possible. We have to make our own the cry, 'Lord, I believe: help my unbelief' (Mark 9:24). For very many of us this will remain our constant prayer right up to the very gates of death."[47]

Thus, reason, searching out difficult questions, and wrestling with doubt are essential elements in the journey of faith. Karl Rahner, known for his rigorous thinking and spiritual depth, called many in the twentieth century to reflect on the question: "What is a Christian, and why can one live this Christian existence with intellectual honesty?" He posits that as we reflect on the fact of our Christian existence, we "want to justify it before the demands of conscience and of truth by giving an 'account of our hope' (1 Pet 3:15)."[48] For some, this may involve entering into dialogue with various philosophies, or historical, sociological, and natural sciences.[49] The life of the mind and life in the Spirit are unified as we seek to know Jesus and make him known, with intellectual honesty and integrity.

Life in the Holy Spirit, the substance of the spiritual life, draws from our reasoning capacities, the limited tools of human language, socially shaped intellect, and moral awareness.[50] Yet we are well aware of our cognitive limitations. "We have limited competency to see even ourselves honestly, much less the whole of history," or to understand the infinite Creator of the

---

46. Oden, *Systematic Theology*, I:340.

47. Ware, *The Orthodox Way*, 16. Ware adds: "For faith implies not complacency but taking risks, not shutting ourselves off from the unknown but advancing boldly to meet it ... [As Bishop J.A.T. Robinson says,] 'The act of faith is a constant dialogue with doubt.'"

48. Rahner, *Foundations of Christian Faith*, 2.

49. For all his deep reflection and desire to be intellectually rigorous and honest, Rahner admits: "All clear understanding is grounded in the darkness of God." *Foundations of Christian Faith*, 22.

50. Oden, *Systematic Theology*, I:340.

universe.[51] With Immanuel Kant and other philosophers, we acknowledge the limits of human reason.[52] Nonetheless, we know that Christian teaching "is not a knowledge that is magically induced or piped into consciousness through a heavenly channel. Human intelligence must work to attain it." Spiritual growth "requires intellectual effort, historical imagination, empathic energy, and participation in a vital community of prayer."[53] Christian spirituality does not shy away from the full engagement of human reason. The mind, with all its reasoning capacities, is a gift from God. Therefore, we seek to "love the Lord with all our mind . . .," as Jesus taught.

Creative Tension

Christian Scripture, Christian tradition, Christian experience, and Christian reasoning exist as responses to God's historical revelation in his people Israel and his Son Jesus Christ. These four sources and guidelines are to be held in creative tension. "All are responses to the revealed word. When the word becomes written, we appropriate it amid changing cultural experiences, reflect on it by reason, and personally rediscover it in our own experience."[54] Our knowledge and love of God develop as we maintain a functional and interdependent equilibrium of these four sources. "The overstress on any one of the four ends in imbalance, like that of a chair with uneven legs." To utilize "only one source is as precarious as the balancing act of a pole-sitter."[55] Inspired by the Christian spiritual classics, we seek to walk in the way of Jesus as it is revealed in Scripture, illumined by tradition, vivified in personal experience, and confirmed by reason.[56] Fullness of life in the Spirit involves each of these four sources. Undergirding these four sources is the life-giving power of prayer, to which we now turn.

---

51. Oden, *Systematic Theology*, I:340.
52. See the informative article by Williams, "Kant's Account of Reason."
53. Oden, *Systematic Theology*, I:340.
54. Oden, *Systematic Theology*, I:331, 341.
55. Oden, *Systematic Theology*, I:341.
56. *The Book of Discipline of The United Methodist Church*, 1996, ¶68, 74.

CHAPTER 5.

Prayer: The Mother of Spiritual Virtues

"Lord, teach us to pray..."
—Luke 11:1

"Prayer is the test of everything; prayer is also the source of everything; prayer is the driving force of everything; prayer is also the director of everything."
—Theophan the Recluse, "What Is Prayer?"

"Abba Macarius was asked, 'How should we pray?' The old man said, 'There is no need to use a lot of words; just stretch out your hands and say, *Lord, as you will and as you know best, have mercy*. And if the conflict grows fiercer, say *Lord, help!* He knows very well what we need and he shows us his mercy.'"
—*Sayings of the Desert Fathers*

Prayer is "an intimate sharing between friends...taking time frequently to be alone with Him who we know loves us."
—Teresa of Avila, *Life*

"Mindfulness of God, or noetic prayer, is superior to all other activities. Indeed being love for God, it is the chief virtue."
—Gregory of Sinai, *Philokalia* 4:282

A LUMINOUS LIFE IS a life of prayer. While there are many rich sources on prayer in various Christian traditions, the following chapter brings together three that have been particularly informative and formative in my understanding of prayer. The first is Madame Jeanne Guyon (1648–1717), a French Catholic who taught a simple method of developing intimacy with God through praying the Scriptures. Second is the *Philokalia*, the Orthodox compendium of classics on prayer and the spiritual life. Finally is Teresa of Avila's teaching on the four waters in the life of prayer.

The beauty and reward of reading these three sources alongside each other will become evident as the chapter unfolds. In short, each source complements and builds on the other. Guyon proffers a simple yet profound way of encountering the Lord through Scripture. The *Philokalia* provides practical advice on biblically rooted, trinitarian-Christocentric prayer, including the Jesus Prayer. Teresa offers helpful perspective, a big picture, of what happens as we grow in the grace of prayer. Gleaning from these sources *together* yields a helpful vision of prayer, how we develop a life of prayer, and what God accomplishes in and through us in prayer. It also reminds us of how the Holy Spirit has taught the saints to pray over the centuries and across various traditions.

Prayer: Types and Essence

There are many ways to define prayer. The New Testament speaks of different types of prayer: supplications, intercessions, thanksgivings (1 Tim 2:1). Outside of the Psalms, which form an entire prayer book, the Bible records 650 prayers.[1] A common thread that emerges in these many prayers is the intimate interaction and communication between God and human beings. In its most basic terms, this is what prayer is: conversation and communion with God. Through prayer, God and human beings share intimate thoughts and feelings.

Praying Creatures

When we ponder the teaching on prayer in the Bible and the Christian spiritual classics, we understand more clearly that we are indeed *praying creatures*. We are created to pray, to commune with God, with words and in silence. Our "innermost constitution has been designed for dialogue . . ."

---

1. See Lockyer, *All the Prayers of the Bible*. This classic on prayer offers concise commentary on all the biblical prayers.

We were created to be hearers of the Word. We are creatures with a mystery in our heart that is bigger than ourselves.[2] Prayer is our spiritual instinct. Something in us longs for more. Deep calls to deep. We yearn for something, for Someone beyond the natural, visible world. Prayer is the means to fulfill this self-transcendent desire. Prayer brings us into contact with the living God.

"Yes" to God's Grace

Prayer, as some ancient writers say, is the mother of spiritual virtues.[3] That is, through prayer, the Spirit of God conceives and births Christlike character within us. Like Mary, we respond to the grace of God through prayer. It is our "yes" to God's invitation. Prayer is our way of saying, "Here am I, the servant of the Lord; let it be with me according to your word" (Luke 1:38). Prayer is our response to God, with whom nothing is impossible. It is the primary way we cooperate with the transformative power of God that works within us (Eph 3:20).

Personal and Interpersonal

Prayer awakens us to communion with the Holy Trinity. In prayer, we approach the throne of the gracious God of the universe, emboldened by the love of the Son, and filled with the power of the Holy Spirit. Through prayer, we are drawn into the very life of God, the community of the Holy Trinity. The transcendent God who indwells us through the Spirit, draws us into ever deeper communion. Through prayer, we learn to trust God and become the friends of God (Jas 2:23). Through prayer, our friendship with Jesus grows, and the spirit of revelation rests on us (Eph 1:17): "I have called you friends, because I have made known to you everything that I have heard from my Father" (John 15:15).

The act of prayer is, therefore, *personal*. We enter into the secret place with God, where we have been raised with Christ above, where our life is hidden with Christ in God (Col 3:1–3). We enter the inner sanctuary where Christ dwells in the depths of our heart. For we are the temple of the Holy

---

2. Balthasar, *Prayer*, 22.

3. Mark the Ascetic says: "Prayer is called a virtue, but in reality it is *the mother of the virtues: for it gives birth to them through union with Christ.*" *Philokalia* 1:128.

Spirit. Through prayer, we encounter the High Priest, who lives to make intercession for us, in the holy place of our hearts.

Yet the act of prayer is also *interpersonal*. When we pray, we join countless others who are also seeking the face of God. We fellowship with those who are fellowshipping with God. Thus, prayer joins us to our elder brother Jesus, and to our sisters and brothers who are in the worldwide family of God. Because prayer is conversational, personal, and relational, we can grow in prayer. Relationship is at the root of prayer. Through prayer, our relationship with God and with one another can be deepened and broadened. The following is one of the main ways to converse with God and grow in prayer, whether alone or with others.

Biblical Meditation

John Cassian, among the most influential writers on prayer and the spiritual life, says that meditation on the Bible is the chief way to grow in prayer, and cultivate friendship with God and purity of heart. Meditation on Scripture draws together the conversational, personal, and relational elements of prayer. For we can meditate on the Bible alone or share meditation with someone else or even a group. But for many of us the idea of meditation may seem strange, impractical, or unattainable. Biblical meditation or meditation on the Scriptures, unfortunately, has become a lost art. Like an invaluable book that somehow slipped behind all the others in a large bookcase, the lost art of biblical meditation has been gathering dust, and must be rediscovered.

Meditating Creatures

As stated above, we are creatures of prayer. More specifically, all of us are meditators. We are *meditating creatures*.[4] Our minds and hearts are, figuratively speaking, organs for meditation. As the physical heart pumps blood through the body, our minds pump thoughts through our inner

---

4. Some might question the notion that we are meditating creatures. Consider this simple illustration. Have you ever had a bill you cannot pay? All you can do is think about the bill. The bill is on your mind first thing in the morning, throughout the day, and in the night. Or how about an unhealthy image that is lodged in your mind? It crops up time and time again, drawing your inner attention. You find yourself "meditating" on the bill or unhealthy image.

life. Therefore, the key is to meditate on the right things, and to do this by rediscovering the life-changing power of Christian meditation taught in Scripture and the spiritual classics.

Transformed through Meditation

The Psalms, the prayer book for Jews and Christians, illustrate the beauty and power of meditation: "I *meditate* on you in the watches of the night" (63:6); "I think of God . . . I *meditate* . . . on all your work" (77:3, 12); "May my *meditation* be pleasing to God" (104:34); "Oh how I love your law! It is my *meditation* all day long" (119:97).[5] The Scriptures assert that we can be transformed by the renewing of our minds (Rom 12:1–2). This occurs through meditation: on the presence of God, the Word of God, and the works of God. The Scriptures also teach that the indwelling Holy Spirit enables us to gaze prayerfully upon the glory of the Lord Jesus, to be transformed into his image and likeness, and to experience freedom as beloved children of God (2 Cor 3:16–18). As meditating creatures we are called *and* empowered to have luminous minds, inner lives suffused with the light, love, and glory of God.

A French Mystic on Biblical Meditation

In studying the Scriptures, both the Old and New Testaments have much to say about meditation, its fruits, and how to do it.[6] Other voices in the Christian tradition provide wise teaching on Christian meditation. One of them is Madame Jeanne Guyon, a French Catholic mystic whose teaching on prayer influenced Catholic archbishop and theologian, François Fénelon, as well as the founder of Methodism, John Wesley.[7] While there

---

5. The Old Testament word for meditation (*hâgâh*) suggests musing and murmuring, thinking and speaking quietly. Biblical meditation involves pondering the Word of God, speaking it under one's breath, keeping it in the heart and mouth, letting it permeate all of life (cf. Deut 6:4–9; 30:14).

6. There are good articles and books on biblical meditation, but I recommend praying through the Scriptures that speak of meditation. Using a concordance, look up the verses that mention "meditation" ("meditate" or other related words), then pray and memorize some of them, ask God to teach you about meditation. Meditate on Psalm 119. It is an extended meditation on David's love for God and the life giving Law.

7. For further information on Guyon, see Ward, "Madame Guyon (1648–1717)" and Ward, *Experimental Theology in America*. Guyon was swept into a theological

are numerous classic teachers regarding meditation on Scripture or *lectio divina* (Latin for "divine reading")[8] there is something compelling about the simplicity and clarity of Guyon's teaching. Her influential book, *Experiencing the Depths of Jesus Christ*, has instructed many about prayer and meditation, especially meditation on Scripture as a means to encounter the Lord's presence. Her method, which she says is simple enough for *anyone* to learn, entails a few steps. Before discussing the steps, she says that the Father's arms of love are wide open to *all* of us; *all* of us are called to a deep relationship with Jesus, through the indwelling presence of the Holy Spirit. She writes to help us discover how to experience this. She explains that *prayer* is the key.

Praying Scripture

Guyon teaches that there are two ways to come to the Lord in prayer. The first is *praying the Scripture*. Choose a simple, practical passage from the Bible (something like John 15:1–11 works nicely).[9] Before reading it, turn to the Lord, inwardly, quietly, and humbly. Carefully read the passage. Take it in, as if tasting good food, and digest each word as you read. Sense the heart of what you are reading. Extract the deeper sense. Guyon explains: "If you read quickly, it will benefit you little. You will be like a bee that merely skims the surface of a flower." Rather, "in this new way of reading with prayer, you must become as the bee who penetrates into the *depths* of the flower. You plunge deeply within to remove its deepest nectar." If you follow this approach, little by little you will "come to experience a very rich prayer that flows from [your] inward being."[10] This requires practice. Take the long view. It does not come overnight. Good things come to those who persist. The grace of God energizes you as you cooperate with the operations of the indwelling Spirit (1 Cor 15:10; 2 Cor 12:9).

---

controversy known as quietism, which was unfortunate. Nonetheless, her writings on biblical meditation are insightful and practical. As with reading any spiritual writing, we read with discernment, ingesting the nutritious meat, and spitting out the bones.

8. For further information on *lectio divina* see Pennington, *Lectio Divina*; Hall, *Too Deep for Words*; and Casey, *Sacred Reading*.

9. John 15:1–11 is about abiding in Jesus, his word, and his love. Try praying through these eleven verses, focusing particularly on vss. 3–5, and 7–11. Read a phrase out loud, pause, use the words to dialogue with Jesus who indwells you through the Holy Spirit. Ask him to teach you how to abide in him, his word, and his love.

10. Guyon, *Experiencing the Depths*, 8.

Beholding the Lord

A second kind of prayer is what Guyon calls "beholding the Lord" or "waiting on the Lord." Again, a brief passage of Scripture is used to quiet your mind and bring you into God's presence, or to bring you into contact with the indwelling presence of the Lord. Come to the Lord by faith, giving thanks for the love and grace of God. Read the passage again, pause, savor and ingest the spiritual food it provides. Set your mind on the indwelling Holy Spirit, focus your mind inwardly on Jesus. If your mind begins to wander, quietly pray the Scripture again, turning your attention back to the inward parts of your being. The Lord is found within your spirit, "in the recesses of your being, in the Holy of Holies; this is where He dwells." For the Lord has promised "to come and make His home within you (John 14:23). He promised to there meet with those who worship Him and who do His will." The Lord "will meet you in your spirit. It was St. Augustine who once said that he had lost much time in the beginning of his Christian experience by trying to find the Lord outwardly rather than by turning inwardly."[11]

As you practice this form of prayer, you will become more aware of the Lord's presence. Your mind and outer senses will be calmed. When you are distracted, when your mind wanders, bring your attention back to the indwelling presence of the Lord. Guyon explains: "When your mind has wandered, don't try to deal with it by changing what you are thinking." If you "pay attention to what you are thinking, you will only irritate your mind and stir it up more. Instead, *withdraw* from your mind! Keep turning within to the Lord's presence." In doing this, "you will win the war with your wandering mind and yet never directly engage in the battle!"[12] Keep practicing, giving thanks for the grace and power of God. Remind yourself that the Lord longs to be gracious to you (Isa 30:18), and receive that grace. God wants you to grow in prayer more than you do.

Becomes Easier: With Practice, by Grace

Guyon says that when you begin this form of prayer, you will discover that it is difficult to bring your mind under control. It is accustomed to wandering all over, in an undisciplined manner. The key is to form a new habit. "Be

---

11. Guyon, *Experiencing the Depths*, 9, 11.
12. Guyon, *Experiencing the Depths*, 12.

assured that as your soul becomes more accustomed to withdrawing to inward things, this process will become much easier." Why? For two reasons: "One is that the mind, after much practice, will form a new habit of turning deep within," and two, because we "have a gracious Lord!" For the "Lord's chief desire is to reveal Himself to you and, in order for Him to do that, He gives you abundant grace." The Lord graces you with "the experience of enjoying His presence. He touches you, and His touch is so delightful that, more than ever, you are drawn inwardly to Him."[13] Over time, this begins to transform the way you view God, yourself, and others. You become increasingly aware of God's affection for you. Your love for God and others grows. Old patterns of thinking and old habits are expelled. New ways of thinking and new, life-giving habits form.

The *Philokalia*: Unceasing Prayer

Along with Guyon, the *Philokalia* offers rich instruction on prayer. A bit of background will help to understand the spiritual wisdom of the *Philokalia*. The *Philokalia*, as noted earlier, is a collection of spiritual writings on prayer and the spiritual life by thirty-six authors, from the fourth to fifteenth century. The *Philokalia* was published in Venice in 1782. St. Nikodimos of the Holy Mountain (1749–1809) and St. Makarios of Corinth (1731–1805), the editors who put together the writings in the *Philokalia*, sought to retrieve the spiritual theology and practice of the early church fathers. They wanted to provide these life-changing teachings to all Christians, not just monks living in monasteries. They believed that Paul's instruction to "pray without ceasing" (1 Thess 5:17) is intended not just for monks in monasteries, hermits in caves, or contemplatives on mountain tops. It is a universal command accompanied by all-embracing grace. The best belongs to everyone.[14] All Christians are invited to learn to pray without ceasing and to experience the deifying power of the Holy Spirit. Through prayer, believers are drawn into communion with the Holy Trinity, conformed to the image of Jesus, and inspired to serve others.

---

13. Guyon, *Experiencing the Depths*, 12, 13.

14. From Ware, "The *Philokalia*." Communion with God through unceasing prayer, according to Nikodimos and Makarios, is for *all* Christians, for those married with families, for farmers, merchants, lawyers, even for kings and courtiers living in palaces.

The *Philokalia* provides practical teaching on how to actualize this communion with the Holy Trinity and experience transformation into the image of Jesus. Its authors suggest, among others, three prayerful activities.

Guarding the Inner Kingdom

The first is called "the guarding of the intellect" (*nepsis* in Greek).[15] The *Philokalia* underscores what Jesus taught in the gospels: that the kingdom of God is within you (Luke 17:21), and that the treasure of the kingdom is hidden in the field of the heart (Matt 13:44). Therefore, guarding the intellect, being watchful over the inner kingdom is crucial. This all-embracing watchfulness, attentiveness, and keeping guard over the inner life enables you to fend off spiritual attack and cultivate intimate friendship with the King who dwells within our heart.

One author in the *Philokalia* who writes extensively on watchfulness or the guarding of the intellect is St. Hesychios (eighth or ninth century). He says that the inner kingdom of the heart is like a city that must be guarded. The "guarding of the intellect is a watchtower commanding a view over our whole spiritual life."[16] We are sentinels, keeping watch at the gate of our hearts. Throughout our daily activities, various thoughts seek entry into our mind and heart. Watchfulness acts like a doorkeeper, allowing only thoughts that please the Lord and bring us life to gain entry. This accords with what Paul teaches about taking every thought captive to the obedience of Christ (2 Cor 10:5).[17] As thoughts seek entry to the inner kingdom, we examine them thoroughly before allowing them in. Moreover, St. Hesychios explains:

---

15. In the glossary of the *Philokalia*, the intellect is described as the highest faculty in human beings, through which—as it is increasingly purified—one knows God by means of direct apprehension or spiritual perception. Unlike reason, "from which is must be carefully distinguished, the intellect does not function by formulating abstract concepts and then arguing on this basis to a conclusion reached through deductive reasoning, but it understands divine truth by means of immediate experience, intuition or 'simple cognition' (the term used by St. Isaac the Syrian). The intellect dwells in the 'depths of the soul'; it constitutes the innermost aspect of the heart . . ." It is "the organ of contemplation" or the "eye of the heart." *Philokalia* 2:384.

16. *Philokalia* 1:175.

17. Likewise, Nikitas Stithatos (c. 1005–c. 1090) suggests that watchfulness, silence, and guarding the five senses are like sifting and sorting the various ideas swimming in the sea of thought. *Philokalia* 4:85–86.

> Just as salt seasons our bread and other food and keeps certain meats from spoiling for quite a time, so the spiritual sweetness and marvelous working which result from the guarding of the intellect effect something similar. For in a divine manner they season and sweeten both the inner and outer self, driving away the stench of evil thoughts and keeping us continually in communion with good thoughts.[18]

Watchfulness engenders numerous positive results. It helps us guard the purity of our inner life, so that we can commune with Christ who indwells us through the Holy Spirit. Watchfulness also seasons and sweetens our entire life, freeing us from evil thoughts, and empowering us to welcome and cultivate good thoughts.

Inner Stillness

A second theme in the *Philokalia* related to meditation is "inner stillness" (*hesychia* in Greek). Watchfulness and inner stillness are intrinsically connected. This stillness is "a state of inner tranquility or mental quietude and concentration which arises in conjunction with, and is deepened by, the practice of pure prayer and the guarding of the heart and intellect." It is not "simply silence, but an attitude of listening to God and of openness towards Him."[19] This inner stillness and attentiveness to God is similar to what Guyon described in her method of prayer.

Another author in the *Philokalia* cited previously, Evagrius, teaches that inner stillness involves "pure prayer," "prayer in which the intellect is 'naked' and free from all images and discursive thinking." Inner stillness "is a shedding of thoughts," according to St. Gregory of Sinai.[20] This might seem abstract to some. Think of it in terms of learning to present your mind and heart to the Lord in prayer as a blank canvas. While some forms of prayer encourage the use of mental images from the Bible and other sources, this kind of imageless (and sometimes wordless) prayer is different. One may begin this form of prayer with images, but the goal is to leave them behind, to dwell in the Lord's presence without mental images, in silence before the holy mystery of God. "Be still . . . and silent . . . and know that I am God" (Ps 46:10). Perhaps Elijah's experience of God in sheer silence evinces this kind of prayer (2 Kgs 19:11–13).

18. *Philokalia* 1:177.
19. *Philokalia* 1:365.
20. *Philokalia* 4:278.

Invocation of the Holy Name: The Jesus Prayer

Origins

How are we to practice *watchfulness* and attain *inner stillness*? Thankfully the *Philokalia* offers immensely practical teaching on *how* to do this. It involves "continual invocation of the Holy Name," or the Jesus Prayer: "Lord Jesus Christ, Son of God, have mercy on me." Some later traditions add "have mercy on me *a sinner*," but the original form lacks this. The Jesus Prayer is a combination of prayers found in the Gospels. In Luke 18:10–14, where Jesus discusses true, humble prayer, the publican or tax collector prays, "Lord, have mercy on me, a sinner." In Mark 10:47, the blind beggar named Bartimaeus hears that Jesus is approaching and shouts, "Jesus, Son of David, have mercy on me!"[21] Bringing together these two petitions, the Jesus Prayer draws us to Jesus in humility and ardent love. St. Nikodimos explains that the Jesus Prayer was revealed by the Holy Spirit, and is a powerful means of grace:

> The Spirit . . . revealed to the Fathers a method that is truly wonderful . . . whereby grace can be rediscovered. This was to *pray continually to our Lord Jesus Christ the Son of God*, not simply to pray with the intellect and the lips alone . . . but to turn the whole intellect towards the inner self, which is a marvelous experience; and so inwardly, within the very depths of the heart, to *invoke the all-holy Name of the Lord and to implore mercy from Him*, concentrating our attention solely on the bare words of the prayer, not allowing anything else to gain entry from within or from without, but keeping the mind totally free from all forms and colors.[22]

Power

The Jesus Prayer is powerful in many ways. By using it we can drive out evil thoughts and resist temptation. Hesychios even calls the Jesus Prayer a spiritual weapon, a powerful sword with which we strike down demonic thoughts and protect our inner heart. "Whenever we are filled with evil thoughts, we should throw the invocation of our Lord Jesus Christ into

---

21. See Kallistos of Diokleia, *The Power of the Name*; Gillet, *On the Invocation of the Name of Jesus*; Hausherr, *The Name of Jesus*; and Cunningham, "The Place of the Jesus Prayer in the *Philokalia*."

22. *Philokalia* 1:xx; from Ware, "The *Philokalia*," 13.

their midst. Then, as experience has taught us, we shall see them instantly dispersed like smoke in the air."[23]

When distracting or tempting thoughts present themselves to us, Hesychios explains that the Jesus Prayer is a means of counterattacking or counter-speaking. The truth and power of Jesus' name counters the trickery of the enemy. As Jesus counterattacked Satan when tempted in the desert (Luke 4:1–13), the Jesus Prayer is a form of speaking against temptations or negative thoughts. Jesus wielded the sword of Scripture to rebuff Satan. We wield the written word of God *and* invoke the living Word of God to come to our aid. Maximus says that those who pray and put into practice the words of God "have power to speak and dissolve demons and build their hearts into temples of God."[24] Evil forces are driven away because we are filled with the presence of God.

Furthermore, the Jesus Prayer turns our inward attention *away* from the enemy and *towards* the presence of Jesus within our hearts. It is like *spiritual judo*. An evil thought comes against you; you turn its energy against itself by turning to Jesus, calling out for his mercy and help. You are able to turn your opponent's force against him. If you practice this, even moments of spiritual attack become opportunities to turn to Jesus and cultivate intimate friendship with him. The power of the enemy is weakened, the lure of temptation withers, and you draw closer to the King who dwells within.

It is an immensely practical and useful form of prayer. It is not meant to be said in rote or mechanical fashion. It is simply a very accessible prayer that can be prayed at any time, to center us on Jesus when our mind is idle, or to fend off negative thoughts. When prayed from the heart, it puts us in contact with the living Jesus. It is actually a trinitarian prayer. We are invoking Jesus: who is Lord, Christ, Messiah, anointed by the Holy Spirit, and Son, who is one with the Father. Together the Father and Son grant mercy to us through the Spirit.[25]

---

23. *Philokalia* 1:189; 1:179. Gregory of Sinai (1260–1346) speaks further about the power of God over evil for those who call on God: "God is a fire that cauterizes wickedness. The Lord is prompt to help, and will speedily come to the defense of those who wholeheartedly call on Him day and night." *Philokalia* 4:277.

24. *Philokalia* 2:207.

25. The Jesus Prayer can also inspire other trinitarian prayers based on biblical texts. For example: "Abba Father, Almighty God and Creator of all, have mercy on me," or "Holy Spirit, Lord and Giver of life, have mercy on me."

Physical Practices

Some link the Jesus Prayer to certain physical practices, in order to engage additional aspects of the human person. For example, while saying the Jesus Prayer, some bow their heads to focus on the kingdom within the heart; others connect the Jesus Prayer to the rhythm of breathing. These are simply ways to involve physical aspects of ourselves, because Christian spiritual practices, including meditation, are holistic ventures.[26] We give ourselves completely to God: body, soul, and spirit. All that we are belongs to the Father, Son, and Holy Spirit. Our bodies, individually and collectively, are the temple of the Holy Spirit (1 Cor 6:19). We present our bodies as a living and holy sacrifice, acceptable to God, which is our spiritual service of worship (Rom 12:1). Holding up our hands in prayer, or other physical actions, are found throughout Scripture, and may help us feel more engaged and open to the presence of God.

God-Given Equilibrium

Hesychios explains that when we practice watchfulness, invoke the name of Jesus, and seek inner stillness, "a certain God-given equilibrium is produced in our intellect." We call upon the Lord Jesus with a burning heart, he comes to our aid, and the power of his name intercedes for us. The key is *persistence*. "In virtue as in vice, constancy is the mother of habit; once acquired, it rules us like nature." Through persistent prayer and dependence on Jesus, old habits die, and new habits emerge.[27]

Additionally, the inner equilibrium these practices cultivate becomes fertile soil for the seeds of God's word to be planted. Inner stillness prepares us to hear God's voice. "When the heart has acquired stillness it will perceive the heights and depths of knowledge; and the ear of the still intellect will be made to *hear* marvelous things from God."[28] Therefore, prayer, meditation, and other spiritual practices, are means to overcome temptation, to cultivate purity of heart, to attain inner stillness, and to grow in our ability to hear the voice of God.

---

26. See Ware, "Ways of Prayer and Contemplation."

27. The dynamic of love taking root, growing, and pushing out sinful habits can be seen in various traditions and eras. For example, see the classic sermon by the Scottish theologian, Thomas Chalmers (1780–1847), *The Expulsive Power of a New Affection*.

28. *Philokalia* 1:178; 1:185.

Prayer

Teresa of Avila: The Four Waters

Along with Guyon and the *Philokalia*, Teresa of Avila offers insightful teaching on prayer. As Guyon teaches, we pray the Scriptures, and contemplate the glory of the Lord through them. Through the *Philokalia*, we learn unceasing prayer, watchfulness, stillness, and the transformative power of the Jesus Prayer. Teresa provides a picture of what happens when we seek and encounter God through these practices. As we saw previously (in chapter 3), where Teresa discussed the seven dwelling places of the interior castle, she has a penchant for using images from the natural world to describe spiritual realities. In her autobiography (known as the *Life*), Teresa suggests the metaphor of a garden to describe progress in the life of prayer. It is a vivid image that helps us picture the process of growth in prayer, which at its core is friendship with God. She says that those beginning in prayer should view themselves as:

> making a garden in which the Lord is to take his delight, but in a soil unfruitful and abounding in weeds. His Majesty roots up the weeds and plants good seed . . . With the help of God we, as good gardeners, have to see that the plants grow, and to water them carefully so that they do not die but produce blossoms that shall send forth much fragrance, refreshing to our Lord, so that he may come often for his pleasure into this garden and take delight in the midst of these virtues.[29]

Garden of Prayer and Communion

The aim of prayer is to cultivate intimate friendship with Jesus, to delight and be delighted by him. With the Lord's help, the soil of our heart becomes a prayerful garden. He lovingly uproots the weeds and plants good seed. Working with him, we cultivate the garden, growing in prayer, love, and other virtues. Because of his gracious help, and our diligent cooperation, our heart is transformed from weed-infested dirt to a vibrant, fragrant garden, a place where we daily commune with him.

---

29. From McGinn, ed., *The Essential Writings of Christian Mysticism*, 112.

First Water

Teresa explains that there are four ways that the garden obtains the life-giving water of the Spirit, each one representing how a person interacts with God through prayer. The first is drawing water by hand from a well. It is the work of beginners in prayer and is an arduous affair. Teresa says: "This process is very laborious ... [Beginners in prayer] must tire themselves out in keeping the senses recollected, and this is a great labor because the senses are accustomed to distractions."[30] Training the senses, particularly guarding over what is heard or seen, is key, just as we observed in the *Philokalia* and Madame Guyon. Praying the hours (set times of prayer rooted in Jewish and early Christian practice) helps direct the senses to the Lord's presence.[31] Prayer in solitude, meditating on the life of Christ in the Scriptures, and examining our lives also keep the senses in check and centered on Jesus. This is strenuous, but Teresa asserts that as the beginner in prayer does these things, the grace of God energizes the work, preserving the budding flowers in the garden, and making the virtues grow. God grants tears as one labors, tears because of our weakness and God's mercy. These tears water the garden.[32]

Second Water

The second way of drawing water is by using a waterwheel and buckets, drawn by a windlass (or a crank). By using a waterwheel and buckets, Teresa explains, "The gardener may be able to draw more water with less labor and is able to take some rest without being continually at work." She says that the kind of prayer experienced at this point is "the prayer of the quiet." After the diligent work of drawing water by hand from a well, here the soul recollects itself, consistently centering its attention on the Lord within, and touching what Teresa calls "the supernatural." She says that the water level rises, less labor is needed to draw it, and the supernatural power of grace "reveals itself more distinctly to the soul." The will becomes occupied with love for Jesus, to the extent that it is "the captive of him it loves." Teresa exclaims: "O Jesus and my Lord, how valuable is your love to us here! It binds our own love so closely that it is not in its power at this moment to

---

30. McGinn, ed., *The Essential Writings of Christian Mysticism*, 112.
31. Regarding praying the hours, see Tickle, *The Divine Hours*.
32. McGinn, ed., *The Essential Writings of Christian Mysticism*, 112–13.

love anything else but you." The hard work of prayer begins to pay off. More water is drawn with less effort. The Lord touches the soul with "consolations," which at times may be rapturous. Through prayer, the soul is quiet before the Lord, content to look upon his face in love and faith with the eyes of the heart. Tears occur here as well, but they are joyful tears, a gift of God's grace.[33]

Third Water

The third way in which the garden is watered is that of running water coming from a river or brook. Here the garden is watered more easily, though some effort is required to direct the flow of the water. It is a grace-empowered irrigation of sorts. "In this state," Teresa says, "our Lord desires to help the gardener in such a way that he may almost be said to be the gardener himself, since he does all the work." As seen in *The Interior Castle*, here a transition occurs. The soul at work in prayer, drawing from the well and utilizing a waterwheel and buckets, comes to fully rest in the Lord through prayer. The faculties of the soul "sleep," as she described with the silkworm analogy in the *Castle*. "The pleasure, sweetness, and delight are incomparably greater than in the former state of prayer because the waters of grace have risen up to the neck of the soul so that it can neither advance nor retreat . . . it seeks only the enjoyment of exceeding bliss."

Cooperation with the energizing power of God's grace is necessary, but the water level rises, carrying the pray-er into new experiences of delight in God. The soul is so overwhelmed with the river of God's presence that "it doesn't know whether to speak or be silent, whether to laugh or weep. This prayer is a glorious folly, a heavenly madness, in which true wisdom is acquired . . ." In the apostle's words, one becomes a fool for Christ (1 Cor 4:10), embracing the crucified Lord, and learning true spiritual wisdom (1 Cor 1:18). When writing this, Teresa says that she had been experiencing this kind of prayer for about five or six years, yet still struggled to describe it. She also explains that in this mode of prayer, the soul is enabled to unite Mary (who represents contemplation) and Martha (who represents activity).[34] We will return to this idea of harmony between the contempla-

---

33. McGinn, ed., *The Essential Writings of Christian Mysticism*, 113–14.

34. McGinn, ed., *The Essential Writings of Christian Mysticism*, 114–15. For the story of Martha and Mary, see Luke 10:38–42.

tive and active life in chapter 12. This leads to Teresa's description of the final water.

Fourth Water

Regarding the fourth water, Teresa says that it is the most difficult to explain. The sense of God doing much of the work during prayer, as in the third water, is even more apparent here. The gardener (or pray-er) finds that the act of prayer is accompanied with such bliss and consolation that "the work is not felt as work but as bliss." Unlike the working of the bucket, the waterwheel, or the flowing stream, here "heavenly water . . . in its abundance soaks and saturates this entire garden . . . This water from heaven often comes when the gardener is least expecting it."[35] The pray-er, surprised by the water, experiences a consuming enjoyment of God that transcends feelings and understanding: "In this fourth state there is no feeling, only enjoyment without any understanding of the thing [in] which the soul is rejoicing." The soul "understands that it is enjoying some good in which all good is gathered together, but this good is incomprehensible." The senses of the pray-er "are all occupied in this enjoyment in such a way that not one of them is at liberty to be able to attend to anything else, either outward or inward . . ." The soul is ravished by the love, goodness, and beauty of the Lord. All other things fade into the background.

Just before writing about this, Teresa says she received the Eucharist and was experiencing this type of prayer. Pondering what the soul experiences in this kind of prayer, Teresa heard the Lord say, "[The soul] dies wholly to itself, my daughter, in order that it may give itself more and more to me. It is not itself that lives, but I. As it cannot comprehend what it understands, it understands by not understanding." The words of the Apostle Paul come to mind when he says that he has been crucified with Christ, and he no longer lives, but Christ lives in him (Gal 2:20). In this type of prayer, the soul (and the will and the whole inner self) is united to God, undergoes spiritual death, and is raised to new life and new dimensions of prayer. The will is "fully occupied in loving," but it does not understand how it loves to this degree. As with many other masters in mystical theology, it is a struggle to adequately describe this state of prayer.[36]

35. Teresa, *Life*, 161.

36. Teresa, with a sense of humor, says: "when I began to write about this last water it seemed impossible to know how to speak of it without making it sound like Greek." Teresa, *Life*, 160.

Prayer

One understands by not understanding. It is a profound paradox.[37] Experiencing the transcendent mystery of God within oneself, as in this fourth water, shatters all barriers and limitations of human knowledge and language. The soul is simply aware that it is joined to God, enveloped in the flames of love, united to the One who is a consuming fire. But creature always remains creature; Creator remains Creator.

Intimacy, Love, and Grace

Teresa's insights on prayer remind us, first and foremost, that prayer is about cultivating an intimate relationship with the Lord Jesus. The Lord loves us deeply, and is more intent on revealing himself to us than we could ever imagine or desire. The Lord is abundantly gracious, wooing us each day, at every stage. Yet this grace, freely given and lavishly poured out, awakens and empowers us to accomplish the hard work of prayer and spiritual growth. As this metaphor of the garden illustrates, the life-giving water of God's presence, love, and grace is there, waiting for us to receive. We grow in communion with the Lord through praying the Scriptures, watchfulness, stillness, and the Jesus Prayer. As we utilize the bucket, the waterwheel, the irrigated stream, or receive the saturating rain, we are compelled to seek the presence of God within our hearts all the more.

Simultaneously, we are satisfied and left longing for more. We, as apprentices of the great Gardener of souls, learn to cooperate more and more with God as our hearts become fragrant gardens where the Lord dwells. Like gardening, it involves hard work. But the Lord brings astounding growth in spite of our meager efforts. "Consider the lilies of the field, how they grow . . . ," Jesus reminds us (Matt 6:28). Through prayer the Lord graciously deepens our friendship with him. Along with prayer are other spiritual practices that the Lord uses to cultivate spiritual growth, including fasting, to which we now turn our attention.

---

37. See Nicholas of Cusa (1401–1464) on the hiddenness, knowability, and unknowability of God, in Nicholas of Cusa, *Selected Spiritual Writings*, 36–42.

CHAPTER 6.

Fasting: Self-Denial for a Greater Good

"Whenever you fast..."
—Matt 6:16

"Is this not the fast which I choose, to loosen the bonds of wickedness, to undo the bands of the yoke, and to let the oppressed go free and break every yoke? Is it not to divide your bread with the hungry and bring the homeless poor into the house; when you see the naked, to cover him?"
—Isa 58:6–7 (NASB)

"As the fathers have said, all extremes are equally harmful. It is as dangerous to fast too much as it is to overfill the stomach..."
—John Cassian, *Philokalia* 1:107–8

"Fasting gives birth to prophets and strengthens the powerful; fasting makes lawgivers wise. Fasting is a good safeguard for the soul, a steadfast companion for the body, a weapon for the valiant, and a gymnasium for athletes. Fasting repels temptations, anoints unto piety; it is the comrade of watchfulness and the artificer of chastity. In war it fights bravely, in peace it teaches stillness."
—Basil of Caesarea, *First Homily on Fasting*

Attainable, Balanced Fasting

Fasting is a challenging topic and practice for many Christians. Just last week, I had a conversation about fasting with a friend. She explained that in recent weeks, she had sensed a renewed call to fast and pray. Over the course of our conversation, we discussed various extremes regarding fasting. On one hand, among certain Christians, fasting is largely ignored. It is viewed as part of the "old covenant," "legalistic," or simply "too difficult." On the other hand, among some Christians, fasting is practiced excessively, without healthy guidelines or practical instruction. My friend and I reflected on some of the biblical teaching on fasting, along with the seasoned wisdom found in the Christian spiritual classics by John Cassian and others. We agreed that when fasting, it is best to avoid extremes, of both avoidance and excess, as the Cassian quote above suggests.[1]

In light of this conversation with my friend, which touches on a few challenging points, the aim of this chapter is to make fasting more understandable, accessible, and doable. We will explore what fasting is, some of the reasons for and benefits of fasting, and various types of fasting.

Fasting as Spiritual Athletes

Put simply, fasting is abstaining from something in order to pursue or cultivate something else. It is self-denial for a greater good or higher purpose. As we will see, throughout history fasting has been practiced by individuals, communities, and at times entire nations.[2] Fasting is part of a broader Judeo-Christian tradition known as *asceticism*. The word *asceticism* is based on an ancient Greek term, *askēsis*, which is related to "athlete" or "athletics."[3] Therefore, those who practice asceticism are like spiritual athletes who discipline their bodies and souls to perform at optimum levels.

Like Olympic athletes who prepare themselves to compete with excellence, Christians can engage in certain ascetic practices, like fasting, to increase their spiritual fitness and run the race of faith more effectively. The New Testament employs this kind of metaphorical language to encourage

---

1. Cassian's teaching on fasting underscores the importance of moderation at every turn: "Better is a reasonable and modest daily repast [supply of food] than harsh and lengthy fasts every now and again. Immoderate fasting is capable not only of destroying the steadfastness of the mind but also, due to bodily weakness, of emasculating the efficacy of prayer." *Institutes*, ch. IX, 122.

2. For a helpful historical overview, see Arbesmann, "Fasting and Prophecy in Pagan and Christian Antiquity."

3. There are expressions of asceticism in numerous religions of the world. Distinctive and common elements can be discerned in these ascetic traditions. For an informative overview of scholarly discussion on Christian asceticism, see the article by Krawiec, "Asceticism."

Christians to train through spiritual exercises, develop spiritual fitness, be prepared to overcome spiritual opposition, and attain victory for the glory of God. For example, in 1 Corinthians 9:24–26, Paul urges the church to run the race to win, to exercise self-control as athletes do, to compete like runners and boxers with focus and purpose, as he does, and to discipline their bodies to qualify for the race.

Apostolic Christianity versus Gnosticism

The New Testament also warns against excessive asceticism or ascetic exercises that cut against the grain of the grace of God, the goodness of all creation, and the saving work of God in the incarnation of Christ. In the New Testament writings, we find glimpses of what would become one of the key theological conflicts during the first three hundred years of the church: apostolic Christianity versus a series of multifaceted movements with "Gnostic" tendencies.[4] In short, apostolic Christianity encouraged spiritual life rooted in the teachings of Scripture. The Old Testament portrayed the world and all that God has made as "good." According to the New Testament, the God of Abraham, Isaac, and Jacob is a God of love who saves human beings through the life, death, and resurrection of Jesus Christ. The gift of the Holy Spirit, operating in the church as the body of Christ, works redemptively in the material world, indwells human beings, and is making all things new to the glory of God.

Conversely, the many expressions of what some scholars later called "Gnosticism" challenged these biblical views. The New Testament provides glimpses into what these "proto-Gnostic" groups taught. Influenced more by ideas within Greek philosophy than Jewish Scripture, they taught that the material world was inferior to the spiritual world. Therefore, the idea that God would enter the material world through the incarnation was unacceptable. Salvation was acquired through knowledge (*gnosis* in Greek), not through faith in the saving work of God in Christ.

Along with obtaining knowledge, one must help the soul "escape" the entanglements of the "fallen material world," through rigorous ascetic

---

4. I understand that the term "Gnosticism" is problematic for various reasons, and recommend the essay by Marjanen, "Gnosticism." Perhaps "Gnosticism" is best understood as "a heuristic category which functions as 'a simple typology for organizing several religious innovations and new religious movements'" that posed challenges to early Christianity and its normative identity formation (209).

practices, including fasting. The goal was, in the words of Platonic philosophy, to liberate the soul, the "most important" element of human existence, "from the prison house of the body." Thus, when we read particular New Testament passages in light of this growing controversy and debate in the first-century, we can discern some of the issues at stake in the early churches. Jesus Christ was the divine Word who took on human flesh (John 1:14). Through faith in the life, death, and resurrection of his flesh, Jesus provides salvation to human beings (1 Cor 15). Salvation is received by grace through faith, not by human knowledge and ascetic achievement (Eph 2:8–9).

Love, Faith, Grace

In light of the various Gnostic ideas and teachings that developed over the centuries and persist to this day, it is important to keep the following biblical ideas in mind before engaging in a fast or other spiritual exercises.

1. *God is a loving Creator.* All that God has made is good, including our bodies, our bodily needs, and the (healthy) food we eat. Maximus explains that nothing about our creaturely existence is evil, except the misuse of good things God has given us:

> It is not food which is evil but gluttony, not the begetting of children but fornication, not possessions but greed, not reputation but vainglory. And if this is so, there is nothing evil in creatures except misuse, which stems from the mind's negligence in its natural cultivation.[5]

2. *We are saved by a loving God, through faith in Jesus Christ, who took on human flesh in order to redeem us, and transform our body and soul into his image.* Athanasius writes:

> The reason of his coming down was because of us, and that our transgression called forth the loving-kindness of the Word, that the Lord should both make haste to help us and appear among men . . . For he was made man that we might be made God

---

5. Maximus, *Four Hundred Chapters on Love*, III:4; in Berthold, trans., *Selected Writings*, 62. Jürgen Moltmann asserts that hope for the resurrection of the body "permits no disdain and debasement of bodily life and sensory experiences; it affirms them profoundly, and gives greatest honour to 'the flesh,' which people have made something to be despised." (Cf. 1 Cor 15:42–44; *The Coming of God*, 65–67.)

[literally, "He was humanized that we might be deified"]; and he manifested himself by a body that we might receive the idea of the unseen Father . . .[6]

3. *Our salvation is based on the grace of God in Christ, not because of our good works or rigorous ascetic achievements.* "For by grace you have been saved through faith, and this is not your own doing; it is the gift of God—not the result of works, so that no one may boast" (Eph 2:8–9). Mark the Ascetic adds: "The kingdom of heaven is not a reward for works, but a gift of grace prepared by the Master for his faithful servants."[7]

Knowing these truths frees us up to fast with purpose, in the spirit of love and grace, and in accordance with the doctrines and practices found in the Old and New Testaments. We fast, not to help our soul escape the prison house of the body, but to cooperate with the energizing grace of the Holy Spirit who is transforming us body and soul into the image and likeness of the Lord Jesus Christ.

Reasons for Fasting

The Scriptures teach many reasons for fasting. Before considering some of them, I want to make something abundantly clear: *God does not need us to fast.* In fact, God does not need anything from us. That is the beauty of the Christian spiritual life. We depend on the almighty, limitless, generous God who overflows with love, grace, and goodness for each of us.[8]

Fasting, like other spiritual exercises, is about reordering our priorities, affections, and pursuits. Fasting is one way to make more room in our lives for the presence of God. Fasting is, as Diadochos of Photiki (c. 400–486) says, "simply a tool for training"[9] that can be used in a variety of ways, with the underlying goal of deepening our relationship with God and being transformed by the grace of the Lord Jesus.

---

6. Athanasius, *On the Incarnation of the Word*, 58–59, 107.

7. St. Mark the Ascetic, "On Those Who Think that They are Made Righteous by Works," *Philokalia* 1:125.

8. To this point, Maximus the Confessor says that God is a "boundless, astonishing sea of goodness," and we are created to long for and depend on this goodness, *Philokalia* 2:100.

9. *Philokalia* 1:267.

Fasting

Intercessory Prayers

One reason for fasting is to intensify intercessory prayer.[10] There are examples of this in the Old Testament. When Nehemiah, the fifth-century BCE leader who went on to help rebuild the walls of Jerusalem, heard the report of survivors in Jerusalem who were suffering, he "sat down and wept, and mourned for days, fasting and praying before the God of heaven" (Neh 1:4). When Mordecai and Esther learned of Haman's plans to destroy the Jews, they led "great mourning among the Jews, with fasting and weeping and lamenting..." (Esth 4:3). After studying the words of Jeremiah, Daniel "turned to the Lord God, to seek an answer by prayer and supplication with fasting and sackcloth and ashes" (Dan 9:3). Sometimes fasting is the best response to dire circumstances or serious challenges, as these stories illustrate. It can intensify our prayers and fuel our sense of urgency.

Repentance

A second reason for fasting is repentance. Again, we do not fast to get anything from God, to twist God's arm, to get God's attention, or to earn forgiveness. Fasting as a sign of repentance is just that, an act that signifies earnestness. We see this in other biblical examples. In response to Samuel, when he called Israel to return to the Lord and leave behind worshiping other gods, the people "gathered at Mizpah, and drew water and poured it out before the Lord," then "fasted that day, and said, 'We have sinned against the Lord...'" (1 Sam 7:6). The people of Nineveh, after hearing the call to repent through the prophet Jonah, "believed God; they proclaimed a fast, and everyone, great and small, put on sackcloth" (Jonah 3:5).

Fasting, along with the other symbolic actions in these passages, is an outward demonstration of an inward reality. Pouring out water before the Lord may have signified purification, a moment of renewal and forgiveness.[11] Putting on sackcloth symbolized mourning and humbling oneself before God. Sometimes clothing reflects inward states or attitudes, as when people wear black to a funeral. Fasting is a way of expressing that we mean business with God, that we are serious about turning from our sinful ways to seek the face of God, and to live in ways that please God. The prophecy

---

10. See the helpful treatment of fasting by Grudem, *Systematic Theology*, 390–91; and Piper, *A Hunger for God*. These sources informed this section on fasting.

11. Barton and Muddiman, eds., *The Oxford Bible Commentary*, 204.

of Joel says, "Even now, declares the Lord, 'return to me with all your heart, with fasting and weeping and mourning'" (Joel 2:12).

Therefore, in our spiritual journeys there may be moments of fasting, whether individually or collectively, to signify repentance. The point is not to grovel before God through fasting and repentance, as if God is angry or slow to forgive. God is love. God is good. God is quick to forgive and restore. From the beginning of the Old Testament narrative, the character of the Lord was revealed as merciful, gracious, slow to anger, abounding in steadfast love, faithfulness, and forgiveness (Exod 33:19; 34:6–7).

Worship

A third reason for fasting is worship. In the opening pages of Luke's Gospel, when Mary and Joseph bring Jesus to the temple, we hear about this wonderful older woman named Anna. As a widow at the age of eighty-four, Anna "never left the temple but worshiped there with fasting and prayer night and day" (Luke 2:37). She is a vivid example of the role of fasting in worship and prayer. Maximus the Confessor says that some fast out of love for God.[12] This seems to be true of Anna. She was so hungry for the presence of the Lord that she skipped eating at times, in order to feast on the goodness of God. Her fasting prepared her to recognize the coming of the Messiah.

In Acts, which is the second part of Luke's narrative, we find the church at Antioch doing what Anna did. The community, including prophets and teachers, was "worshiping the Lord and fasting" (Acts 13:2). The Holy Spirit spoke to them in this context of worship, fasting, and prayer, instructing them to set apart and send off Barnabas and Saul. Therefore, fasting, worship, prayer, and mission are intrinsically connected.

Guidance

A fourth reason for fasting is to seek guidance. In a well-known text on fasting, which we will consider further below, we read that there is a kind of fasting that God endorses, one that prepares us to receive the Lord's guidance (Isa 58:6, 11). As we just saw in Acts 13, fasting has historically been part of seeking guidance in preparation for missionary activity. In Acts 14,

---

12. *Philokalia* 2:57.

we also see Paul and Barnabas appointing elders for each church in Lystra, Iconium, and Antioch, "with prayer and fasting" (14:23).

Thus, fasting is linked to seeking guidance in preparing for missions and appointing church leadership. As in the early church, contemporary fasting clears our minds and hearts, sensitizing us to the voice of the Spirit, and helping us cooperate with the Father, as Jesus did (John 5:19-20).

Revelation and Visions

A fifth reason for fasting, as seen in the Scriptures, is preparation to receive revelation and visions. In the context of the covenant being renewed between the Lord and the people of Israel, Moses ascends Mount Sinai. The Lord instructs Moses to record the words of the covenant for the people to learn and live by. The passage explains that Moses "was there with the LORD forty days and forty nights; he neither ate bread nor drank water . . ." (Exod 34:28). Moses prepared to receive revelation from the Lord. Even though Moses had walked with God for many years, and knew the Lord "face to face" as an intimate friend, he longed for more of God. Moses longed for the Lord to show him his glory (Exod 33:11, 13, 18). In preparation to encounter the Lord, Moses consecrated himself through fasting. He soon found himself swept up into the glorious presence of God, feasting on the presence of the Lord.

In another story that echoes Moses's experience on Mount Sinai, we see Elijah fasting and praying before encountering God. After the dramatic episode on Mount Carmel, where the Lord was revealed as the true God who answers by fire (1 Kgs 18:16-45), Elijah flees to escape the threat of Jezebel. Before embarking on his next journey, Elijah eats bread and water provided by the angel of the Lord. "Strengthened by that food, he traveled *forty days and forty nights* until he reached Horeb, the same mountainous area where Moses met the Lord. There he went into a cave and spent the night" (19:8-9).

The parallels to the story of Moses are striking. Like Moses, Elijah goes forty days and forty nights without food before his encounter with God. The account suggests that the cave may have been the cleft of the rock, or one like it, where Moses hid as the Lord passed by (cf. Exod 33:22). After a series of theophanies or manifestations of divine power, the Lord comes to Elijah in a gentle whisper, in sheer silence (1 Kgs 19:11-12). For both Moses and Elijah, an extended fast was part of their preparation for encountering the Lord. As Evagrius says, fasting "prepares you for God's presence."[13]

Longing for Christ's Return

A sixth reason for fasting is to express longing for the return of Jesus. The disciples of John asked Jesus, "Why do we and the Pharisees fast often, but your disciples do not fast?" Jesus answered, "The wedding guests cannot mourn as long as the bridegroom is with them, can they? The days will come when the bridegroom is taken away from them, and then they will fast" (Matt 9:14–15). While fasting was customary for Jews on the Day of Atonement (Lev 23:26–32), the Pharisees were known to fast twice a week. John the Baptist and his followers were also known for their ascetic rigor. However, Jesus answers using metaphorical language found in the Old Testament that describes the Lord as the groom and his people as the bride (e.g., Isa 62:5). Jesus explains that while he, the bridegroom, is with his followers, the wedding guests and bride, it is not a time for mourning and fasting, but for celebration. When he leaves, then they will fast, longing to see him again. Likewise, when disciples fast today, they are conveying their desire to be with Jesus, to see him, and to be with him forever, as his beloved bride.

Benefits of Fasting

Closely connected to the various reasons for fasting are a number of benefits. Reflecting on the following benefits will further inform our understanding of fasting.

1. Increase humility and dependence

One value of fasting is that it can increase humility and dependence on the Lord. For example, upon the return of the Jews from Babylon, and with the intent to rebuild the temple in Jerusalem, Ezra proclaimed a fast. Ezra explains that he called the fast "so that we might humble ourselves before our God and ask him for a safe journey for us and our children, with all our possessions" (Ezra 8:21, NIV). Likewise, when the opponents of King David rose up against him, he says, "I put on sackcloth and humbled myself

---

13. *Philokalia* 1:36.

with fasting" (Ps 35:13, NIV). Accordingly, fasting can be an act of humility before God, as we seek divine protection for our life journey, our children, and our belongings. And in the face of opposition, we can humble ourselves before the Lord with fasting, seek his face, and find strength through dependence on his power.

2. More Attention to Prayer
A second outcome of fasting is that it allows more attention to prayer. Because we are not spending time normally given to acquiring, preparing, or eating food, we can invest extra time in prayer or more intently focus our inward attention on the presence of God. If you are responsible for preparing and serving food to others, perhaps you can pray while doing it. In the spirit of the French Carmelite monk, Brother Lawrence (1614–1691), we can learn to practice the presence of God in the kitchen or other places related to serving food or cleaning up. I encourage you to craft certain prayers based on your reading of Scripture that can assist you along these lines. For example, at times when you would normally be eating, you could pray the words of Jesus: "My food is to do the will of him who sent me and to complete his work" (John 4:34). Our hunger can serve as a reminder to turn to the Lord, to abide in his love for us, and to express our affection for him.

3. Self-Discipline
A third benefit of fasting is that it exercises our self-discipline. In the passages considered earlier, we saw that athletes are so devoted to their sport that they are willing to discipline themselves—body and soul—in order to perform well. They are willing to give up certain foods or practices that might inhibit their training, development, and performance. They are willing to lift weights or run laps while others are lounging. There is, no doubt, a measure of pain and sacrifice as athletes feel the burn of muscles or lungs during workouts.

Like spiritual athletes, we are training ourselves for the long race of faith. Wise, moderate fasting may be part of that workout routine. If we train ourselves to voluntarily embrace "the small suffering of fasting,"[14] we will be better equipped to accept other forms of suffering as we seek to live righteous lives. As spiritual athletes, we train our will to turn away from those things that entice us to sin, and exercise our will to turn to the presence of Jesus within our hearts. If we learn to control our physical appetites

---

14. Grudem, *Systematic Theology*, 390; cf. Heb 5:8 and 1 Pet 4:1–2.

through spiritual exercises like fasting and prayer, then we will be more inclined to control our thoughts, words, and actions. We are body and soul. There is a symbiotic relationship between what we do with our body and what we think or do in the depths of our soul. The inner and outer life is organically united. Spiritual athletes understand this holistic perspective and live accordingly.

Self Discipline and the Passions

On this note, I want to touch on a theme related to exercising self-discipline. In the spiritual classics, there is an ongoing debate over the human passions or desires. The Greek word for passion, *pathos*, basically means something that happens to a person or thing.[15] It is an experience that is undergone passively, including an appetite or impulse such as anger or desire. Some of the Greek Fathers view the passions as something intrinsically evil. For example, John Klimakos (c. 579–649) says that God is not the creator of the passions, they are unnatural, and alien to humanity's true self.

Other Greek Fathers, such as Isaiah the Solitary (c. 431–491), see the passions as impulses that were implanted in human beings by God from the very beginning. The passions are fundamentally good, though they are distorted by sin. Therefore, the passions are to be transfigured, not suppressed; to be educated, not eradicated; to be used positively, not negatively.

Why is this discussion on the passions important or related to fasting? For one, it clarifies that hunger and other natural desires or appetites, when transformed by grace and used in positive ways, are good. The key is to direct the passions toward the Lord and good things; because the glory of the Lord is a person fully alive, as Irenaeus (c. 130–200) said, not a person whose passions are uprooted.[16] The passions are like wild horses inside us that need to be trained properly. The goal is not to be broken and dispirited, but vibrant and full of the life of the Holy Spirit.[17]

---

15. The section on "passion" in the glossary of the *Philokalia* 1, informed my discussion here, 363–64

16. Irenaeus, *Against Heresies*, Book 4, 20:7.

17. In the dialogue *Phaedrus* (sections 246a–254e), Plato develops an allegory of a chariot and two horses to describe the relationship between the rational and irrational impulses within the soul. The aim is to direct, harmonize, and align the two horses, so the chariot can move forward.

4. Heightens Alertness

A fourth outcome of fasting is that it heightens our spiritual and mental alertness. When we focus less on eating and digesting food, we are freed up to focus on spiritual realities. Those who fast learn that there is a sharpness and clarity of mind that occurs during fasting. We become more sensitive to the inner workings of our mind and heart, and to the movement of the Holy Spirit in our lives. Further, some medical doctors and scientists have conducted research on fasting, and concluded that intermittent fasting can be good for your brain, your mental alertness, and aid your body in fighting off neurological diseases.[18]

5. Increases Spiritual Strength

A fifth benefit of fasting is that it increases our spiritual strength and power. Fasting can empower us to overcome temptation and walk in the power of the Holy Spirit. The life of Christ illustrates this:

> Jesus, full of the Holy Spirit, returned from the Jordan and was led by the Spirit in the wilderness, where for forty days he was tempted by the devil. He ate nothing at all during those days, and when they were over, he was famished . . . Then Jesus, filled with the power of the Holy Spirit, returned to Galilee (Luke 4:1–2, 14).

In Scripture, the wilderness symbolizes a place of testing, temptation, and spiritual battle. As Jesus entered the wilderness, where he was enticed by the devil, he fasted, prayed, and overcame temptation. Jesus prepared himself for spiritual battle. Along with fasting, Jesus countered each temptation with a specific truth from Scripture. After overcoming the temptation of the enemy, Jesus was invigorated with fresh power from the Holy Spirit. He returned to Galilee, where he preached and healed, and news about him spread.

Fasting also increases spiritual power to drive out demons. In Mark 9, a father brings his son to the disciples, so they can drive an evil spirit from the young man. They were unsuccessful. Jesus, using this as a teaching moment, drove the evil spirit from the boy, explaining that this kind of evil spirit "can come out only by prayer *and fasting*" (9:29). Some ancient manuscripts do not include the words, "and fasting." But we know that Jesus, the early church, and the people of God throughout history have fasted to increase spiritual power and authority. Therefore, there may be times to

---

18. For example, see Dr. Mark Mattson, a professor of neuroscience in the Johns Hopkins School of Medicine, "Are There Any Proven Benefits to Fasting?"

fast and pray, in order to overcome temptation, break the power of an evil spirit, and experience a fresh impartation of the power of the Spirit.

6. Expresses Earnestness and Urgency

A sixth benefit of fasting is that it helps us express earnestness and urgency in prayer. At a basic, physiological level, if we continued to fast, eventually we would die. In a symbolic way, therefore, fasting communicates to God, "We are prepared to lay down our lives for this situation to change, rather than see it continue as it is now."[19] The prophet Joel illustrates fasting as a way to infuse prayer with earnestness and urgency:

> Yet even now, says the LORD, return to me with all your heart, with fasting, with weeping, and with mourning; rend your hearts and not your clothing. Return to the LORD, your God, for he is gracious and merciful, slow to anger, and abounding in steadfast love, and relents from punishing (Joel 2:12-13).

Here fasting conveys a wholehearted return to the Lord. Rather than tearing their clothing, a custom that symbolized repentance or deep sorrow, the people are told to rend their hearts. Instead of an outward display, the Lord seeks genuine inward repentance, a turning back to the Lord within the heart. This earnest return to the Lord is met with, and made possible by, the grace, mercy, patience, and love of God.

7. Minister to the Poor

A seventh benefit of fasting is that it provides us with the opportunity to minister to the poor. Isaiah 58 is a key text on fasting. It describes fasting that pleases the Lord, in contrast to fasting to show off for others or to try and manipulate God into doing what pleases us. Speaking through Isaiah, the Lord says:

> Is not this the fast that I choose: to loose the bonds of injustice, to undo the thongs of the yoke, to let the oppressed go free, and to break every yoke? Is it not to share your bread with the hungry, and bring the homeless poor into your house; when you see the naked, to cover them, and not to hide yourself from your own kin? Then your light shall break forth like the dawn, and your healing

---

19. Mahatma Gandhi was known for his extended fasting to express urgency and desire for change among the people of India. Gandhi said that, along with other religious leaders, Jesus served as an example for him, especially in fasting, nonviolence, and love for one's enemies.

shall spring up quickly; your vindicator shall go before you, the glory of the LORD shall be your rear guard (Isa 58:6–8).

The kind of fasting God chooses involves acting justly, setting free the oppressed, sharing food with the hungry, providing shelter to the homeless, providing clothing to those without it, and taking care of relatives. Sometimes when we fast, we do not think about taking the opportunity to share with those in need. We could take food and clothing to someone, or to a food and clothing bank; or we could work at a homeless shelter or soup kitchen. As Diadochos of Photiki says, when we fast, "we can give to the poor what remains over, for this is the mark of sincere love."[20] The point is to care for others. Fasting helps us focus on the needs of others, and perhaps even identify with those who live hungry much of the time. When we fast in the way God has prescribed, the light of God's glory shines through us, we experience healing, and the Lord vindicates and protects us.

8. Receiving the Father's Rewards

An eighth and final benefit of fasting is that it opens the door to receive the Father's rewards. These rewards are found in Jesus' teaching on prayer and fasting in the Sermon on the Mount:

> Pray then in this way: Our Father in heaven, hallowed be your name. Your kingdom come. Your will be done, on earth as it is in heaven (Matt 6:9–10).

> And whenever you fast, do not look dismal, like the hypocrites, for they disfigure their faces so as to show others that they are fasting. Truly I tell you, they have received their reward. But when you fast, put oil on your head and wash your face, so that your fasting may be seen not by others but by your Father who is in secret; and your Father who sees in secret will reward you (Matt 6:16–18).

One reward is the privilege of knowing God as Father, along with sharing in the kingdom of God, and praying for the kingdom and will of God to be manifest on earth. Another reward is the opportunity to fast—not "if" but "*when* you fast"—and develop a secret history with God. The Father, who remains unseen but can be reached through prayer, sees our fasting and rewards us.

---

20. *Philokalia* 1:266.

Length of Fasts

Wisdom and Moderation

There are many biblical and later historical examples that suggest how long we might fast. Before considering these, it is critical to emphasize that *fasting should be practiced with wisdom and moderation*. One of the great teachers on fasting and the ascetic life in general is John Cassian, the Desert Father considered in the previous chapter. He writes: "as the fathers have said, all extremes are equally harmful. It is as dangerous to fast too much as it is to overfill the stomach . . ." Cassian knew some "who were not defeated by gluttony, but were undermined by immoderate fasting and lapsed into gluttony because of the weakness caused by this fasting. Indeed, I can remember having experienced this once myself."[21] Avoiding extreme fasting is as important as avoiding gluttony.

For some of us, moderation, or walking the middle way, can be very challenging. We seek moderation in all our spiritual practices. Knowing that we are holistic organisms, we understand that spiritual health is the result of caring for body and soul together. Evagrius, the mentor of Cassian, asserts that we should "act as if [we are] going to die tomorrow; yet [we] should treat [our] body as if it was going to live for many years." The first "cuts off the inclination to listlessness," and makes us more diligent; the second "keeps [our] body sound and [our] self-control balanced." In this, we are harmonizing the *carpe diem* ("seize the day" in Latin) and the "life is a marathon" perspectives. We live with passion and with wisdom. When fasting, or engaging in any spiritual exercise, we use common sense, discernment, and practical wisdom. We treat our bodies with respect, taking care of them. We balance "appropriate discipline" and "adequate nourishment" of the body.[22] Avoiding burnout and excessive austerity, we are looking to build a vigorous spiritual life *based on sustainable practices*.[23]

---

21. *Philokalia* 1:108. Cassian goes on to detail the problem that arose from his excessive fasting and concludes, "Thus I was in greater danger because of my immoderate fasting and insomnia than I was from gluttony and too much sleep."

22. Diadochos of Photiki, *Philokalia* 1:266.

23. When I first started fasting thirty years ago, I wish I would have had more sound advice from experienced "fasters," like John Cassian.

Not Fasting

Along with moderation, I want to add that *some should not fast at all*. Ideally, you will have a spiritual director in your life (which we will discuss at length in chapter 10), someone with significant experience in the spiritual journey who can offer you sound advice and guidance. That person could help you think through if fasting is a good option or not. You may have a medical doctor who says that fasting is not viable for you because of health reasons. Maybe you are taking medication that requires food every day. Maybe you are pregnant or trying to get pregnant. Maybe you have struggled with an eating disorder. Anorexia, bulimia, and other eating disorders are serious matters. I have seen too many young people either develop or intensify an eating disorder because of unwise fasting. Listen to the advice of professionals. The wisdom of God comes to us through the wise counsel of others, whether they are doctors, therapists, nutritionists, or physical trainers. Frankly, it is foolish to not heed the advice of those who are professionally trained, who spend their lives taking good care of others—body, soul, and spirit.

It may be frustrating to hear that fasting is not a viable option for you. Believe it or not, this may be an opportunity to practice a different kind of spiritual discipline or utilize spiritual wisdom. I have had seasons in my spiritual life, over the past thirty years, when I could not fast for health reasons. I "fasted from fasting." Knowing the benefits of fasting, it was difficult to not fast. If only I had read some of the practical teaching from the *Philokalia* or other vital sources earlier on! John of Karpathos (c. seventh century) says that if you try to fast "and cannot do so because of ill health, then with contrition of heart you should give thanks for Him who cares for all and judges all." Practical wisdom acknowledges that health reasons may keep some of us from fasting. Yet we can still engage God at the deepest levels of our heart, give thanks, and entrust ourselves to the One who cares for us. John adds:

> Understanding the Lord's will, then, do not be discouraged because of your inability to practice asceticism, but strive all the more to be delivered from the enemy through prayer and patient thanksgiving. If thoughts of weakness and distress force you to leave the city of fasting, take refuge in another city (cf. Mt. 10:23)—that is, in prayer and thanksgiving.

If you are unable to fast, direct your energy into prayer and patient thanksgiving. The disciplines of prayer and *patient* thanksgiving—that is, giving thanks in all things, including your inability to fast—will deliver you from the enemy. This may even take you even deeper into facets of the spiritual life than you can imagine. Being unable to fast, and perhaps rely on it in ways that lead to subtle pride, you will find new resources for experiencing the grace, presence, and power of God. Be mindful of your own weaknesses and limitations. You may have to leave the more familiar ground of fasting and discover how to connect with God in new ways through prayer and thanksgiving.

How Long? How To?

If fasting is feasible for you, there are many options on how long to fast and how to do it. One is a twelve to sixteen hour fast. After eating dinner the night before, you skip breakfast the next day, and eat lunch. You can skip lunch as well, then eat an early dinner. This is one of my preferred ways to fast. Because of my history of stomach and digestive issues, this approach works well. It cultivates a fasting mentality and some of the benefits of fasting without the susceptibility to problems with stomach acid or diarrhea that may occur with longer fasts.

One day, while reflecting on shorter versus longer fasts, an image came to mind. It was a pendulum moving back and forth over the surface of some soil. Each time it swung, the pendulum skimmed off a thin layer of soil. Over time, the grazing of the pendulum dug a deep well. This was a picture of the subtle effects of shorter fasts. They are different than extended, more rigorous fasts, which are like digging a well with a shovel. I urge you to keep in mind the inconspicuous effects of a twelve- to sixteen-hour fast. The results may be less noticeable in the short term, but over time a deep well is dug in your heart. Consistent, shorter fasting may, for many reasons, be more advantageous and sustainable.

Before looking at other options for fasting, it is good to remind ourselves that the goal of all fasting and other spiritual disciplines is to cultivate intimacy with the Lord. We are focusing our attention, with our body and soul, on the indwelling presence of Jesus. If we lose sight of him as the goal and reward of all our spiritual training, we slip into religious activity that can leave us prideful, empty, or burned out.

Another shorter fast is the one day or twenty-four hour fast. Typically this involves skipping three meals. Cassian again provides practical wisdom on this. He discusses controlling the stomach, avoiding gluttony, and gauging how to fast based on physical strength, age, sickness or health, and fragility of body. Cassian says that the Holy Fathers "found a day's fast to be more beneficial and a greater help toward purity than one extending over a period of three, four, or even seven days." How so? Because someone "who fasts for too long . . . ends up eating too much food. The result is that at times the body becomes enervated [or fatigued] through undue lack of food and sluggish over its spiritual exercises;" yet "at other times, weighed down by the mass of food it has eaten, it makes the soul listless and slack."[24] A one-day fast, then, based on the extensive experience of the Desert Fathers, is more profitable in the spiritual journey than longer fasts. Shorter fasts are more conducive to an attainable and consistent practice of fasting and other spiritual exercises. It helps us avoid becoming fatigued while fasting or overeating when we are not fasting. To stay physically fit, we do better to walk or jog one to two miles three times a week, rather than running twenty miles every two weeks. So it is with fasting.

Other options for the length of fasts, as mentioned by Cassian and seen in Scripture, are numerous: from two to forty days. We have already seen examples of forty-day fasts in the lives of Moses, Elijah, and Jesus.[25] The key is to pray for wisdom, discern what is best for your body and soul, and to heed the advice of wise counsel.

Other Options for Fasting

Besides duration of fasts, there are various options regarding things from which we can fast. Pondering this is important, especially for those who are unable to fast in more common ways. A biblical model for another type of fasting is found in Daniel 1. As servants in the palace of King Nebuchadnezzar, Daniel and his comrades did not want to defile themselves with the royal rations of food and wine. They requested to eat vegetables and drink water for ten days. At the end of the ten days, they appeared to be healthier than those who had been partaking of the royal rations. Subsequently, this model has been called a "Daniel fast." The Daniel fast can also be practiced

---

24. *Philokalia* 1:73.

25. There are many fasts in Judaism. One of the more prominent is Yom Kippur, the Day of Atonement (cf. Lev 23:26–32).

in other ways. Instead of vegetables and water for ten days, you could eat fruit or bread or something else. Some people fast using blended drinks of vegetables or fruit. This is not a diet, but a fast. Our aim is to seek the face of God, to commune with the indwelling presence of Jesus through the Holy Spirit, and to be transformed by the grace of God. The focus is not to lose weight, as in a diet, though you may lose some weight during the fast. Again, the key is to be smart, use common sense, and do what is best for your overall health.

Over the years, I taught a college seminar on the *Philokalia*. During the course, some of my students and I discussed different ways they might fast in order to cultivate a contemplative lifestyle. Some of them had eating disorders, other health issues, or took medication that did not allow fasting from food. They came up with other excellent alternatives. One student said she would give up chocolate for two weeks; another gave up a particular game on her phone; another said she would "fast from negativity," turning from negative thoughts and abstaining from negative words. Their ideas were inspiring, and so were the reports of their fasting experiences. They came up with creative and healthy approaches to fasting. The methods best suited where they were in life. They demonstrated to themselves (and their professor!) that fasting can be creative, rewarding, and not miserable.[26] As you can see, the alternatives are limitless. Any of us could benefit from a fast from negative thoughts and words over a week or two: turning from negative thoughts to meditate on positive promises from Scripture, or by praying the Jesus Prayer, and making positive statements to and about others (and ourselves). Doing this for a week would help us cultivate inner strength, deepen our relationship with Jesus, and empower us to speak encouraging words. In the next chapter, we consider another spiritual practice, solitude.

---

26. See Appendix for further discussion and practical suggestions regarding fasting.

CHAPTER 7.

Solitude and Community: Retreat to Re-Engage

"But Jesus Himself would often slip away to the wilderness and pray."
—Luke 5:16 (NASB)

"Acquire inward peace, and thousands around
you will find their salvation."
—St. Seraphim of Sarov

"If you live entirely on your own . . . whose feet will you wash?"
—Basil of Caesarea

"Let him who cannot be alone beware of community . . . Let him who is not in community beware of being alone . . . Each by itself has profound perils and pitfalls. One who wants fellowship without solitude plunges into the void of words and feelings, and the one who seeks solitude without fellowship perishes in the abyss of vanity, self-infatuation and despair."
—Dietrich Bonhoeffer, *Life Together*

Solitude and silence—why are these two words so foreign, even intimidating, to some Christians? One explanation is that many of us are connected to digital devices, or viewing other screens, the majority of our waking hours. Some of us are distracted and overstimulated by them; others are outright addicted. The idea of being alone in the presence of the

Lord, seeking his face in silence, is daunting to some. What's more, some of us are so lonely, so disconnected from community, that the thought of more time alone is stifling. Our aim in this chapter is to reconsider solitude and silence, to view them in a more positive light, and to explore practical ways to cultivate these revitalizing exercises in our daily lives.

The Call to Solitude and Silence

One way to approach solitude and silence from a more positive angle is to recognize that these related spiritual practices enable us to connect more deeply with God and with others. We are called to solitude *and* community, to retreat in order to re-engage. The truth is, we are summoned to be alone while never being alone. We are baptized into the church of Christ, the family of God. The Father pours out his love into our hearts through the Holy Spirit who is given to us. We are the dwelling place of the Holy Spirit. Christ dwells in the depths of our hearts. We are never alone. We are simply called to learn to be *alone yet not alone*. We observe this in the Old Testament, the life of Jesus, his first-century followers, and his disciples throughout history.

Solitude and Silence in the Old Testament

Jacob, the Old Testament patriarch whose twelve sons became the founders of the twelve tribes of Israel, spent the night alone while his family stayed on the other side of the River Jabbok. He wrestled with a mysterious figure until daybreak. After being blessed by him, Jacob called the place Peniel, explaining that he had seen God face to face, yet lived (Gen 32:22–30).

After the exodus event, Moses used to pitch the tent of meeting outside the camp, far away from the bustling activity, where he would meet with the Lord, and the Lord would "speak to Moses face to face, as one speaks to a friend" (Exod 33:7–11). And as we saw in the previous chapter, Elijah encountered the Lord while being alone, and heard the Lord through the gentle whisper of silence, rather than through startling theophanies in the wind, earthquake, or fire (1 Kgs 19:9–18). Sometimes the Lord is revealed to us when we are alone. We experience the presence of God when no one or no thing is around to divide our attention.

Further, when we are alone with the Lord, we are drawn into a state of silence and stillness, two postures that are often interrelated in the Old

Testament. Moses told the Israelites, as they prepared to cross the Red Sea with the Egyptians advancing on them, "The LORD will fight for you, and you have only to keep still" (Exod 14:14). Silence is a crucial part of intimacy with God. In silence and stillness, we witness the love and power of God working to defeat our spiritual enemies. Through silence and stillness we enter into a realm of worship untouched by words or activity. "Be still, and know that I am God! I am exalted among the nations, I am exalted in the earth" (Ps 46:10).

In stillness, we encounter the Great I Am, the self-existent Creator of the universe, the God and Father of our Lord Jesus Christ. The scales fall from our eyes. We see that God truly is exalted among the nations, over the earth, and over the turmoil of our lives. In quietness before God we experience salvation and strength: "For thus said the LORD God, the Holy One of Israel: In returning and rest you shall be saved; in quietness and trust shall be your strength . . ." (Isa 30:15). It seems that silence is one of the purest expressions of worship, as we join all of creation in acknowledging the holiness, majesty, and sovereignty of the Lord: "But the Lord is in his holy temple; let all the earth keep silence before him!" (Hab 2:20).

Solitude and Silence with Jesus and His Followers

Jesus and his followers further illustrate the important role of solitude and silence in the spiritual life. Jesus liked to get up early in the morning, find a solitary place, and seek the Father: "In the morning, while it was still very dark, he got up and went to a deserted place, and there he prayed" (Mark 1:35). Jesus embraced the desert, where he was led by the Spirit, sought the face of God through fasting and prayer, and emerged filled with the power of the Spirit (Luke 4:1–2, 14). This marked the beginning of his ministry, but it was also an ongoing practice as the reach of his ministry expanded. The word about him spread, crowds gathered to hear him and be healed, and Jesus retreated in order to re-engage: "But Jesus often withdrew to lonely places and prayed" (Luke 5:16). After withdrawing to pray, Jesus began teaching again, crowds came to hear, "and the power of the Lord was with him to heal" (Luke 5:17).

Jesus knew the secret of solitude, silence, and seeking the face of the Father. This was the place of intimacy with the Father, where he heard and saw what the Father was doing (John 5:19–20). In solitude, those "lonely places," Jesus communed with God, was filled with the Spirit, replenished with spiritual vigor, and prepared for each new ministry venture. Perhaps we do not meditate on this reality enough. Jesus, fully God and fully man, needed to pray as we do. If this was not the case, then he was not fully human. But he was and is fully human, and models for us how vital it is to learn to be with the Father in solitude and silence. We can imagine that there were times in those solitary places, perhaps under a desert moon or at the break of day, when Jesus would be still, know that his Father was God, and that God was being exalted through him.

The Gospels demonstrate that this is the power behind his life and ministry, and he drew his disciples into it: "Jesus took with him Peter and James and his brother John and led them up a high mountain, by themselves. And he was transfigured before them, and his face shone like the sun . . ." (Matt 17:1–2). He shared his solitude with these three friends. Like Moses, he went up a high mountain to meet with God. Unlike Moses, he took three companions. He shared this revelatory moment with them. The glory of God blazed from his face. It was like looking into the sun at noon. He was transfigured before them. This was a materialization of what happened with Jesus on those many mornings and nights in the desert. They were able to see what happened between Jesus and the Father. The glory of God washed over him, radiated from his face, and left the disciples stunned. The interaction he shared with them was one of love. Of all the things the Father could have said, it was, "This is my Son, the Beloved; with him I am well pleased; listen to him!" (Matt 17:5).

This was the transfiguration of the unique Son of God, however, it is also a model of prayer for the disciples of Jesus, then and now. Longing to be like him in every way, we too can ascend the mountain of prayer with Jesus. The same glory that transfigured him now transfigures us. He draws us into the fire of holy love that courses between the Father and Son. The Father speaks over us the same words, "You are my beloved son, my beloved daughter; with you I am well pleased." In solitude and silence, these words sink deep within. The love of God is poured out into our hearts, through the Holy Spirit (Rom 5:5).

Monks in the Desert

Following the example of Jesus, the apostles, and others in Scripture, early Christians sought the Father in solitude and silence. This is particularly evident in fourth-century monasticism. Scores of people, women and men, left cities and villages for the desert. There they sought to leave behind the trappings and distractions of city life in order to give themselves to God in undivided devotion. Some of them were excessive, treating their bodies harshly and avoiding contact with other people at all costs. But there were others who sought the Lord in solitude and silence in more moderate ways, as we saw previously with John Cassian and his approach to fasting and other ascetic exercises.[1] Since they lived in solitude, and spent more time reflecting on it than most of us, we can glean insights from those balanced teachers within the monastic traditions.[2]

1. Deepens Our Relationship with God

First and foremost, like all other spiritual disciplines, the aim of solitude is to deepen our relationship with God. Spending time alone with God, as was the custom of Jesus, enables us to focus more intently on the presence of God. Alone with God, we can turn our full attention to the presence of the Holy Spirit within us, meditate on Scripture, sing songs of worship, pour out our hearts in prayer, and listen to the Lord in silence. Often times when spending time alone with the Lord, I thank him for loving me, tell him I love him, and ask for help to grow in love for him and my neighbor. Solitude, from start to finish, is a space to focus on the love of God, an exercise in clearing the mind and heart, and a time for the Lord to kindle love within us.

2. Clarifies Distractions

Second, solitude helps us gain clarity on what distracts us from communion with God, purity of heart, and love for others. Columba Stewart, a

---

1. Some might argue that the whole enterprise of Christian monasticism that began in the fourth century was problematic, removing people from society where they would act as salt and light and leaven in the world. But this is not the place to consider that debate. Regardless of whether or not you agree with monasticism, there is much spiritual wisdom on solitude that has been developed by monastic writers. For those interested in learning more about monasticism, see Chitty, *The Desert a City*.

2. Writers in the *Philokalia* speak of being a monk *inwardly*. The word *monk* (from *monachos* in Greek, which means "solitary" or "alone"). The word suggests aloneness, singleness of devotion, oneness, and other things. Outward actions and external characteristics are not the signs of a true monk. Maximus says that whoever is freed from impassioned conceptual images, and has been granted uninterrupted, pure, and spiritual prayer, has the "mark of the inner monk," *Philokalia* 2:106. Perhaps each of us has the spirit of an inner monk. With action rooted in love and energized by grace, we can develop the inner monk through friendship with Christ.

Benedictine monk and respected authority on John Cassian, elucidates the function of solitude in Cassian. For Cassian, solitude is a primary way to exercise self-restraint, particularly in sexual areas. Through solitude one can address past and present fantasies of others, wean themselves of unhealthy images of faces and bodies, and allow the purifying love of God to cleanse the mind and heart.[3] In solitude and silence, we avail our hearts and minds to Holy Spirit who searches all things, and helps us weed out that which hinders communion with God.

3. Prepares for Healthier Engagement
Solitude actually prepares us for healthier engagement with others. In Cassian's view, solitude is therapeutic. Time alone in the presence of God can bring healing. Additionally, the goal of solitude is not isolation, but healthy relationship. In fact, Cassian devotes an entire section of his teachings (*Conference* 16) to friendship, something he knew well from personal experience. Having spent most of his life in the company of his friend from childhood, Germanus, Cassian speaks at length on the value of human partnership and healthy relationships in the monastic quest.

Cassian also explains that the sign of a mature, patient, and caring monk is that they are aflame with the love of God, something that draws others to them. Refusing to receive and show hospitality to others might actually reveal irrational strictness and spiritual lukewarmness. As Cassian's mentor Evagrius instructs, one is to "flee lust but pursue hospitality." Mature spiritual teachers actually *become* hospitality. They learn to discern that some apparent "interruptions" to solitude may actually be opportunities to love. Stewart explains: "We know from Cassian and other monastic writers that many of the most perfect anchorites [spiritual recluses] ended up in community, where they could be more available to the needs of others."[4]

Thus, solitude is an invitation to prayer, worship, and stillness in the presence of God. In solitude we encounter the love of God. In solitude the grace of God heals us, deepens our capacity for healthy friendships, transforms us into hospitable people, and prepares us for service in community.

---

3. Stewart, *Cassian the Monk*, 74–75.
4. Stewart, *Cassian the Monk*, 75.

SOLITUDE AND COMMUNITY

Moderation, Balance

As with the other spiritual exercises we are considering, moderation and balance are requisite. Mark the Ascetic writes, "[I]t is dangerous to isolate oneself completely."[5] Bonhoeffer warns, "Let him who cannot be alone beware of community . . . Let him who is not in community beware of being alone . . . Each by itself has profound perils and pitfalls."[6] To avoid these dangerous extremes, we follow the example of Jesus, engaging others, sharing and showing the kingdom, working hard, and regularly pulling away to pray and be with the Father.

Cultivating Solitude and Silence

Could it be that because of all the wonderful things that solitude and silence open for us, our spiritual enemy seeks to divert us from engaging in them? More time on our devices, more newsfeeds, more advertisements, more images, more enticements to pornography, more social networking . . . Do not get me wrong: I am not against technology, our devices, or the like. Technology, when properly used, can be very positive. I am questioning *our use* of technology and our devices.[7] Do we control them or do they control us? Are we moderate in the use of our devices? Do they restrict meaningful connection with God and those around us? If so, we do well to be mindful of how much time we spend on our devices. We can regain control, get our priorities straight, and establish daily rhythms of solitude and silence. The dividends will be innumerable.

Cultivating moments for solitude and silence is not a burden, another item to check off the spiritual "to do" list. It is an invitation, to be loved, to love, to grow in love. It is attainable. If we examine our daily lives, there are plenty of opportunities to practice solitude. It does not have to always include a walk in the woods or traveling to a remote place. We can find brief moments of solitude that already exist in our busy schedules. It might be time in the car without the radio; time in the shower or bathroom; a walk or jog around the block; the walk from one office to another. Examine your routines. Find thirty to sixty seconds each day to practice solitude in

---

5. *Philokalia* 1:158.

6. Bonhoeffer, *Life Together*, 77–78.

7. Some argue that technology and digital devices are leading to new addictions, like "digital drugs." See the bracing article by Dr. Nicholas Kardaras, "It's 'Digital Heroin.'"

silence. It will probably leave you wanting more.[8] Then you can find additional bits of time to retreat then re-engage. Remember, in solitude we are alone yet not alone. The Lord is with us. The Lord is within us.

Created for Community

Throughout our reflections, we have seen that solitude is connected to community. We are created in the *imago Dei*, the image of God, as Genesis 1:26 says: "Then God said, 'Let us make humankind in our image, according to our likeness . . .'" More specifically, the Christian tradition posits that we are created in the *imago Trinitatis*, the image of the Trinity.[9] God is Trinity: three divine Persons, one divine substance. The Church Fathers used the Greek word *perichoresis* to describe the relationship between the Father, Son, and Holy Spirit. There is a reciprocal relationship, a deep unity, a communion between the divine Persons. We catch a glimpse of this in John 17:21, when Jesus prays to the Father on behalf of his followers: "that they may all be one. As you, Father, are in me and I am in you, may they also be in us, so that the world may believe that you have sent me." There is a *perichoresis*, a coinherence, a community shared by the Father, Son, and Spirit. Members of the body of Christ are drawn into this perichoretic unity, into the very communion of the Holy Trinity.[10] We are created in the image of the Trinity, and called to share in community with God and with one another. We are created for community, not isolation. Solitude only deepens our experience of this divine and human community.

Images of Community

Christian spiritual life is lived out in community. Various biblical metaphors of the church express this.

---

8. For some, thirty to sixty seconds a day of silence and solitude may not seem very long. For others, who are constantly with children, friends, or colleagues, or who are connected to various forms of technology, it is a significant step to take. I often step into our garage, with the lights off, say the Jesus Prayer with my hands held out, and stand for a few moments of silence. Each of us can find our own "quiet cave," as Elijah did, to encounter the Lord's presence in silence (1 Kgs 19:9–18).

9. See Nonna Harrison, *God's Many-Splendored Image*, 170–177; and Miroslav Volf, *After Our Likeness*, 67–82, 191–220.

10. See Ware, "The Human Person as an Icon of the Trinity"; Moltmann, *The Trinity and the Kingdom*, 1–20, 94–96; and Twombly, *Perichoresis and Personhood*, 8–46.

Body of Christ

We are individual members that make up the whole body of Christ. "For just as the body is one and has many members, and all the members of the body, though many, are one body, so it is with Christ" (1 Cor 12:12). Through baptism we are joined to the body of Christ. "For in the one Spirit we were all baptized into one body—Jews or Greeks, slaves or free—and we were all made to drink of one Spirit" (1 Cor 12:13). The sacrament of baptism, as Jesus instructed, draws together disciples from all nations into the one mystical body of Christ (Matt 28:19–20). Through baptism all that could potentially divide us—ethnic, racial, gender, socioeconomic, or other barriers—is overcome. We are washed in the same waters of baptism, enabled to drink of one Spirit, and given new life together.

Reflecting on Galatians 3:28 and other related passages, Maximus explains that through faith in Christ we transcend our differences and are made one in the Holy Spirit:

> All are born into the Church and through it are reborn and recreated in the Spirit. To all in equal measure it gives and bestows one divine form and designation, to be Christ's and to carry his name. Thus to be and to appear as one body formed of different members is really worthy of Christ himself, our true head, in whom says the divine Apostle, "there is neither male nor female, neither Jew nor Greek, neither circumcision nor uncircumcision, neither foreigner nor Scythian, neither slave nor freeman, but Christ is everything in all of you."[11]

However, Maximus adds, in this union with Christ and one another, we do not lose our particular identities. As we are united to God without losing our creaturely identity, we are united to one another without confusing or losing our particular personhood. For Maximus, the two unconfused natures of Christ—the divine and human—serve as the paradigm for unity in diversity within the church:

> [T]he holy Church of God is an image of God because it realizes the same union of the faithful with God. As different as they are by language, places, and customs, they are made one by it through faith. God realizes this union among the natures of things without

---

11. Maximus, "The Church's Mystagogy," 187.

confusing them but in lessening and bringing together their distinction . . . in a relationship and union with himself . . ."[12]

Temple of the Holy Spirit

We are the temple of the Holy Spirit. "Do you not know that you are God's temple and that God's Spirit dwells in you?" (1 Cor 3:16) "Or do you not know that your body is a temple of the Holy Spirit within you, which you have from God, and that you are not your own? For you were bought with a price; therefore glorify God in your body" (1 Cor 6:19–20). This is the heart of the spiritual life, being indwelt by the Spirit of God; being made holy because of the Holy One who lives within us. It is an inside-out endeavor. We have been redeemed by the One who redeemed the Israelites from Egypt. Through the death and resurrection of the Son, we are saved, and now belong to God. This is a holistic salvation, soul and body, all that we are, all that we have. Worship in spirit and truth takes place within us (John 4:24). We glorify God in our body. We present our body as a living sacrifice, holy and acceptable to God (Rom 12:1). Our minds are transformed by the renewing work of the Spirit who dwells within us (Rom 12:2). God is at work in us, individually and collectively, building us into a spiritual house, where we serve as holy priests, offering spiritual sacrifices to God through Jesus Christ (1 Pet 1:4–5).

Family of God

We are the family of God. "See what love the Father has given us, that we should be called children of God; and that is what we are . . ." (1 John 3:1). God loves us beyond comprehension. God is the paradigm of a loving parent. Human parents, male and female, created in the image of God, reflect to a limited degree the parental love, skills, and capacities of our Maker. But God is the ultimate loving parent. Scripture speaks of God in the symbolic language of both Father and Mother.[13] We are more familiar with the

---

12. Maximus, "The Church's Mystagogy," 187–88; cf. McIntosh, *Discernment and Truth*, 251–55.

13. Ware explains: "In itself the Godhead possesses neither maleness nor femininity. Although our human sexual characteristics as male and female reflect, at their highest and truest, an aspect of the divine life, yet there is in God no such thing as sexuality. When, therefore, we speak of God as Father, we are speaking not literally but in symbols." *The Orthodox Way*, 33.

metaphor of the Father, but we cannot ignore the symbols that portray God as a Mother who is like: a mother eagle protecting her young in the nest (Deut 32:11–12), a nursing mother who shows compassion to the child she would never forget (Isa 49:15), and a mother bear who protects her cubs (Hos 13:8).

We will discuss this further in the next chapter when we consider the symbolic nature of language about God. What we are underscoring here is that God is a good and loving Father, and that by receiving Jesus and believing his name, we are given power to become children of God (John 1:12). Because we "are children, God has sent the Spirit of his Son into our hearts, crying, 'Abba! Father!'" (Gal 4:6). Like Jesus, we have access to the Father. We can relate to him as "Papa" or "Daddy," as Jesus did. What's more, the Father works for the good of his children, who love and are loved by him, and who are called according to his purpose. He has determined that we should "be conformed to the image of his Son, in order that he might be the firstborn within a large family" (Rom 8:28–29). Loved by God; brought into his family through faith in Jesus; filled with the Spirit of his Son; transformed into the image of his Son; and living as a daughter or son in the worldwide family of God. This is community. This is spiritual life.

Early Church Community Practices

Spiritual life, as we are seeing, involves following the example of Jesus. He spent time with the Father in solitude, time with others in ministry, and time with his disciples in community. He would retreat in order to re-engage. The early church observed these patterns and practices, as the book of Acts illustrates. In the upper room, the hundred and twenty waited on God in prayer. They anticipated the promise of the Father—the coming of the Spirit—who would clothe them with power from on high to be witnesses of Jesus to the ends of the earth (Acts 1:8). Gathered together to celebrate the day of Pentecost, the Holy Spirit filled them, as the new temple of God, and empowered them to declare God's deeds of power (Acts 2:1–4, 11).

Peter, as a freshly anointed witness of Jesus, shared a message that cut to the heart of many, and three thousand people were added to the church (Acts 2:14–41). How did they welcome and integrate these new disciples? "They devoted themselves to the apostles' teaching and fellowship, to the breaking of bread and the prayers" (Acts 2:42). These four activities convey the inner life of the early church, providing a perennial model for Christian community. As they did, we devote ourselves to these four things.

The Apostles' Teaching

First, we devote ourselves to the apostles' teaching. The apostles' teaching, *didaché* in Greek, includes "all that Jesus did and taught" (Acts 1:1).[14] This entails the message of the kingdom of God proclaimed by Jesus, as well as the demonstration of the kingdom through his miracles, healings, and other works of power. The teaching of Jesus became the teaching of the apostles; the teaching of the apostles becomes the teaching of disciples from all nations (Matt 28:19–20).

The revelation of who Jesus is and all that he does is the foundation of the church. It is the content of the church's proclamation to outsiders and the formation of insiders. It is the elucidation and application of the incarnation, life, death, resurrection, and ongoing mission of Jesus through his church. The apostles' teaching is an invitation to enter into a living relationship with Christ and his church, to join the family of God, and to be filled with the Holy Spirit. Studying the apostles' teaching, the dynamic doctrine of the early church, is a vital part of church community and spiritual life. We are to be avid students of the Word. But this is not just data to learn; it is a relationship with the living Word; it is a story to enter, a way of living.

Fellowship

Second, we devote ourselves to fellowship. The Greek word *koinónia* denotes partnership, communion, and fellowship. As we discussed, the Holy Trinity is the ultimate image of partnership, communion, and fellowship. Through the grace of God, the church shares in this communion. Our fellowship is with the Father (1 John 1:3), Son (1 Cor 1:9), and Holy Spirit (2 Cor 13:14). We share this communion with one another. Christian fellowship is a manifestation of the Spirit's presence, a fruit of Pentecost. Through faith, baptism, and the gift of the Holy Spirit, we share in the mystical body of Christ (1 Cor 10:16). We share or participate in the gospel of Christ (Phil 1:5).

---

14. See Keener, *Acts*, 1000–11.

Through *koinónia*, the love of God is revealed in the world. The Spirit empowers the church to manifest the kingdom of God through the love of sisters and brothers, their deeds, words, and generosity. The fellowship of a Spirit-empowered community is an apologetic, an ongoing incarnation and explanation of the life of Christ in our world. As we face increasing numbers of post-religious people, Christian fellowship may at times be more compelling than rhetoric or argument. In a world of lonely and atomized individuals, people are hungry to see and experience the life of Christ in community. Many are looking for spiritual family, friendship, and mentorship.

Breaking of Bread

Third, we devote ourselves to the breaking of bread. Like *koinónia*, the breaking of bread is a social practice. For early Christians, this involved sharing a meal in one another's homes (Acts 2:46), perhaps the main meal later in the day, according to Jewish custom. Luke-Acts pays special attention to the significance of sharing meals or "table fellowship," as some say. Jesus shared meals with people on the margins, those labeled by the religious leaders as "sinful" or nonreligious (Luke 5:30, 33), with religious leaders (Luke 7:36), with the five thousand he miraculously fed (Luke 9:17), and with his disciples before his crucifixion (Luke 22:14–20).

This final meal, "the last supper," becomes the model for how we break bread together. It is a shared meal rooted in Old Testament salvation history. Prior to the exodus from Egypt, the Israelites shared the Passover meal. As Jesus shared his final meal with the disciples, he spoke of a new covenant based on his body and blood. Through his life, death, and resurrection, a new exodus was taking place, a liberation of the enslaved and oppressed. God was entering into a new covenant with believers from all nations. Jesus was the full realization of the Passover. This final meal foreshadowed the eschatological banquet of the kingdom of God.

Luke reinforces the significance of breaking bread in the final chapter of his Gospel. The two disciples on the road to Emmaus do not recognize the One walking with them. It is only at the table, when the bread is broken, that they discern who he is. "When he was at the table with them, he took bread, blessed and broke it, and gave it to them. Then their eyes were opened, and they recognized him . . ." (Luke 24:30–31).

Today, when we break bread with one another in each other's homes, we give thanks for the food and drink we share, and we enjoy the presence of others and of the Spirit of Jesus among us. Our shared meals, as in the early church, are times of friendship, worship, and community. It is a "eucharistic" moment, when we give thanks for the love of God expressed through Jesus. We acknowledge that there is something very special about sharing food together. Feasting together is as sacred as fasting. Christ is among us when we break bread. May our eyes be opened to recognize him, and may our hearts burn within us as he reveals himself to us.

Prayers

Fourth, we devote ourselves to the prayers. "Prayers," the plural of prayer, is used because the early Christians prayed in the Jewish temple, typically three times per day. Regular prayer throughout the day is illustrated in the life of Daniel, who prayed three times a day (Dan 6:10), and David, who speaks of praising the Lord seven times a day (Ps 119:164). For ancient Jews and Christians, these traditional prayers, rooted in Scripture, were not to be prayed in mechanical fashion, but served as reminders to turn attention to the Lord. Praying these prayers together, in the temple and in homes, was a vital part of fellowship. The early church, with its roots in Judaism and its leader a rabbi, was a praying community. Luke-Acts portrays this.

Jesus was a man of prayer, a model for his disciples to follow. He often went to the desert and prayed (Luke 5:16). He prayed with his disciples and taught them to pray (Luke 11:1–13). Prayer was the prelude to Pentecost (Acts 1:14). Prayer was the lifeblood and power source for the early church, which experienced an ongoing Pentecost (Acts 4:23–31). Prayer was a mark of the apostolic church, as Paul urged them to pray without ceasing (1 Thess 5:17). This was (and is) not a yoke to bear, but a promise to obtain. Hidden within the injunction to pray continually is an assurance that it can be done, through the grace and power of the Holy Spirit.

Inspired by this promise and the example of the early church, we can devise creative ways to turn to the Lord throughout the day and grow in prayer. With others in our community, we can pray the Scriptures together, pray "the hours" using *The Book of Common Prayer* or Phyllis Tickle's books, or share silence before an icon of Christ or other work of art that helps us focus our attention and affections on the Lord.[15] Therefore, devo-

---

15. See Nouwen, *Behold the Beauty of the Lord*; Forest, *Praying with Icons*; and Verdon, *Art and Prayer*.

tion to each of these four themes and practices enriches our relationship to the triune God and to other Christian sisters and brothers. We also share community with others, as we will see.

Varieties of Friendships

Solitude and silence deepen our relationship with God and with other believers. As we are seeing, God is relational, and those in relationship with God share relationships with one another. For Christians, this is the case especially in Christian community. However, our relationships are not limited to other Christians. Practicing solitude and silence, and cultivating prayerful community with other followers of Jesus, opens our eyes to all those around us. Time in the presence of God, alone and with others, sensitizes us to our neighbors and coworkers. Much of our life is spent with colleagues at work, school, or in some other context. The rhythm of retreat and re-engagement, of prayer and the active life, strengthens our love for those around us. In these relationships, how can we through our words and actions demonstrate the kingdom of God, carry the fragrance of Christ, and share the life of the Holy Spirit? Solitude and Christian community stoke the inner flame, so that we can be light in the world.

Friendship, which flows from the very heart of God, is to be shared with everyone in the various circles of our lives. This includes people from other faith traditions. Of course this includes Christians from traditions or denominations different than our own, but it also includes people from other religions. In a world where the media often demonizes and Balkanizes people from various religious traditions, Christians have the opportunity to show the love of Christ to others. Thankfully, in our day there are growing movements that build interfaith friendship between Christians and other traditions.[16] Unlike previous movements in the 1960s,

---

16. In college seminars, I have used materials by those involved in Scriptural Reasoning, a movement founded by the Jewish scholar and professor at the University of Virginia, Peter Ochs, as well as the Christian scholar and professor at Cambridge University, David Ford. Also helpful are some of the books and materials published by the Muslim scholar and activist Eboo Patel, and the organization he established, Interfaith Youth Core. Both of these movements are known for calling students to deeper commitment to their own faith tradition through dialogue and friendship with people from other traditions. The deeper you sink your roots into the soil of your own tradition, the more empowered and inspired you are to branch out in friendship with people of other traditions. The Holy Spirit compels Christians to engage with others—in friendship and mission—always in the spirit of love.

these groups emphasize friendship in the midst of differences. It is not spiritual "Kumbaya," where Christians circle up with people from other religions, focus on all the "similarities" of their traditions, and neglect the distinctives. These movements train people to learn more about their own religious beliefs and practices through friendship and dialogue with others. Particular beliefs and practices are not homogenized nor mixed into a pluralistic stew. Differences and distinctives are discussed and respected.

As Christians dialogue with Jews, Muslims, Hindus, Buddhists, and others, they learn more about themselves, their Christian roots, and how to live the life of Christ in ways that spread love in the face of bigotry and hate. Engaging in interfaith friendship can be a challenging endeavor. Some would rather remain safe and secure behind the walls of their church. This endeavor would take them too far outside their comfort zone. For others, interfaith friendship is an opportunity to be challenged and to grow in new ways.

The Community of Creation

Christians are called and empowered to carry friendship with God into every sphere of life. This includes fellow Christians, neighbors, colleagues, people from other faith traditions, and the broader "community of creation."[17]

Recent decades have witnessed increased discussion on the theological and spiritual facets of human respect for all of creation, and our place in the broader community of creation. For example, Jürgen Moltmann

---

17. Regarding this, Christians in the United States can learn from Native American traditions. Leading Native American theologians speak of "the circle," a multivalent symbol that signifies the family, the clan, the tribe, and ultimately all of creation. The circle indicates the egalitarian nature of all that exists. There is a deep connection between all God's creatures. "All of creation is filled with our relatives; thus all of creation is alive." This wisdom stands as a corrective to misinterpretations of Genesis 1:26, which speaks of humans "having dominion" over all other creatures. Some understand the notion of "ruling" over all creation as license to exploit nature. They argue that because we are "at the top" of the hierarchy or pyramid, humans can do as they wish with all creatures and the natural world. The symbol of the circle reminds us that all of God's creatures "participate together, each in their own way, to preserve the wholeness of the circle." Human beings, knowing our rightful place in the world and the sacredness of creation, are to live appropriately, fulfilling our responsibility as part of the created whole. The key word that conveys our posture, according to American Indian culture, is "respect," a respect for trees and plants, for each other, for all of life, for all of creation. See Kidwell, Noley, Tinker, *A Native American Theology*, 50–51.

published his influential book, *God in Creation: A New Theology of Creation and the Spirit of God*, in 1985. Moltmann writes:

> The title expresses the book's intention: not to go on distinguishing between God and the world, so as then to surrender the world, as godless, to its scientific "disenchantment" and its technical exploitation by human beings, but instead to discover God *in* all the beings he has created and to find his life-giving Spirit *in* the community of creation that they share. This view—which has also been called panentheistic (in contrast to pantheistic)—requires us to bring reverence for the life of every living thing into the adoration of God. And this means expanding the worship and service of God to include service for God's creation.[18]

Moltmann illustrates the theological and spiritual significance of this conversation. Drawing from "the ecological wisdom" of the Old Testament, the New Testament, and classic Christian spirituality, Moltmann's work inculcates a God-centered, doxological view of creation. The Spirit of God (*Ruach Elohim* in Hebrew) broods over all of creation, fills human beings, and animates all creatures with life. Human beings perceive the world as "creation," a gift of love from God, and enter into a "community of creation." We participate in this community, rather than exploit it. In fact, we are called to serve as "eucharistic beings" in the community of creation. We do not

> merely live in the world like other living things. [We do not] merely dominate the world and use it. [We are] able to discern the world in full awareness as God's creation, to understand it as a sacrament of God's hidden presence, and to apprehend it as a communication of God's fellowship. That is why the human being is able consciously to accept creation in thanksgiving, and consciously to bring creation before God again in praise.[19]

We have a eucharistic calling—to give thanks and praise—in the community of creation. We view the world not as a thing to be dominated or exploited, but as a beautiful gift from the Creator. Creation is a visible sign of the love, goodness, and generosity of God. The heavens declare the glory of God; the voice of creation shouts how wonderful the Creator is! (Ps 19:1–4). As eucharistic creatures made in the image of God, we receive creation with thanksgiving, live within it with reverence and joy, and join

---

18. Moltmann, *God in Creation*, xi–xii.
19. Moltmann, *God in Creation*, 70–71.

one another in worship and praise of the God who graces us with the gift of life, new life in Christ, and community in the body of Christ. In the next chapter we explore two ways of approaching the knowledge of this God who dwells in community and calls us into community.

CHAPTER 8.

Cataphatic and Apophatic Spirituality: The Positive and Negative Ways

> "Ever since the creation of the world his eternal power and divine nature, invisible though they are, have been understood and seen through the things he has made."
> —Rom 1:20

> "No one has ever seen God..."
> —John 1:18 (cf. Exod 33:20; 1 John 4:12)

> "It is easier for us to get to know God than to know our own soul ... God is nearer to us than our soul, for He is the ground in which it stands ... so if we want to know our own soul, and enjoy its fellowship, it is necessary to seek it in our Lord God."
> —Julian of Norwich, *Revelations*

> "You are beyond our mind."
> —Symeon the New Theologian

THE CHRISTIAN TRADITION SPEAKS of two ways or approaches to the knowledge of God. These "ways" of knowing, experiencing, and communicating about God complement one another. One is the cataphatic or "positive way," also known as the "way of affirmation."[1] This approach seeks the knowledge of God through affirmations or positive statements about God. For example, God *is* a strong tower (Ps 61:3), or God *is* a rock (Deut 32:18).

---

1. Cataphatic comes from the Greek word *kataphasis*, which means "affirmation."

The cataphatic is the approach "with images." This way "affirms that truths about the Almighty are disclosed via biblical teaching, the sacraments, and other symbols of the faith."[2]

The second is the apophatic or "negative way." This approach seeks the knowledge of God through negations or negative statements about God.[3] For instance, God is *not* actually a strong tower. God is *not* a rock. God is *beyond* or more than the meager symbol of a tower, rock, or any other object within creation. The apophatic is the approach "without images." Advocates of the negative way explain "that the divine Reality, dwelling in a realm beyond human comprehension, cannot be known by ideas, images, and language. Rather, God is known in the darkness by detachment, prayerful silence, and contemplation."[4]

Both Ways Are Significant

Both of these approaches are equally significant for knowing, experiencing, and communicating about God. However, contemporary Christians, at least in the West, tend to be more familiar with the cataphatic way. Therefore, this chapter will focus more attention on the apophatic way. Exploring the apophatic way, clarifying how it functions, and considering examples from the Christian classics, will deepen our theological reflection and enrich our practice of spirituality.

An Apophatic Corrective

Alister McGrath says that the apophatic approach steers Christians away from the dangers of idolatry. "The apophatic tradition within Christian theology and spirituality offers a corrective to the use of imagery..."[5] McGrath

---

2. "Cataphatic spirituality is prevalent in Augustine, Luther, Calvin, the spiritual exercises of Ignatius, and the teachings, liturgy, and art forms of the Catholic and Protestant traditions. Both apophatic and cataphatic ways direct sincere seekers to God and spiritual life." Nassif and Demarest, eds., *Four Views on Christian Spirituality*, 19.

3. Apophatic comes from the Greek word *apophasis*, which means "denial."

4. "Proponents appeal to Moses' approach to God in 'thick darkness' (Exodus 20:21), as well as in a 'cloud' (Exodus 24:15). Robust apophatic spirituality is found in Gregory of Nyssa (c. 335–c. 395), Meister Eckhart (c. 1260–c. 1328), *The Cloud of Unknowing* (fourteenth century), John of the Cross (1542–1591), and Eastern Orthodoxy." Nassif and Demarest, eds., *Four Views on Christian Spirituality*, 19.

5. McGrath, *Christian Spirituality*, 118.

cites the treatise *On the Incomprehensibility of God* by the Archbishop of Constantinople, John Chrysostom (347–407). Chrysostom emphasizes the limits to all creaturely knowledge (human and angelic) and comprehension of God:

> Let us invoke him as the inexpressible God, incomprehensible, invisible and unknowable. Let us affirm that he surpasses all power of human speech; that he eludes the grasp of every mortal intelligence; that the angels cannot penetrate him; that the seraphim cannot see him clearly; that the cherubim cannot fully understand him. For he is invisible to the principalities and powers, the virtues and all creatures, without exception. Only the Son and the Holy Spirit know him.[6]

The cataphatic tradition, with its positive statements about God, helps us know God to a limited extent. But, as Chrysostom asserts, God is ultimately inexpressible, incomprehensible, invisible, and unknowable. God outstrips all of our symbols, languages, and intellectual capacities. McGrath adds: "Apophatic theology identifies and stresses the limitations of human knowledge of God, and especially the ability of human ideas and images to convey the full reality of God." The apophatic tradition "reminds us that there are limits to what can be known about God, and that a distinction must always be drawn between the images of God and the reality of God."[7] In short, God *is always more*. If we would could fully conceive of God, then that would be no God at all, as Augustine and other theologians claim.[8] Pondering the fact that God is a transcendent mystery, and that no human intellect or theological system can capture this mystery, keeps us humble.

The apophatic tradition does not discourage us from using our minds and words to seek, describe, and worship God. Quite the opposite is true. Orthodox theologian Bradley Nassif states: "The apophatic way ... does not negate the use of the mind. On the contrary, the church fathers recognized that rationality is perhaps the noblest feature of God in humans. Christ died so that we may lose our sins, not that we may lose our minds." The apophatic tradition "creates a posture of profound reverence in the heart"

---

6. Chrysostom, *On the Incomprehensibility of God*, 3; in McGrath, *Christian Spirituality*, 118.

7. McGrath, *Christian Spirituality*, 118.

8. God always remains a mystery that transcends human intellect and words: "If you understood him, it would not be God" (St. Augustine, *Sermo* 52, 6, 16 and *Sermo* 117, 3, 5).

of Christians, helping them "understand that God is and they are not."[9] The cataphatic and apophatic ways work together. The cataphatic way uses a wide variety of images, words, and symbols to help us know God and make God known. The apophatic way reminds us that all these images, words, and symbols are limited when it comes to describing the fathomless mystery of God.

The Apophatic and Aquinas

A story about Thomas Aquinas, whether legendary or historical, illustrates the interplay between the cataphatic and apophatic ways. Aquinas spent nearly a decade writing his masterful *Summa Theologica*. These volumes provide a wide-ranging summary of theological questions and answers. In the *Summa*, Aquinas commends both the cataphatic and apophatic ways. The *Summa* itself is an exercise in the cataphatic way. Aquinas invests nearly ten years of his life recording detailed reflections on God, creation, humanity, Christ, salvation, and the sacraments.

The story says that while celebrating Mass in 1273, Aquinas received a revelation that affected him so deeply he ceased writing. His friend and secretary, Brother Reginald, asked Aquinas why he stopped writing before completing his *Summa*. Aquinas explained that after the revelation he received, his writings seemed like straw. This masterful exposition of Christian doctrine—which went on to become a classic of theology and philosophy—was like rubbish compared to the glory of God it sought to describe. All the nuanced articulation of who God is came to a screeching halt when Aquinas encountered God in this revelation.

The cataphatic approach brought Aquinas to new vistas of God's infinite character. A revelation struck him like lightning. God was much more than Aquinas could ever imagine or communicate. The master theologian and philosopher was brought to silence. Cataphatic theology is "concerned with what we affirm about God: apophatic theology is concerned with our understanding of God, when, in the presence of God, speech and thought fail us and we are reduced to silence."[10] Aquinas's encounter with God at Mass that day illustrates this beautifully.

---

9. Nassif and Demarest, eds., *Four Views on Christian Spirituality*, 42.
10. Louth, *The Origins of the Christian Mystical Tradition*, 160.

Cataphatic and Apophatic Spirituality

Biblical Foundations of Apophatic Spirituality

As we are seeing, both the cataphatic and apophatic approaches to the knowledge of God are integral. Apophatic spirituality, like the cataphatic, is based on biblical stories and insights. The following are just a few examples illustrating that God is beyond all our symbols, concepts, and theologizing. Chrysostom said, God "eludes the grasp of every mortal and angelic intelligence." The Bible itself, as revelatory and marvelous as it is, is like God condescending to our level to convey a limited amount about himself and his ways, as John Calvin (1509–64) suggests:

> For who even of slight intelligence does not understand that, as nurses commonly do with infants, God is wont in a measure to "lisp" in speaking to us? Thus such forms of speaking do not so much express clearly what God is like as accommodate the knowledge of him to our slight capacity. To do this he must descend far beneath his loftiness.[11]

As a nurse speaks baby talk to an infant, so God adapts to our limited capacity to understand. The voice of God in Scripture, Calvin humorously claims, is like the "goo goo ga ga" of a loving mother or a nurse to a child. God descends to us in the written words of Scripture just as God descends to us in the incarnation as the living Word. God is exalted, inexpressible, incomprehensible, invisible, and unknowable, according to Calvin and Chrysostom. The apophatic thread that runs through Scripture can be seen in the following passages. Take a moment to read them and ponder the apophatic qualities.

Exodus 3:1–14: *The angel of the Lord appears in fire, God speaks to Moses, revealing the divine name as "I Am Who I Am"*
The angel of the Lord appeared to Moses in a flame of fire out of a bush. God called to Moses from the bush. Moses hid his face because he was afraid to look at God. God told Moses that he is the God of Abraham, Isaac, and Jacob. God also said to Moses, "*I Am Who I Am.*"

Exodus 33:20: *No human can see God and live*
The Lord said to Moses, "You cannot see my face; for no one shall see me and live."

---

11. Calvin, *Institutes of the Christian Religion*, Ch. XIII, Section 1, p. 121.

1 Kings 19:11–13: *Elijah encounters the Lord in silence*
Elijah encounters the Lord in silence, not in wind, earthquake, or fire.

Job 36:26: *God is beyond understanding*
"How great is God—beyond our understanding! The number of his years is past finding out" (NIV).

Isaiah 6:1–2: *Even angels who dwell in the presence of the Lord cover their faces*
"In the year that King Uzziah died, I saw the Lord sitting on a throne, high and lofty; and the hem of his robe filled the temple. Seraphs were in attendance above him; each had six wings: with two they covered their faces, and with two they covered their feet, and with two they flew."

John 1:18: *No one has ever seen God; only the Son makes God known*
"No one has ever seen God. It is God the only Son, who is close to the Father's heart, who has made him known."

Ephesians 3:18–19: *The love of Christ surpasses knowledge*
"I pray that you may have the power to comprehend, with all the saints, what is the breadth and length and height and depth, and to know the love of Christ that surpasses knowledge, so that you may be filled with all the fullness of God."

Philippians 4:6–7: *The peace of God surpasses all understanding*
"Do not worry about anything, but in everything by prayer and supplication with thanksgiving let your requests be made known to God. And the peace of God, which surpasses all understanding, will guard your hearts and your minds in Christ Jesus."

1 Timothy 6:16: *God dwells in unapproachable light and has never been seen*
"It is he alone who has immortality and dwells in unapproachable light, whom no one has ever seen or can see; to him be honor and eternal dominion. Amen."

1 John 4:12: *No one has ever seen God*
"No one has ever seen God; if we love one another, God lives in us, and his love is perfected in us."

Cataphatic and Apophatic Spirituality

Revelation 8:1: *Silence in response to divine action*
"When the Lamb opened the seventh seal, there was silence in heaven for about half an hour."

Because God is beyond and ultimately unknowable to us, Scripture reveals a measure of who the triune God is. The apophatic tradition is based on biblical passages like those above. We could turn to numerous voices in the Christian East or West to learn more about apophatic spirituality, but two are particularly important.

Insights from the Past

Gregory of Nyssa: The Life of Moses

One classic Christian theologian who further illustrates apophatic spirituality is Gregory of Nyssa. One of Gregory's goals was to build a bridge between Greek (or Hellenistic) culture and the Jewish Scriptures.[12] He sought to help educated Greeks read, understand, and live the Scriptures. His work *The Life of Moses* demonstrates this goal. Gregory's contemplative exposition of the story of Moses, as detailed in the book of Exodus, presents Moses as a paradigm of mystical ascent to God. Gregory's treatise is organized around three theophanies[13] or manifestations of God to Moses. The first theophany is when Moses sees God in the light of the burning bush (Exod 3:1–15). The second theophany occurs when God is revealed in both light and darkness, in the pillar of cloud and fire that guides the Israelites in the desert (Exod 13:21). The third theophany is when Moses meets God in the thick darkness at the summit of Mount Sinai (Exod 20:21).

What is especially important in this is how Gregory views the spiritual life as a journey into the mystery of God. Like Moses, believers ever-increasingly encounter God in the darkness of unknowing. Gregory explains that as we progress on the spiritual ascent to God, we understand more clearly that aspects of God's nature are uncontemplated:

> For leaving behind everything that is observed, not only what sense comprehends but also what the intelligence thinks it sees, it keeps on penetrating deeper until by the intelligence's yearning for

---

12. See Meyendorff, the preface to Gregory of Nyssa, *The Life of Moses*, xii.

13. A theophany (from the Greek *theos* "God" and *phainein* "to show") is a visible manifestation of God.

> understanding it gains access to the invisible and the incomprehensible, and there it sees God. This is the true knowledge of what is sought; this is the seeing that consists in not seeing, because that which is sought transcends all knowledge, being separated on all sides by incomprehensibility as by a kind of darkness. Wherefore John the sublime, who penetrated into the luminous darkness, says, *No one has ever seen God* [John 1:18], thus stating that knowledge of the divine essence is unattainable not only by men but also by every intelligent creature.[14]

Gregory says that we yearn to know more of God. This desire takes us to new spiritual heights, where we come to know and encounter the invisible and incomprehensible God. But this true spiritual knowledge is not a full comprehension of God, as if we could ever analyze God under our theological microscope. We actually see God by not seeing God. God, who makes darkness his hiding place (Ps 18:11), transcends our human intellectual capacity. Only as the Holy Spirit purifies our heart and illumines our mind can we increasingly know the God who dwells in darkness.

Kallistos Ware says that the spiritual journey proceeds from light to darkness. "We go out from the known to the unknown, we advance from light into darkness." We do not simply journey "from the darkness of ignorance into the light of knowledge, but we go forward from the light of partial knowledge into a greater knowledge which is so much more profound that it can only be described as the 'darkness of unknowing.'" In this darkness, we begin to realize "how little we understand," as Socrates suggested. Gregory of Nyssa declares: "God's name is not known, it is wondered at."[15] Ware adds, "God is not so much the object of our knowledge as the cause of our wonder." The apophatic journey from light to darkness inspires us to wonder at the name, glory, and beauty of God.

Pseudo-Dionysius: The Mystical Theology

A second classic theologian who describes apophatic spirituality in great detail is Pseudo-Dionysius, an unknown author who scholars think lived in the sixth century, possibly in Syria.[16] His work *The Mystical Theology*

---

14. Gregory of Nyssa, *The Life of Moses*, 95.
15. Ware, *The Orthodox Way*, 13–14.
16. The name "Pseudo-Dionysius" is a combination of two words. Dionysius, the unknown character mentioned in Acts 17:34, who listened to Paul's speech about Jesus

is a concise yet challenging treatise on apophatic spirituality. In this five-chapter work, we glean a handful of insights into apophatic spirituality.

The Holy Trinity

First, apophatic spirituality centers on the Holy Trinity. At the beginning of chapter one, Dionysius prays:

> Trinity!! Higher than any being, any divinity, any goodness! Guide of Christians in the wisdom of heaven! Lead us up beyond unknowing and light, up to the farthest, highest peak of mystic scripture, where the mysteries of God's Word lie simple, absolute and unchangeable in the brilliant darkness of a hidden silence.[17]

While transcending all being and human understanding, the Holy Trinity is immanent, guiding Christians into wisdom, leading us into the divine presence, and opening to us the mysteries of God's Word. Our quest is for God: the Father who created us, the Son who saves us, and the Spirit who indwells and transforms us. As Dionysius says, we "strive upward as much as [we] can toward union with him who is beyond all being and knowledge."[18] Our goal, for which we strive energized by grace, is to know and experience the Holy Trinity.

Affirmation and Negation

Second, apophatic spirituality involves the related acts of affirmation and negation. This means making positive statements about God, as seen earlier, then making negative statements. Dionysius suggests, because God "is the Cause of all beings, we should posit and ascribe to it all the affirmations we make in regards to beings, and, more appropriately, we should negate all these affirmations." Again, the point of this is that God is beyond privations, every denial, and every assertion.[19]

---

at the Areopagus in Athens; and Pseudo, because the author uses the name Dionysius as an alias or pseudonym. In scholarly circles, he is also called Dionysius the Areopagite or Denys for short.

17. Pseudo-Dionysius, *Complete Works*, 135.
18. Pseudo-Dionysius, *Complete Works*, 135.
19. Pseudo-Dionysius, *Complete Works*, 136.

God in the Darkness

Third, apophatic spirituality urges us to seek God in the darkness. Like Gregory of Nyssa, Dionysius views Moses as a model for this apophatic journey. Following the example of Moses, we are purified by the work of the Spirit, enabled to pass beyond the summit of every holy ascent, leave behind every divine light, every voice, every word from heaven, and "plunge into the darkness where, as Scripture proclaims, there dwells the One who is beyond all things."[20] On the summit of the mountain, Moses "does not meet God himself, but contemplates, not him who is invisible, but rather where he dwells," encountering the unimaginable presence of the Transcendent One. Moving further, Moses breaks free of what is seen, and "plunges into the truly mysterious darkness of unknowing. Here, renouncing all that the mind may conceive, wrapped entirely in the intangible and the invisible, he belongs completely to him who is beyond everything." Here Moses "is supremely united to the completely unknown by an inactivity of all knowledge, and knows beyond the mind by knowing nothing."[21] Moving beyond the visible, the transcendent God is encountered in "the cloud of unknowing," as the fourteenth-century anonymous writer said in the same-titled work.[22] After contemplating and praising the many facets of God's character, like Moses we encounter God beyond our knowing faculty, united with God in love. Here God does not "belong" to us, as if we could objectify or capture the Transcendent One; rather, we belong to God.

Language Falls Short

Fourth, apophatic spirituality teaches us that the higher we ascend in the spiritual journey, the more language falters. Dionysius explains:

> The fact is that the more we take flight upward, the more our words are confined to the ideas we are capable of forming; so that now as we plunge into that darkness which is beyond intellect, we shall find ourselves not simply running short of words but actually speechless and unknowing . . . [T]he more [the intellect] climbs, the more language falters, and when it has passed up and beyond

---

20. Pseudo-Dionysius, *Complete Works*, 136.
21. Pseudo-Dionysius, *Complete Works*, 137.
22. Walsh, trans., *The Cloud of Unknowing*.

Cataphatic and Apophatic Spirituality

the ascent, it will turn silent completely, since it will finally be at one with him who is indescribable.[23]

We use words to describe the glory and greatness of the Holy Trinity (the cataphatic approach), but the closer we get to God, the more we realize how our language falls short of adequately glorifying God (the apophatic approach). Silence becomes the most appropriate response to the holy presence of God. Entering the thick darkness, we realize that the apophatic way of unknowing and worshipful silence "brings us not to emptiness but to fullness. Our negations are in reality super-affirmations." Negative in outward form, "the apophatic approach is affirmative in its final effects: it helps us reach out, beyond all statements positive or negative, beyond all language and all thought, towards an immediate experience of the living God."[24] In this encounter, we respond as Elijah, the seraphim of Isaiah 6, and Job did when confronted by the numinous presence of God. "The Lord is in his holy temple; let all the earth be silent before him" (Hab 2:20).

God Is Beyond All

Fifth, apophatic spirituality reminds us that, as Dionysius puts it, God is ultimately beyond all perception and conception. That is, God is beyond what we can sense (see, hear, touch) and what we can understand. God, who is the Cause of all, "is above all and is not inexistent, lifeless, speechless, mindless." God "is not a material body, and hence has neither shape nor form, quality, quantity, or weight . . . is not in any place and can neither be seen nor be touched . . . is neither perceived nor . . . perceptible."[25] The essence of who God is transcends our senses; God is beyond all human perception.

Further, God is not soul or mind, nor does God "possess imagination, conviction, speech, or understanding . . ." God "cannot be spoken of and . . . cannot be grasped by understanding." Dionysius of course does not ignore the reality of the incarnation, when the Word takes on human flesh and dwells among us. He speaks of the incarnation, of the eternal Word who "became a being with true human nature."[26] What he is discussing

---

23. Pseudo-Dionysius, *Complete Works*, 139.
24. Ware, *The Orthodox Way*, 15.
25. Pseudo-Dionysius, *Complete Works*, 140, 141.
26. Pseudo-Dionysius, *Complete Works*, 139.

here is the unseen and unknown essence of God, as John's Gospel says: "No one has ever seen God. It is God the only Son, who is close to the Father's heart, who has made him known"(John 1:18). God the Father "is beyond assertion and denial." We make assertions and denials of what is next to God, but never of God, for God is "beyond every assertion" and "beyond every denial."[27]

God, therefore, transcends all human conception. As we have seen from Scripture, Gregory of Nyssa, John Chrysostom, Pseudo-Dionysius, and John Calvin, God exceeds all human intellectual capacities. God is always more. God bursts the confines of even the most sophisticated theological thinking and systems.

The Son is the image of the Father, the invisible God. That Christ would indwell us is a great mystery of divine grace: Christ in us, the hope of glory. Christ indwells us through the Holy Spirit. We are the temple of God. In this sense, God is more than immanent. In God we live and move and have our being. Yet the apophatic tradition balances this perspective. The immanent God is also the transcendent God. Embraced by the love of the Father, abiding in the love of the Son, and filled with the Holy Spirit, we acknowledge with Symeon the New Theologian and others in the apophatic tradition, "You are beyond our mind."[28]

Implications of the Apophatic Approach

Drawing from the Scriptures we considered, along with Gregory of Nyssa and Pseudo-Dionysius, this final section brings together four implications regarding the two ways, the cataphatic and apophatic traditions.

1. Cultivates humility.

Together the cataphatic and apophatic traditions remind us that God is infinitely beyond our limited intellectual capacities. Based on careful and prayerful study of Christian Scripture, tradition, and history, we make positive statements about God to help us relate to God, but we acknowledge that God is always more than these affirmations. There is always more to discover about the mystery of God. As my students and I have said many times, God blows our minds! This was the case when the Lord confronted Job from the whirlwind (Job 38–42). The Lord reminded Job that he was

---

27. Pseudo-Dionysius, *Complete Works*, 141.
28. In McGinn, ed., *The Essential Writings of Christian Mysticism*, 328.

the sovereign Creator of the universe, and that Job was a mere creature. After this powerful encounter, in which the great works of the Lord were recounted, Job replied:

> See, I am of small account; what shall I answer you? I lay my hand on my mouth. I have spoken once, and I will not answer; twice, but will proceed no further (Job 40:4–5).

> I know that you can do all things, and that no purpose of yours can be thwarted. "Who is this that hides counsel without knowledge?" Therefore I have uttered what I did not understand, things too wonderful for me, which I did not know (Job 42:2–3).

The greatness of God and his works left Job humbled, speechless, and convinced that he did not really understand God or his ways. Job's response has an apophatic quality, one of deep humility before the Almighty.

2. Engenders worship.
The cataphatic and apophatic traditions remind us of the greatness of God and his works, which produces humility. Closely related to this, these traditions engender worship. 1 Timothy 6:16 says, "It is he alone who has immortality and dwells in unapproachable light, whom no one has ever seen or can see; to him be honor and eternal dominion. Amen." Because the Lord has immortality or unceasing life that overpowers death, and dwells in radiant glory that blinds all creatures, no one can see him or comprehend who he is. The proper response to these truths about the Lord is worship: Paul exclaims, "To him be honor and eternal dominion!"

This verse also parallels what we saw in the other passages: no one has seen or can see the Lord. Even the seraphs, angelic beings who dwell in the presence of the Lord, covered their faces (Isa 6:1–2). The holiness of the Lord is too much for any creature to behold. At times, when we encounter the numinous presence of the Lord, we are struck by *mysterium tremendum*, the tremendous mystery. It can, at times, simultaneously be overwhelming and gentle, shattering and soothing, terrifying and attractive. "It may become the hushed, trembling, and speechless humility of the creature in the presence of—whom or what? In the presence of that which is a *mystery* inexpressible and above all creatures."[29] Integrating cataphatic *and* apophatic approaches to prayer into our spiritual life elicits further

---

29. Otto, *The Idea of the Holy*, 12–13.

worship from our hearts. In the face of divine mystery—who God is and what God does—we worship.

3. Safeguards against idolatry.

The cataphatic and apophatic traditions cultivate humility, engender worship, and safeguard against idolatry. The apophatic tradition serves as a spiritual tool—an "apophatic hammer"—that shatters potential idols. Catholic theologian Elizabeth Johnson explains that an idol is not necessarily a false god shaped like an animal, a golden calf or small statue carried by a devotee, as we see in the Old Testament.

> Rather, any representation of the divine used in such a way that its symbolic and evocative character is lost from view partakes of the nature of an idol. Whenever one image or concept of God expands to the horizon thus shutting out others, and whenever this exclusive symbol becomes literalized so that the distance between it and the divine reality is collapsed, there an idol comes into being. Then the comprehensible image, rather than disclosing the mystery, is mistaken for the reality.[30]

The apophatic way reminds us that all our symbols fall short when it comes to describing God. When we literalize a particular symbol, focus exclusively on that symbol while ignoring others, and lose the sense of distance between that symbol and the mystery of God, we are on thin ice. We do well to meditate on the wisdom of Chrysostom and affirm that the Lord "surpasses all power of human speech . . . and eludes the grasp of every mortal intelligence."

Johnson continues her reflection, quoting Calvin:

> The mind of man is, if I may be allowed the expression, a perpetual factory of idols . . . the mind of man, being full of pride and temerity, dares to conceive of God according to its own standard and, being sunk in stupidity and immersed in profound ignorance, imagines a vain and ridiculous phantom instead of God.[31]

The human mind is inclined to fashion false images of God. It is part of our nature, a bent toward arrogance, audacity, and foolishness, as Calvin claims. We are made in the image of God. Yet somehow we turn this around, seeking to make God in our image. We must remind ourselves, on

---

30. Johnson, *She Who Is*, 39.
31. Johnson, *She Who Is*, 39.

Cataphatic and Apophatic Spirituality

a regular basis, that the mystery of God cannot be captured by our theological formulations. Our minds are to be transformed from perpetual factories of idols into temples of unceasing prayer and praise. Part of this process involves the hammer of apophatic theology and spirituality. Johnson references C. S. Lewis: "My idea of God is not a divine idea. It has to be shattered time after time. He shatters it Himself. He is the great iconoclast. Could we not almost say that this shattering is one of the marks of His presence?" Lewis adds that "most are offended by the iconoclasm; and blessed are those who are not."[32] In worship and humility, we subject our minds, hearts, and theological formulations to the idol-shattering force of apophaticism.

Because of the symbolic nature of our theological formulations, based on the teachings of Scripture, and the councils and traditions of the church, we employ the positive and negative ways of theologizing. We need the cataphatic and the apophatic approaches together, as Kallistos Ware states:

> We need to use negative as well as affirmative statements, saying what God is *not* rather than what he is. Without this use of the way of negation, of what is termed the apophatic approach, our talk about God becomes gravely misleading. All that we affirm concerning God, however correct, falls far short of the living truth ... So the way of affirmation is balanced by the way of negation. As Cardinal Newman puts it, we are continually "saying and unsaying to a positive effect." Having made an assertion about God, we must pass beyond it: the statement is not untrue, yet neither it nor any other form of words can contain the fullness of the transcendent God.[33]

Everything that we affirm about God, based on what has been articulated about God over the centuries, *falls far short of the living truth*. Therefore, drawing from the wisdom of the cataphatic and apophatic traditions, we "say and unsay" in our pursuit of God. This rhythm of affirmation and denial safeguards us against idolatry and aids us in our upward ascent into the luminous darkness.[34]

4. Enriches our prayer life.

At the heart of the spiritual life is the experiential knowledge of God. Prayer is an integral part of this ongoing pursuit and encounter. Cataphatic and

---

32. Quoted in Johnson, *She Who Is*, 39.
33. Ware, *The Orthodox Way*, 14.
34. Ware, *The Orthodox Way*, 15.

apophatic spirituality enriches our pursuit of God in prayer. Through prayer we explore the expansive terrain of God's character. We are reminded of the astonishing nature of who God is. Kallistos Ware gives a vivid description:

> The Greek Fathers liken man's encounter with God to the experience of someone walking over the mountains in the mist: he takes a step forward and suddenly finds that he is on the edge of a precipice, with no solid ground beneath his foot but only a bottomless abyss. Or else they use the example of a man standing at night in a darkened room: he opens the shutter over a window, and as he looks out there is a sudden flash of lightning, causing him to stagger backwards, momentarily blinded. Such is the effect of coming face to face with the living mystery of God: we are assailed by dizziness; all the familiar footholds vanish, and there seems nothing for us to grasp; our inward eyes are blinded, our normal assumptions shattered.[35]

In prayer we meditate on the word of God. We ponder the names of God, the facets of God's character, and the glory of God's works. The Spirit reveals to us the love of God and the grace of the Lord Jesus. We use the images of Scripture to bring us into living contact with God. We become closer, more intimate friends with God. Yet God remains an awesome, expansive mystery. Apophatic spirituality inspires us as we stand on the edge of the precipice, looking over the bottomless abyss. God is always more. Apophatic spirituality encourages us as we are struck by the lightning of God's holy presence. God is the ray of darkness that blinds us. What appears to be darkness is actually the blazing white light of divine glory. We are silent, still, and set ablaze with the fire of love. In the next chapter, we consider the darkness and glory of the cross, the supreme symbol of the love of God in Christ.

---

35. Ware, *The Orthodox Way*, 13.

CHAPTER 9.

The Cross: Suffering and the Crucified Life

"Very truly, I tell you, unless a grain of wheat falls into the earth and dies, it remains just a single grain; but if it dies, it bears much fruit."
—JOHN 12:24

"Through the cross joy has come into all the world."
—HYMN TO THE RESURRECTION, IN THE ORTHODOX CHURCH

"All visible realities need the cross..."
—MAXIMUS THE CONFESSOR, *PHILOKALIA* 2:127

"There is no other path but through the burning love of the crucified."
—BONAVENTURE, *THE SOUL'S JOURNEY TO GOD*

"The mercy of God is hidden in sufferings not of our choice..."
—ST. MARK THE ASCETIC, *PHILOKALIA* 1:136

Follow Me

WHEN JESUS CALLS US, he calls us into a life of love: to receive the love of the Father, to respond to the Father's love as beloved children, and to share this love with others. He also urges us: *"Take up your cross and follow me."* This phrase is deep in meaning, can be understood in various ways, and has multiple applications. A common theme that runs through all these rich understandings is that following Jesus involves suffering.

Christian life is cruciform. Christian spirituality is cross-centered. Whether we are Catholic, Orthodox, or Protestant, our chief symbol is the cross of Christ. This multivalent symbol signifies for us the life, death, and resurrection of the Lord Jesus. The cross symbolizes the extravagant love of God in Christ. At the same time, the cross, and the suffering it represents in the life of Jesus and his followers, can be a difficult subject. I certainly do not feel adequately equipped to elucidate the mystery of the cross of Christ and the suffering of his followers. It is holy ground, and it reduces any author to humility.

The following are meditations on suffering, mere fragments, not a systematic argument or exposition. They are starting points for study, reflection, prayer, and conversation. We proceed prayerfully, asking the Lord for mercy, humility, revelation, and insight into the mystery of the cross and suffering.

1. Suffering is part of human life. All of us suffer, in varying degrees.
Many of us come into the world crying. Our mother experienced the pain of childbirth. Suffering, pain, and tears, from that moment on, are part of life. Catherine of Siena (1347–1380), the only woman other than Teresa of Avila to be granted the title of Doctor of the Church, said, "No one born into this life passes through it without suffering of body or spirit."[1] Suffering is a reality of life. There are many manifestations of suffering and reasons for it. This is not the place to address all this in great detail, but it is important to acknowledge the reality of suffering, glean a few insights to help us develop perspective on it, and discuss how cultivating our spiritual life might strengthen us to endure suffering and pain.

The Jewish and Christian traditions teach that the genesis of suffering is human rebellion against God, what the Bible calls "sin." It involves the misuse of freedom, will, and all that being made in the image of God entails. Genesis 1–3 narrates this "fall" from what God intended. Human rebellion against God sends fractures through the rest of the created order.[2] Human beings and all of creation are groaning to be redeemed. Christian spirituality gives voice to this groaning. In our praying, meditating, fasting, serving, and other Spirit-empowered activities, we are cooperating with God in the divine drama of redemption. Therefore, the rest of the story, from Genesis to Revelation, recounts the numerous ways God delivers,

---

1. Catherine of Siena, *The Dialogue*, 91. This reality is conveyed in other spiritual traditions. Buddha taught that to exist is to suffer.

2. Maximus speaks of the human being as microcosm and mediator. Through the incarnation of the Word, and his ongoing incarnation in human beings, the divisions in creation that were caused by sin are healed. See Thunberg, *Microcosm and Mediator*; Balthasar, *Cosmic Liturgy*.

saves, and restores human beings along with the broader community of creation.

Suffering is part of life. It is also relative. There is always someone else who is suffering more than you are. My father has endured great suffering the past fifteen years. We actually keep a legal pad of the numerous sicknesses, injuries, and surgeries he has had over the years. It is stunning. We have written over four pages of them so far, from the fifteen surgeries on his broken frame, to his recent battle with cancer. This helps him keep a sense of humor through it all. He will tell you how important laughter is in the midst of suffering. He says it keeps him sane. One day when he was sitting in the waiting room, to see the doctor for problems with his degenerating spine, he observed others seated around him. One man was an amputee; another was hunched over and writhing in pain. My father thought to himself: There are others who have it worse than I do. We are joined in our suffering. I respect them for their endurance. I am grateful to be able to drive myself here to this appointment. It could be worse. He looked at the black leather bracelet my brother gave him, which he wears on his right wrist. It has a slender silver plate that reads: "This too will pass." The phrase does not encourage him to have an escapist mentality, holding on to the idea that one day Jesus will "take him out" of all his pain and suffering, so that until then, he is just going to hang on. Rather, it encourages him to endure, to keep going, knowing that there will be an end to his, and all, suffering. He knows that suffering is part of life. He happens to have more of it than many of us. But he realizes that there are others who have it much worse than he does. Some are completely paralyzed. Some have been severely burned and are bedridden. Some have been abandoned by their parents, feeling lost and unloved in a cruel world.

Suffering, as we know, can be experienced in the body or soul. Tending to the spiritual life, growing in our relationship with God, is a vital way to bear up under the weight of suffering. "Life is not possible without an opening toward the transcendent; in other words, human beings cannot live in chaos. Once contact with the transcendent is lost, existence in the world ceases to be possible . . ."[3] We need the transcendent God. We either suffer with God or without God. We were made for relationship with our Creator, to draw strength from the living presence of God, especially when we feel empty and broken. Through contact with God, we can face chaos and endure. Through prayer and other spiritual exercises, our inner life

---

3. Eliade, *The Sacred and the Profane*, 34.

is nourished. Whether we face suffering in body or soul, friendship with Jesus empowers us to keep going. It is friendship formed in battle. The old story of the dream, "Footsteps," is set on a beach. Jesus carries the suffering person along the shore. Perhaps a more appropriate setting would be a battlefield. He carries us from foxhole to foxhole, through enemy lines, to the medic's tent. Life is hard. It is full of ups and downs. The story of Jesus and his earliest followers reveals this.

2. Suffering is part of Christian discipleship and life in the kingdom of God.
Second, suffering is part of Christian discipleship and life in the kingdom of God. Jesus warned his first disciples that they would suffer, be hated and persecuted, and even be put to death on account of his name (Matt 10:22; 24:9). Jesus told his disciples that not only would he himself continue to suffer persecution by those who opposed him and his ministry, but he would one day suffer and be put to death (Matt 16:21). He urged them to take up their crosses and follow him, as he traveled on the way to the cross (Luke 9:23). We follow "the crucified carpenter," as Fred Shuttlesworth said.[4] His entire life was cruciform. Jesus knew that there can be power hidden in the pain of suffering. He invited his followers, as little seeds from the same stock as the master Seed, to be planted in the earth, in order to bear much fruit.

Through the cross, Jesus overcame the power of Rome. They hung him on the cross to punish and publicly humiliate him as a political dissident. As James Cone says, Jesus' death on the cross was a first-century lynching.[5] He was known as "the king of the Jews." This did not sit well with the Roman government. They sought to put an end to his subversive behavior. Any challenge to Roman authority was vanquished. However, they did not understand the ways of the God of Israel. Through human weakness, divine strength is displayed. The suffering of Christ on the cross displayed the love of God for human beings, even those who put him to death. It also displayed the power of God to overcome oppressive forces or structures that seek to obstruct that love. Jesus invited his followers to follow him in the way of the cross. Their suffering would join the suffering of their Master, who was planted in the earth. The movement started by Jesus would become unstoppable, overshadowing and outlasting the very Empire that put him to death. "The blood of the martyrs is the seed of the

---

4. In Cone, *The Cross and the Lynching Tree*, 75.
5. Cone, *The Cross and the Lynching Tree*, 30, 161.

church," as the Latin church father Tertullian (c. 155–c. 240) proclaimed.⁶ As followers of Jesus, we are seeds in the hand of God. Plant us where you will, O God, you who bring life from death.

Saul of Tarsus learned that suffering is part of Christian discipleship and life in the kingdom of God. He was actually transformed from persecutor to persecuted, from inflictor of suffering to recipient. Saul watched and approved the martyrdom of Stephen, the church's first martyr (or second, after Jesus). Afterward, he met the resurrected Jesus on the Road to Damascus. The words of Jesus struck him like a lightning bolt: "Saul, Saul, why do you persecute me?" (Acts 9:4). To oppress one of his followers is to oppress Jesus. Saul was tyrannizing Christ himself. Jesus also directed one of his disciples in Damascus, Ananias, to help Saul. Jesus told Ananias that he had chosen Saul to be his instrument, to carry his name, and to suffer for his name. These prophetic, prescient words marked Saul's life as he transformed into the Paul we know. He was changed from fierce opponent of the church to fiery apostle of the church. He suffered much for the name of Jesus. His life, too, became cruciform, as he followed the crucified, resurrected Jesus. Like Jesus, he urged disciples to endure suffering in the power of the Holy Spirit. "There [in Antioch in Syria] they strengthened the souls of the disciples and encouraged them to continue in the faith, saying, 'It is through many persecutions that we must enter the kingdom of God'" (Acts 14:22). As people of the kingdom, we live between the times, between "the already and the not yet," between this age and the age to come. Sometimes dwelling between the already and the not yet feels like a vice grip crushing us from both sides. Christian spirituality, life in the Holy Spirit, enables us to survive the times and seasons with all their hardships and joys.

The letters of Paul continue this theme: that he and other Christians would suffer for the name of Jesus.⁷ He suffered as an apostle of the Lord (2 Cor 11:23–33). It was a mark of his genuine apostleship (2 Cor 4:7–15) and an essential part of his calling (Acts 9:15–16). Paul continually faced suffering and the threat of death, as if he were in the Roman arena or the Roman triumphal procession (1 Cor 15:32; 2 Cor 2:14). Paul saw divine purpose in his suffering. Through his suffering and weakness, the power of God was revealed (2 Cor 12:9–10). Paul interpreted his own suffering in light of the cross. Through his suffering, the reality of the crucifixion and resurrection of Jesus was manifest (Phil 3:7–11). His suffering was an

---

6. Tertullian, *Apologetic*, ch. 50.
7. See Hafeman, "Suffering."

embodiment of the gospel, so that the message of the cross was displayed before the church (Gal 3:1). Paul even goes so far as to say that his suffering completes what is lacking in Christ's afflictions (Col 1:24). In this Paul is not suggesting that his suffering has atoning significance and somehow finishes what Christ did not complete. Paul says elsewhere that Christ's suffering stands alone as unique and sufficient (Col 2:13–14; Gal 1:4; 1 Cor 1:18–31). What Paul seems to be saying here is that his ministry *extends* the knowledge and reality of the crucifixion, resurrection, and power of the Holy Spirit to the Gentile world (Col 1:23; Eph 4:13). Paul's suffering also clarifies the fact that the power of the gospel resides in God not the apostle. The "thorn in the flesh," which remains unknown to readers, kept Paul from boasting in the remarkable revelations he received (2 Cor 12:7). Whatever the "thorn" or "messenger of Satan" was, it kept Paul humble and dependent on God. Paul appealed to the Lord three times, asking that it be taken away. But the Lord replied, "My grace is sufficient for you, for power is made perfect in weakness." Therefore, Paul said, "So, I will boast all the more gladly of my weaknesses, so that the power of Christ may dwell in me. Therefore I am content with weaknesses, insults, hardships, persecutions, and calamities for the sake of Christ; for whenever I am weak, then I am strong" (2 Cor 12:9–10).

Paul called others to imitate him as he followed Christ in the way of the cross. His willingness to suffer on behalf of the churches provided a model of Christlike love, encouraging believers to waive their rights for others, even if this involved suffering (1 Cor 4:8–13; 6:7; 9:1–27; 13). However, Paul does not teach that all believers are called to suffer as he does as an apostle. Instead, Paul acknowledges that all Christians will suffer because of their relationship with Christ (Rom 8:17; Phil 1:29–30; 2 Tim 3:12), and because suffering is part of life in the present age (1 Cor 7:28; 12:26; 1 Tim 5:23).

Further, Paul encouraged his Christian sisters and brothers to endure suffering with joy. Because of the joy set before the face of Jesus, he endured the suffering of the cross (Heb 12:1–2). Paul and other early disciples were able to face suffering with joy because God works providentially when Christians experience affliction, pouring out the Spirit and love to sustain or deliver them when they suffer (Rom 5:3–5; 8:12–39; 2 Cor 1:6). Like the apostle, fellow Christians embody the cross and resurrection as they suffer in life. Paul encourages the churches to be patient and endure in the midst of adversity (Rom 12:12; 2 Tim 4:5), because only those who suffer with

Christ will be glorified with him (Rom 8:17). As their lives participate in the reality of the crucifixion and resurrection, their suffering becomes the pathway to sharing in Christ's glory (Rom 8:35; 2 Cor 4:14; 2 Thess 1:7). This hope fuels strength to persevere in faith (Rom 4:18–25; 8:18–25; 1 Cor 15:20–34, 58).

Much of the suffering mentioned in the lives of Jesus, his early disciples, and Paul is the result of religious persecution, but not all of it. Jesus suffered from loneliness, loss, betrayal by friends, and the suffocating specter of the cross. He actually asked if there was another option (Matt 26:39). Sometimes we do not meditate enough on the humanity of Jesus. He was fully divine *and* fully human. The notion that his humanity was subsumed in his divinity is christological heresy, as is the notion that he only appeared to he human. Jesus was human. He was a flesh and blood man who felt deep pain in his body and soul. Because of this, he can empathize with us. He has been tempted and tested as we are, and walks with us as our sympathetic high priest (Heb 4:15). Note this word, *tempted* or *tested* (*pepeirasmenon* in Greek). This suggests that Jesus was tempted in many ways. These temptations tested him. He came through stronger, like clay fired in the kiln or iron forged in fire. The sufferings of Jesus were many. We do not hear much discussion about how he was tempted as a man who experienced sexual desires, like other men: "tempted *as we are*." He never married, and had to wrestle with the natural, God-given urges that coursed through his body. This was another form of suffering he endured. These were natural feelings, those given to Adam and Eve, which God said were "good" (Gen 1:31). Yet he chose to forego these desires, for the kingdom of God (Matt 19:12; cf. 1 Cor 7:25–40). Anyone who says this was not a form of suffering is glossing over the situation.

Again, the Jesus of Scripture suffered in the deepest places of his soul, in the crucible of desire, to the marrow of his bones. The Gospels, councils, and creeds testify to this. For him, ultimate suffering came in the form of the cross, the electric chair of his day. He was executed publicly, as a criminal. It was painful beyond words, utterly humiliating. But his whole life was marked by suffering: temptation, testing, betrayal, loneliness. Below we will look into how Jesus found joy in all this.

3. Suffering is not inflicted on us by a sadistic God.
Pondering the reality of suffering in the Christian life, we remind ourselves that suffering is not inflicted on us by a cruel God. The God and Father of

Jesus Christ is a God of love. Scripture, tradition, reason, and experience teach us that the Father is good. But we must recognize the seriousness of this issue regarding suffering in the face of a good and loving God. It is one of the central arguments raised against the Christian faith, and understandably so. For example, David Hume (1711–1776), the Scottish philosopher, asks: "Is he [God] willing to prevent evil, but not able? then his is impotent. Is he able, but not willing? then he is malevolent. Is he both able and willing? whence then evil?"[8] These questions are actually part of an extensive intellectual enterprise known as "theodicy," which discusses explanations of evil and suffering in the world.[9] There are numerous responses to Hume's questions offered by Christian theologians, but in the end, we are left with the choice to trust God in the midst of suffering, or not. This is difficult. Christians with spiritual depth understand this and do not trivialize suffering with shallow, sentimental responses. Prayer, study, reflection, community, humility, and persistence help us address suffering in ways more satisfying to us and sensitive to others.

Before reading Hume and other Enlightenment thinkers, I came across certain teaching on suffering that troubled me. One respected teacher spoke on Isaiah 53. During the course of his sermon, he reflected on the verse: "the Lord was pleased to crush Him, putting Him to grief" (Isa 53:10, NASB). He explained that God the Father found pleasure in crushing the Son, because it brought redemption to human beings trapped in sin. Not only was his exegesis questionable, but I was left wondering, "What kind of God would do this to his Son, and actually find pleasure, no matter how one nuanced it?" Later I read biblical interpreters who more skillfully explained Isaiah 53:10, and other theologians who actually claimed that this kind of thinking sounded a lot like child abuse by a sadistic parent.[10] If the Father treated his beloved Son this way, how could one trust God?

---

8. Hume, *Dialogues Concerning Natural Religion*, 244; in Livingston, *The Anatomy of the Sacred*, 247.

9. The word *theodicy* comes from two Greek words, *theos* and *dike*, "God" and "justice," and means "justifying the ways of God" in response to the presence of evil, chaos, and suffering in the world, Livingston, *The Anatomy of the Sacred*, 235. For further reading on theodicy, see the helpful introduction by Livingston, *The Anatomy of the Sacred*, 235–58.

10. For example, Sölle, *Suffering*, 22–28. Sölle critiques aspects of Jürgen Moltmann's interpretation of the cross in his work, *The Crucified God*. Whether one agrees or disagrees with Sölle's argument, it is helpful to read ongoing theological discussions of the cross. For example, see Boyd et al., *The Nature of the Atonement*.

The Cross

Suffering, whether from persecution or affliction from living in a broken world, is difficult. How can we cling to God in the midst of such pain? How can we believe that God is love, that God is good, especially when our body, soul, or overall life circumstances are being crushed under the weight of suffering? Cultivating the spiritual life—developing intimate friendship with Jesus—is one chief way to address these significant questions. As I said earlier, *we can either suffer with God or without God.*

Prayer in times of suffering may be a source of strength. Prayer becomes the groaning of the Spirit within us, when we cannot come up with words (Rom 8:26). At times, it may be hard to even pray. Some undergo dark nights of the soul, seasons of intense anguish, or experience long lives of suffering. There are no easy answers. Sometimes, if we can pray at all, it comes out as, "How long, O Lord?" (Ps 13:1), or "Help!" (Ps 70:1). On the cross, in a moment of horrific pain and suffering, Jesus prayed, "My God, my God, why have you forsaken me?" (Ps 22:1; Mark 15:34; Matt 27:46). He felt deserted, abandoned, completely alone. We know that his passion, his suffering on the cross, brings us salvation, but it also serves as an example of human anguish before God. If Jesus felt forsaken by God and gave vent to it in this manner, we can as well. We also know that his suffering was unique, as the incarnate Word, but again, he was a human as we are. His example frees us to experience our pain and suffering before God, without shame or a sense that we have to hold back our true feelings.

I have walked through seasons of distress and spiritual desolation when much of my prayer was silence before God. I will never forget the time at seminary when I overheard someone "praying" in one of the study rooms late at night, when everyone else had left the building. I heard shouting, crying, and a bit of talking, and saw the young man come out of the room later that night. I got to know him and heard his story a few months later. He had been an outstanding athlete, but broke his back. Since then, he lived in chronic pain. He also had experienced abuse as a child. In college, he encountered the Lord, became a Christian, and was studying for ministry. His life was marked by pain in his body and suffering in his soul, yet he was one of the most joyful, altruistic people I had ever met. I caught a glimpse of his prayer life that night and would never forget it. I had never witnessed anything quite like it. He held nothing back before God. He was a true friend of God. He knew how to pray, in pain, with honesty and transparency in the Lord's presence. His life was a picture of the love and goodness of God. In the midst of his pain and suffering, he found a way to cling to his Maker. I respected him. Some of you live in deep pain and suffering, and have found ways to hold on to God. I respect you, too. This is one reason we share our stories with one another, so we can remind each other that God is not sadistic, but a good and loving Father.

4. Suffering reminds us that one day we are all going to die.
In an age of Botox, the pursuit of the fountain of youth, and every method of resisting aging and death, suffering reminds us that all of our paths lead to the grave. The moment we come out of our mother's womb, the clock is ticking. We move, moment by moment, closer to the end of life. We all suffer. We all die. This can either be morbid and threating, or a fiery incentive to live each day with passion, purpose, and gratitude. Every day is a gift. David says: "The days of our life are seventy years, or perhaps eighty, if we are strong; even then their span is only toil and trouble; they are soon gone, and we fly away . . . So teach us to count our days that we may gain a wise heart" (Ps 90:10, 12). Life is short. Suffering is part of it. Paul exclaims: "I die every day!" (1 Cor 15:31) On Ash Wednesday in some churches, ashes are applied to the forehead, and words are spoken: "You are dust and to dust you will return." This is a symbolic reminder of our death in the context of the death of Christ.

There are ways to harness what could be the threat of suffering and death. One of the most powerful and helpful approaches I have come across is found in the *Philokalia*. Hesychios the Priest introduced me to a powerful exercise. He writes: "The unremitting remembrance of death is a powerful trainer of body and soul. Vaulting over all that lies between ourselves and death, we should always visualize it, and even the very bed on which we shall breathe our last, and everything else connected with it."[11] He encourages readers to continually remember death. In the same spirit, Evagrius wrote some four hundred years earlier: "remember the day of death, visualize the dying of your body."[12] This exercise forms us body and soul. As our body ages, suffers, and aches, we are reminded of death. Our mind ponders this reality and process. We picture in our minds past memories and future scenarios, scenes that make up our lives: healthy, constructive scenes, not sins and regrets. We imagine ourselves lying on our deathbed, the place

---

11. *Philokalia* 1:178. Hesychios adds: "Whenever possible, we should always remember death, for this displaces all cares and vanities, allowing us to guard our intellect and giving us unceasing prayer . . . The hour of death will come upon us, it will come, and we shall not escape it." *Philokalia* 1:189–90.

12. *Philokalia* 1:35.

The Cross

where we will take our final breaths. We picture who might be there around us in those final moments. This exercise is intended to wake us up, to sober us, to cultivate purity of heart, to clear away the trivial things in life that do not really matter.[13] Just think how cultivating this mind-set could positively affect the way we treat others (and ourselves), the way we forgive and move forward, or the way we make things right with God. What matters most? What are we living for? Are our lives prioritized around love for God and others? Who will be there for us in our dying moments? Meditating on death can bring clarity. For some, meditating on death will stoke the coals of desire to live more deliberately. For others, meditating on death will comfort the one ready to die, to escape their broken body. It can help us realize that the sting of death has been removed by the cross of Christ. The death and resurrection of Jesus reconfigure our perspective on our broken bodies, our suffering, and our death. Pondering death can help us make wise decisions on a daily basis. It can empower us to live well and prepare to die gracefully.[14]

5. Perhaps an apophatic approach to suffering might help us endure seasons and lives of suffering.

God is a transcendent mystery, ultimately beyond the reach of human comprehension. We cannot know the essence or inner life of God. Likewise, there are times we do not know the deepest reasons for our suffering or the suffering of those around us. God, and the ways of God, surpass the reach of our limited minds: "For my thoughts are not your thoughts, nor are your ways my ways, says the Lord. For as the heavens are higher than the earth, so are my ways higher than your ways and my thoughts than your thoughts" (Isa 55:8–9). We are humbled before the mystery of God. We are also humbled before the mystery of suffering. The topic of suffering is sacred ground. We address it with humility, in fear and trembling. We weep with those who weep. We avoid lecturing those who are suffering. An arm around the shoulder of someone in the midst of suffering is more helpful than a mouth full of proposed solutions or personal platitudes. An embrace, sharing tears, sitting in someone's pain with them, letting them

---

13. This deuterocanonical passage is quite moving: "In all you do, remember the end of your life, and then you will never sin" (Wis Sir 7:36).

14. The poetic song by Sufjan Stevens, "The Fourth of July," expresses this beautifully: "Well you do enough talk/My little hawk, why do you cry?/Tell me what did you learn from the Tillamook burn?/Or the Fourth of July? We're all gonna die/We're all gonna die . . ." From the album *Carrie & Lowell*.

vent, grieve, express their pain, walking with them during their years of suffering; these are the actions of compassion and friendship. A listening ear is more comforting than quoting Romans 8:28 or some other verse that could feel like salt in a fresh wound. When my mother-in-law died, a well-meaning friend of the family told my wife at the funeral, "The Lord is going to use this for his glory. Remember Romans 8:28, 'the Lord causes all things to work together for good for those who love him and are called according to his purposes.'" Powerful promise. Bad timing.

The truth is, my mother-in-law's life was stolen from her. She was diagnosed with multiple sclerosis at age thirty-six, in the prime of her life, with two preteen daughters. Her energy and passion for life were slowly drained from her body, day by day. The medical treatments did little to push back the ongoing damage caused by the scleroses or scars forming on her brain and spinal cord. Her mind remained sharp, while her body wilted. Eventually, she ended up in a wheelchair, unable to feed herself very easily, or do the usual everyday things she used to do. We had some deep conversations about her MS, her struggles, and why God allows things like this to happen. She knew her Bible, read numerous books on suffering, and worked through many of the arguments and explanations for human suffering. I had no viable answers. She was the master teacher. I was the student. Some of the questions she raised could not be answered by anyone, no matter how brilliant or experienced they might be. Her questions were actually internal meditations that she externalized through conversation. They were diamonds formed under and within the crushing pressure of twenty years of suffering. I listened . . . and learned. What amazed me was her quiet tenacity. She refused to give up: on God, on fighting the MS, on developing her mind, on loving her family. Sure, she had bad days, weeks, and months. She battled depression. Who wouldn't? But I learned from watching her. She dealt with the mystery of suffering in an exemplary, honorable way. Through it all, she clung to the mystery of God and God's ways.

She would have insisted I was overstating it, had I said she embodied what Job declared: "Though he slay me, I will hope in him; yet I will argue my ways to his face" (Job 13:15, ESV). However, a measure of that suffering that broke like waves over Job's life invaded hers as well. The robust life she once had slipped through her fingers as her body succumbed to numbness and sluggishness. MS was "slaying" her day by day, and for some reason this was allowed by the sovereign Creator, but she kept hoping in God. And she continued to ask questions and argue to God's face. Looking back on years

The Cross

of her life, and conversations we had, I can discern an apophatic spirit in her view on suffering. MS changed the trajectory of her life. It took her into "the cloud of unknowing." Though she had serious questions for God, she clung to the crucified Jesus.

Over a decade after her death, I taught a college seminar in which we discussed the book by Nancy L. Eiesland, *The Disabled God: Toward a Liberatory Theology of Disability*. Professor Eiesland suffered from a congenital bone defect and eventually died at age forty-four. In this profound book, Eiesland discusses the journeys of other women who have faced lives of suffering, including Nancy Mairs, who was diagnosed with MS at age twenty-nine. Eiesland quotes Mairs and reflects on her words:

> "Because a difficult life is more complicated than an easy one, it offers opportunities for developing a greater range of response to experience: a true generosity of spirit." It also opens a space for honesty about death as part of an ordinary life... "Taught through intimate relations with disability and death that life, though lugubrious enough, is even more ludicrous and that no one develops fully until she can play and mourn in balance, I had to risk a messenger's death then and still must do: We are all going to die. And it is all right."[15]

While most will not experience the difficult life of MS of which Mairs speaks, she explains that suffering can broaden us, and engender a more generous spirit. A difficult life, and I might add, difficulty in life, cuts through the candy coating that culture tends to spread over suffering and death. Disability, suffering, and death, no matter how hard people try to spin or conceal them, are constituent parts of human existence and Christian spirituality. Can we learn to play and mourn in balance? Will we heed the voice of the messenger who reminds us that we are all going to die... and it is all right? The teachings and practices of Christian spirituality help us grapple with such things. In Scripture, we hear the voice of another messenger, one that calls from the desert. To the desert we now turn.

---

15. Mairs, *Carnal Acts*, 114; and *Ordinary Time*, 216–17; in Eiesland, *The Disabled God*, 46.

CHAPTER 10.

The Desert: Seasons of Dryness, Death, and New Life

"The wilderness and the dry land shall be glad, the desert shall rejoice and blossom; like the crocus it shall blossom abundantly..."
—Isa 35:1, 2

"Christianity in the desert was not about death but about new life."
—Benedicta Ward, *The Desert Fathers*

"There is no enclosure so fenced in that he cannot enter, or desert so withdrawn that he fails to go there."
—Teresa of Avila, *The Interior Castle*

"If you study the history of spirituality or the spiritual life of the Church, you will find that each time that there is a spiritual renewal in the Church, the desert fathers are present."
—Irénée Hausherr, "Pour comprendre l'Orient chrétien"
[To Understand the Christian East]

Reframing the Desert

My wife and I spent seven years in a spiritual desert. It was lonely, miserable, and at times suffocating. We cried out to God for help, for deliverance, for a way out of the desert. But year after year, there was no end to it. As we looked up and within, the desert seemed to stretch out endlessly.

It is no wonder that the desert is often absent from contemporary Christian discourse. It is a difficult subject. But what if avoiding the topic of the desert only limits our spiritual vision or impairs our spiritual progress? Perhaps the image of the desert is one of the more helpful ways to describe the ups and downs of the spiritual journey. What if we were to reconsider the desert, to reframe our understanding of it? This is the aim of this chapter, to let the symbol of the desert speak to us. Through examining images of the desert in Scripture and early Christian spiritual writers, we will seek wisdom that will help us survive *and* thrive in the desert seasons.

Biblical Images of the Desert

Creation

An initial image of the desert is suggested in the creation narrative in Genesis. The text says: "In the beginning when God created the heavens and the earth, the earth was a formless *void* . . ." (Gen 1:2). The Hebrew word for *void* is one of several that is used elsewhere in the Old Testament to describe the desert or wilderness.[1] The text goes on to recount the creation of the garden of Eden, juxtaposing the formless void of the wilderness with the fruitful garden. The God of Israel alone, the Creator of all things, has the power to transform the formless, desolate wilderness into a lush garden, where God and humans walk together in the cool of day (Gen 3:8).

The Exodus

A second biblical image of the desert emerges in the story of Moses. In Exodus, after Moses is outraged at the forced labor of his people under the Egyptians, he kills an Egyptian, and "hid him under the sand" (Exod 2:12). Moses flees, settles in the land of Midian, marries Zipporah, and she gives birth to Gershom (Exod 2:15–22). The desert is the place of hiding, as well as where new life is birthed. Later, Moses is tending a flock in the wilderness, where the angel of the Lord appears to him in the flame of fire out of a bush (Exod 3:1–2). Moses approaches the strange sight, and the Lord speaks: "'Come no closer! Remove the sandals from your feet, for the place on which you are standing is holy ground.'" He said further, "I am the God of your father, the God of Abraham, the God of Isaac, and the God of Jacob.' And Moses hid his face, for he was afraid to look at God" (Gen 3:5–6). The Lord saw the misery of Moses's people, came down to deliver them and

---

1. See the article, "Desert in the Bible."

bring them to another land, the land promised to them. The Lord would send Moses to deliver the people from the Egyptians.

However, Moses questions that he is the right person for the job. The Lord assures Moses that he will be with him and sends him to the Israelites and their leaders in the power of the divine name: "'Thus you shall say to the Israelites, "I am has sent me to you."' God also said to Moses, "Thus you shall say to the Israelites, 'The Lord, the God of your ancestors, the God of Abraham, the God of Isaac, and the God of Jacob, has sent me to you'" (Exod 3:14–15). The desert, therefore, becomes a place of encounter, revelation, and commission. Moses is met by the fiery presence of the Lord, hears the mysterious and powerful name of the Lord, and is sent to deliver the people of the Lord.

Moses is marked by these experiences in the desert. As the story continues, Moses leads the Israelites in the wilderness. Because they did not believe that the Lord would give them the land that they had spied out for forty days, they would have to wander the desert for forty years (Num 13–14). Thus, the desert became the place of discipline for Israel's rebellion and refusal to believe God. It is where they were humbled and tested by God, to see if they would obey and depend on him: "Remember the long way that the Lord your God has led you these forty years in the wilderness, in order to humble you, testing you to know what was in your heart, whether or not you would keep his commandments" (Deut 8:2).

Hebrew Prophets

Elijah

A third image of the wilderness is found in the Hebrew prophets. These are actually various aspects of the desert found in the Old Testament prophetic tradition. One is that the wilderness is the place of quiet encounter with the Lord. Elijah, as we saw earlier in the section on apophatic spirituality, fled to the wilderness after Jezebel threatened to kill him. In the midst of his discouragement and depression, he encountered the Lord in a desert cave near Mount Horeb. The divine presence was not found in the wind, earthquake, or fire, but in sheer silence. Elijah wrapped his face in his mantle and the voice of the Lord spoke to him (1 Kgs 19:11–13).

The Desert

Hosea

Another aspect of the desert is found in the prophet Hosea. Through Hosea, the Lord warns Israel, who has broken the covenant relationship with the Lord. Israel's unfaithfulness to God, Hosea declares, is like adultery. Israel would be punished for leaving God to worship other gods. The Lord will "make her like a wilderness, and turn her into a parched land" (Hos 2:3). The wilderness symbolizes the arid spiritual condition that results from disobedience.

Nevertheless, the symbol of the desert takes on new meaning a few verses later in the passage. After reprimanding Israel for Baal worship, the Lord says: "Therefore, I will now allure her, and bring her into the wilderness, and speak tenderly to her" (Hos 2:14). The meaning of the wilderness shifts from a place of punishment and a condition of spiritual barrenness to a place where God draws Israel to reaffirm love for God and to renew the covenant (Hos 2:16–20).

Isaiah

The prophet Isaiah adds further strokes to the image of the desert. The wilderness, which often signifies a precarious place of wandering, testing, or discipline, is transfigured. Isaiah declares:

> The wilderness and the dry land shall be glad, the desert shall rejoice and blossom; like the crocus it shall blossom abundantly, and rejoice with joy and singing... Then the eyes of the blind shall be opened, and the ears of the deaf unstopped; then the lame shall leap like a deer, and the tongue of the speechless sing for joy. For waters shall break forth in the wilderness, and streams in the desert; the burning sand shall become a pool, and the thirsty ground springs of water (Isa 35:1–2, 5–7).

> Do not remember the former things, or consider the things of old. I am about to do a new thing; now it springs forth, do you not perceive it? I will make a way in the wilderness and rivers in the desert (Isa 43:18–19).

> A voice cries out: "In the wilderness prepare the way of the Lord, make straight in the desert a highway for our God" (Isa 40:3).

The wilderness becomes the context for new life, reinvigoration, miraculous works of God, and fresh revelation. It is no longer threatening. In fact, the Lord actually constructs and travels on a roadway through this once ominous setting. Because the Lord is so faithful and powerful, the desert is transformed and now symbolizes God's ability to bring new life and startling miracles out of barren, hopeless situations. According to Isaiah, the garden of Eden that was lost because of the fall will be recovered. The desert of the post-fall world is the interim between the garden and the new creation, the space between paradise lost and paradise restored.

New Testament

Jesus

Against the backdrop of these Old Testament images of the desert, the New Testament portrays Jesus as someone with roots in the wilderness. Jesus, as an embodiment of ideal Israel, draws together the desert experiences of the exodus and prophets. His life, like Moses, Israel, and the Hebrew prophets, is marked by the desert. He was born in Bethlehem, at the edge of the Judean desert (Matt 2:1). His ministry was announced by John the Baptist, the prophetic voice in the wilderness (Matt 3:1–3). He was tempted in the desert before his public ministry was launched (Matt 4:1). Where Israel failed to trust and obey God in the wilderness, he succeeded. Overcoming the temptations of the enemy with the Torah written on his heart and flowing from his lips, the desert was a place of obedience and victory.

Further, Jesus often slipped away to the wilderness to pray (Luke 5:16). Once the place of testing and spiritual battle with Satan, the wilderness became the place of communion with the Father. Jesus passed along this practice to his disciples, as he took them with him for times of solitude and prayer in the desert (Matt 17:1). For Jesus, his disciples, and the early church, the desert was a place of spiritual retreat, prayer, intimacy with God, and renewal.

Early Christian Desert Dwellers

Influence and Criticisms

With this rich biblical history of experiencing God in the desert, it is not surprising that some Christians felt drawn to seek the face of God in the desert. What transpired in the Egyptian desert in the fourth century

The Desert

became known as the monastic movement. In fact, there were other deserts (in Asia Minor and Syria) where Christians retreated to seek God in prayer and solitude. Some individuals moved to the desert in order to focus on God, live in solitude, and engage in spiritual disciplines. While some lived solitary lives, others gathered in communities. Sometimes disciples would gather around a particular man or woman, to learn from their experience of life in the desert. Eventually these became the first monasteries, and particular leaders were later known as desert fathers and mothers. These various desert movements were, and continue to be, influential on Christianity across the globe.

Yet from the beginning, desert monasticism has had its critics, and it is informative to listen to their objections. Douglas Christie, in his bracing study, *The Word in the Desert: Scripture and the Quest for Holiness in Early Christian Monasticism*, comments:

> Not all observers of the early monastic movement have seen it as a positive force in the world. Its critics have maintained, for a variety of reasons, that the whole movement was deeply flawed, even fundamentally misconceived. Two criticisms of early monasticism have been particularly important. Some have argued that the early monastic movement was antisocial and anticultural, thereby contributing notably to the decay of human culture and civilization in late antiquity. Others have criticized early monasticism as being profoundly unbiblical. They charge that the monks misread the biblical message of salvation, either through ignorance, conscious manipulation, or the influence of heterodox thought.[2]

Considering these two criticisms—that monasticism is antisocial and unbiblical—is part of developing an informed opinion on these desert movements. However, this is not the place to thoroughly review the monastic movements of the fourth century and beyond. Instead, our focus is on the spiritual wisdom that came to light in the Egyptian desert. On this note, Christie adds:

> The retreat to the desert and growth of monasticism in fourth-century Egypt has long been recognized as one of the most significant and alluring moments of early Christianity. In the withdrawal from the mainstream of society and culture to the stark solitude of the desert, *a vibrant and original spirituality was born which had a wide influence on both contemporaries and succeeding generations.*

---

2. Burton-Christie, *The Word in the Desert*, 11.

> It was a rich and varied movement, full of apparent contradictions and paradoxes.³

This is what we are centering on: the vibrant and original spirituality that was born in the desert. Whether one agrees or disagrees with Christian monasticism, there are undoubtedly certain biblical ideas and practices that were retrieved or took on deeper meaning in the fourth-century monastic movements of the desert.

Strangers and Exiles

Prior to the movements of early Christian desert dwellers in the Egyptian desert, Christians in Greco-Roman society often faced exclusion and persecution.⁴ They identified with the Old Testament heroes of the faith who were "strangers and exiles" on the earth; they were seeking a homeland, a better, heavenly country; and God prepared a city for them (Heb 11:13–16). Appropriating the same notion of Christians as resident aliens, Paul says: "So then you are no longer strangers and aliens, but you are citizens with the saints and also members of the household of God . . ." (Eph 2:19); for "our citizenship is in heaven . . ." (Phil 3:20). "This idea, that the world is for Christians, if not a desert, at any rate not their homeland but a foreign country, penetrated deeply into the early Christian consciousness."⁵

---

3. Burton-Christie, *The Word in the Desert*, 3. Italics mine. Also noteworthy is the account of the young man in Milan in 386 who heard the story of Antony being read. Benedicta Ward recounts that this young man was deeply moved by Antony, and his response to the words of Jesus ("Go and sell all that you have and give to the poor and come and follow me"). The young man asked, "What is the meaning of this story? These men have none of our education and yet they stand up and storm the gates of heaven." Ward explains, "In this way, the story of an uneducated Egyptian peasant farmer and his adoption of solitude in the desert for life proved to be the turning point in the conversion of Augustine, the formative theologian of Europe." Ward, *The Desert Fathers*, xix–xx.

4. The chapter, "Desert Fathers," by Louth, in *The Wilderness of God*, has informed my discussion here, 53–70.

5. Louth, "Desert Fathers," 54.

The Desert

Antony the Great: Saint of the Desert

Beginnings

When Emperor Constantine embraced Christianity and decreed tolerance for it in 313 CE, Christians naturally began to feel more at home in the world. Others, including those who would become monks, heard the call and sensed the draw of the desert. For many of "the desert monks refused to participate in the growing establishment of the church under Constantine, choosing instead to live on the margins of society under the direct guidance of the Spirit and the Word of God."[6] One of them was an Egyptian man who was later known as Antony the Great (c. 251–356).

According to the biography of Antony, written by the prominent theologian Athanasius (c. 296–373), he was raised in a prosperous family.[7] In his late teens, his parents died, leaving Antony and his younger sister. One day in church, Antony heard the story of the rich young man. Jesus' words pierced his heart: "If you wish to be perfect, go, sell your possessions, and give the money to the poor, and you will have treasure in heaven; then come, follow me" (Matt 19:21). Antony felt the words were addressed to him, so he sold all the family property and gave the money to the poor. He entrusted his sister to the care of a community of virgins connected to his local church. She later became their leader. Antony placed himself under the tutelage of an older man in a nearby village who had spent his life in solitude and prayer. Over time, Antony migrated from the villages where he grew up to tombs outside the villages, then eventually to the desert, where he lived in solitude in an abandoned fort on the east bank of the Nile for twenty years. This location at Pispir, about fifty miles south of Memphis, became known as his "Outer Mountain."

A Daily Martyr

Antony's reputation grew. Around 306, he and some of the people who followed him went to Alexandria to support Christians who were being persecuted by the Emperor Diocletian. Along with others at the time, Antony longed to die a martyr's death, but this never happened. Instead, as Athanasius wrote, Antony became a "daily martyr in his conscience, ever

---

6. Burton Christie, *The Word in the Desert*, 3.
7. Along with Louth, the classic by Chitty has been helpful, *The Desert a City*, 1–19.

fighting the battles of the Faith."[8] Stories in his biography recount some of the spiritual battles he fought against demons, his spiritual disciplines, temptations he overcame, and miracles God worked through him. Antony became one of the first well-known desert ascetics. As a "spiritual athlete," the desert was the coliseum in which he competed in rigorous spiritual competitions.

We can make several observations about Antony's spiritual wisdom and desert practices. One is that Antony engaged in spiritual warfare by setting his mind on Jesus. When the devil "raised up in his mind a great dust cloud of arguments, intending to make him abandon his set purpose," Antony "*filled his thoughts with Christ* . . . and thus quenched the glowing coal of temptation." The enemy and his temptations were thrust out of his heart. Antony grew "all the more alert in spirit," and "his mind was master of the situation."[9]

Inner Posture

Another observation, which stems from the previous one, is that Antony cultivated an inner posture that repelled demonic attacks and temptations. He consistently rejoiced in the Lord, meditated on the good things God had done and would do, and contemplated the Lord and all that was his. The inner mechanics of this are key:

> The ascetic [Antony] was bent upon reclaiming his conscious life from memories of error, weakness, and indulgence. This he did by *fixing his attention on a range of concepts and of texts* or dicta that could not but exclude those other "thoughts." In this way *he built up a psychic wall* against his past, both cultural and personal.[10]

Antony combatted spiritual attack by "filling his thoughts with Christ." How? By fixing his attention on spiritual themes and texts. Meditation on Scripture was central. When temptation knocked on the inner door of his heart, Antony was prepared. Another guest was already present. Antony communed with the indwelling presence of Jesus. There was no room for intruders. Through continual prayer, biblical meditation, and contemplation

---

8. *Life*, 47; in Louth, *The Wilderness of God*, 56.
9. Jones et al., eds., *The Study of Spirituality*, 126, italics mine.
10. Jones et al., eds., *The Study of Spirituality*, 126, italics mine.

on the Lord and his ways, Antony built up a wall against thoughts, both past and present, that might impede his intimacy with God.

Prayer and Work

A third observation is that Antony sought to balance the contemplative and active elements of the spiritual life. He modeled that prayer and work complement one another. One of Antony's greatest achievements emanated from his unwillingness to recoil from the world: "Far from brooding on his state of soul, he was immensely industrious. He worked to support himself, and to give to the poor. Even in his ultimate retreat he sought out fertile soil to grow his grain, and made baskets to exchange for food from visitors." Antony dialogued with "pagan philosophers," championing "a faith through love that works for Christ." He was generous, and "never found it hard to correlate his daily task with this inner availability."[11]

Road to Paradise

More people gathered to Antony, in order to seek his spiritual counsel or to live the ascetic life under his guidance. In time, Antony retreated more deeply into the desert, to his "Inner Mountain," Mount Colzim, about 100 miles southeast of modern Cairo. At the base of this Inner Mountain "there was water, crystal clear, sweet, and very cold. Spreading out from there was flat land and a few scraggy date palms. Antony . . . fell in love with the place." Antony took to the desert as a fish to the ocean. For him, the desert became a road to Paradise. He spent the rest of his days, to the age of 105, living at times on the Inner Mountain and other times on the Outer Mountain, where fellow monks lived and where non-monastics visited him.[12]

Model of Desert Spirituality

These features of Antony's journey illustrate why he became a model of the spiritual life to many. Antony's desert discipleship began when he heard the words of Jesus to sell his possessions, give to the poor, and follow Jesus. Antony lived the life of a spiritual athlete, training his mind and body

---

11. Jones et al., eds., *The Study of Spirituality*, 127–28.
12. Louth, *The Wilderness of God*, 56.

through persevering prayer, ongoing meditation on Jesus and his words, regular fasting and other ascetic exercises, and uniting worship and work. While some may have questions about the lifestyle and methods of Antony and other monks, desert monasticism "as story and spirituality, caught the imagination of the ancient world, and its appeal has diminished little over the centuries."[13] Like other movements in the history of Christianity, there is much to learn from what transpired in the Egyptian desert in the fourth century.

Desert Experiences Today

DESERT AS ALLEGORY

Origen: desert wandering, crossing the Jordan

Considering the examples in Scripture, Antony, and monasticism, the desert is sometimes a literal place. But this is not always the case. At other times, the desert is an allegory. The desert may be a spiritual experience, a baptism into hardship, death to self-sufficiency, and a realization of dependence on divine grace.[14] One example is found in Origen of Alexandria, where he views the desert wanderings of Israel as an allegory of the Christian life:

> Before the soul comes to perfection, it dwells in the desert, where it can be exercised in the commandments of the Lord, and where its faith may be tried by temptations. Thus when it overcomes one temptation and its faith has been tried in that, it comes to another. And so it passes from one stopping place to another, and when it has gone through what happens there, it goes on yet to another. And thus by passing through all of the trials of life and faith, it is said to have stopping-places, in which the growth in the virtues is the real issue, and there is fulfilled in them the saying of Scripture: "They shall go from strength to strength," until they come to the last, the highest stage of the virtues, and cross the river of God, and receive the promised inheritance.[15]

The spiritual journey of growth in faith and holiness includes time in the desert. In the desert, Christians learn to follow the teachings of Scripture, overcome temptation, pass through many trials, and thereby advance in

---

13. Louth, *The Wilderness of God*, 56.
14. Scorgie, ed., *Dictionary of Christian Spirituality*, 395.
15. Origen, *Homiles on Joshua*, 12; in McGrath, *Christian Spirituality*, 102.

righteousness. Those who rely on the strength and leadership of the Lord proceed from one place of strength to another, until, like the ancient Israelites, they cross the Jordan and enter the promised land.

Rupert of Deutz: manna in the desert

Another example of the desert as an allegory of the spiritual life is found in Rupert of Deutz (c. 1075–1130), an influential Benedictine theologian. In this case, the Lord's gracious provision of manna to Israel in the wilderness is interpreted allegorically to mean that God will provide spiritual nourishment to Christians who journey through the desert:

> As often as the Holy Spirit opens the mouths of the apostles and prophets and even teachers to preach the word of salvation and unveil the mystery of the Scriptures, the Lord opens the gates of heaven to rain down manna for us to eat. As long as we are going through the desert of this world, walking by faith and not by sight, we need these provisions desperately. We are fed in our minds by reading and hearing the word of God. We are fed in our mouths by eating the bread of life from the table of the Lord, and drinking the chalice of eternal salvation. Yet when we finally come to the land of the living, to Jerusalem the blessed, where the God of gods will be seen face to face, we shall no longer need the word of doctrine nor shall we eat the bread of angels under the appearances of bread and wine, but in its own proper substance.[16]

The Lord strengthens the church through the word and sacraments. As apostles, prophets, and teachers preach the Scriptures, it is like manna falling from heaven. The bread of the Scriptures feeds the minds of Christians as they pass through the desert trials of life in this world. Additionally, eating the bread of life and drinking the cup of salvation feeds the church until the day of beatific vision or entering the promised land, when we see the Lord face to face.

George Florovksy: desert and empire

Allegorically speaking, life in this world parallels the desert wandering of ancient Israel. The desert symbolizes life circumstances in which God

---

16. Rupert of Deutz, *de trinitate et operibus eius*; in McGrath, *Christian Spirituality*, 103.

instructs, molds, and transforms us. Orthodox theologian Georges Florovksy (1893–1979) suggested the idea that "the desert is to empire what apocalypse is to history."[17] This can be understood in various ways. On one hand, fourth-century monks aimed to establish new community in the desert, an alternative to both pagan empire and imperial Christianity. Life in the desert broke from the ongoing history of empire building. On the other hand, Florovsky's words can be understood figuratively. As Christian disciples, dwelling in the desert subverts our personal empire building. In the desert we are often deconstructed so that God may reconstruct us. Building on our unhealthy ambitions comes to a halt in the desert. Our visions and desires fall to the ground, and are buried beneath the sand. The desert invades the story of our lives as the apocalyptic vision of prophets crashes into broader human history. Thus, the desert itself is a prophetic place. Prophets were formed there: Moses, Isaiah, Jesus. They still are. Members of the body of Christ, which is the prophetic church, are also formed in the desert. In the depths of the desert, it may seem that we are chiseled down to a nub, nearly reduced to dust, broken beyond repair. But God is at work. Deconstruction is followed by reconstruction. The master builder is at work in the desert . . . rebuilding, sustaining, preparing us for what lies ahead.

Spiritual Renewal and the Desert Fathers

Reflecting on the biblical images of the desert, early Christian desert dwellers, and the allegorical understanding of the desert helps us see some of the ways God works in the wilderness. There is much to glean from those who have journeyed in the desert. "The voice of one calling in the wilderness" continues to speak to us today. When we take time to listen to the voice of the Spirit speaking through the writings of ancient desert dwellers, we can be revitalized. The old becomes new and we are made new. As Irénée Hausherr (1881–1978), a Jesuit scholar, has said: "If you study the history of spirituality or the spiritual life of the Church, you will find that each time that there is a spiritual renewal in the Church, the desert fathers are present."[18] If this is the case, then let us listen again with renewed interest, and with passion for spiritual renewal!

---

17. Florovksy, *Christianity and Culture*, 128; in Jones et al., eds., *The Study of Spirituality*, 594.

18. Hausherr, "Pour comprendre l'orient chrétien," 359; in Burton-Christie, *The Word*

The Desert

The *Philokalia*: A Desert Survival Manual

I know of no better place to turn in the passionate pursuit of God and spiritual renewal than to the *Philokalia*, the compendium of spiritual classics from the Christian East referenced in previous chapters.[19] As mentioned earlier, Saint Nikodimos and Saint Makarios edited this collection of ascetic writings to enrich the spiritual lives of all Christians, both monks and lay people. Many of the writings originated from the desert. They were born in the hearts and minds of fiery desert dwellers, the Desert Fathers. Over the centuries, the fathers of the *Philokalia* have served as travel guides through the arid spiritual wilderness. These thirty-six authors have provided much needed spiritual wisdom and encouragement that have helped Christians from various traditions. Along with countless Christians from Orthodox, Catholic, and Protestant traditions who have benefited from its spiritual wisdom, I recommend the *Philokalia* to those in need of a "desert survival manual," or those simply interested in learning more about desert spirituality. In addition to earlier comments on the *Philokalia*, I would urge others to prayerfully read its writings for the following reasons.

Desert: Part of the Journey

First, the *Philokalia* teaches that the desert experience is part of the spiritual journey. It is normal, not abnormal, to undergo seasons in the spiritual desert, where God works in us, transforming us into the image of Jesus.[20] Kallistos Ware explains that the desert actually exists within each of us. Our aim is to learn to meet Jesus in this desert.[21]

---

in the Desert, 11.

19 The following are helpful resources on and guides to the *Philokalia*: Ware, "The *Philokalia*"; Bingaman and Nassif, eds., *The Philokalia*, especially the chapter by Ware, "St. Nikodimos and *The Philokalia*," 9–35; Louth, "The Theology of *The Philokalia*."

20. *Philokalia* 3:49.

21. From a talk on the Desert Fathers by Kallistos of Diokleia, February 12, 2015; the first in a series of "Thursday Lunchtime Talks" at St. Giles' Church, Oxford, on a "Continuing Journey to the Source: Exploring the Wisdom of the Mystics" (from January 22 to March 12, 2015). In his concluding remarks, he says: "The desert experience means, for many of us, the desert has to be in our own heart. Each of us needs a quiet place in our heart, an inner sanctuary where we can, even if it's only for a few minutes each day, be alone with God. So the desert is not just something physical, it is also something spiritual. And this is why I would say that the sayings of the Desert Fathers is not just a book for monks and nuns, but it is a book for all Christians. I would commend it to you all *because*

Spiritual Practices

Second, the *Philokalia* explains that there are certain spiritual practices that enable us to cooperate with God's work within us during desert seasons. Chief among these is prayer. In fact, the *Philokalia* can be viewed as a practical guide to communion with God through prayer. According to its teachings, prayer is a gracious gift of God, and involves dialogue with God. Prayer is the highest of all spiritual activities, uniting us to God in love, and is to be practiced by all Christians. Prayer involves ongoing remembrance of Jesus (through the Jesus Prayer and meditation on Scripture), becomes a continual practice, and is a weapon in spiritual warfare.[22] In short, prayer is the activity of desert travelers; it is the lifeline to God that keeps us from being swallowed up in desert sand.

A further set of interrelated spiritual practices includes silence and stillness. According to the *Philokalia*, silence is beautiful, and is closely linked to fruitful prayer and inner stillness, particularly when practiced with the Jesus Prayer.[23] Prayer and silence generate and protect one another, leading to humility and deep spiritual understanding.[24] Silence prepares Christians to receive the fire of the Holy Spirit, as on the Day of Pentecost. Silence and stillness, when practiced with psalmody (singing the Psalms) and prayerful reading of Scripture, enable believers to acquire the Spirit, "penetrate the divine darkness" of God, and "perceive the radiance of God's inexpressible beauty and wisdom."[25] In silence, the Lord teaches us to pray continually, while he fights our spiritual battles.[26] As the language of the age to come, "perfect silence alone proclaims Him, and total and transcendent unknowing [through the apophatic or negative way] brings us into His presence."[27]

---

all of us, if we are to be effective in the world, need to have something of the spirit of the desert within us." Accessed online: https://www.youtube.com/watch?v=noVX9lRQkDA.

22. *Philokalia* 1:62, 2:15; 4:181, 4:282; 4:118, 343; 3:72, 1:15; 1:155–56; 1:310, 2:346, 348; 1:301, 316, 3:56, 57.

23. *Philokalia* 1:286, 3:40, 3:56.

24. *Philokalia* 4:233, 235, 239, 272, 285, 1:345.

25. *Philokalia* 4:126, 155.

26. *Philokalia* 4:268, 2:120.

27. *Philokalia* 2:271.

The Desert

Work

Besides prayer, silence, and stillness, the *Philokalia* underscores the importance of work. Work is an integral part of life, spiritual development, and survival in desert seasons. Evagrius teaches:

> Provide yourself with such work for your hands as can be done, if possible, both during the day and at night, so that you are not a burden to anyone, and indeed can give to others, as Paul the Apostle advises (cf. 1 Thess. 2:9; Eph. 4:28). In this manner you will overcome the demon of listlessness and drive away all the desires suggested by the enemy; for the demon of listlessness takes advantage of idleness. "Every idle man is full of desires" (Prov. 13:4).[28]

Desert wisdom suggests that steady work is healthy, creates vital self-sustenance, and enables us to be generous to others, in accord with New Testament teaching. Work is a means to overcome spiritual attack, sluggishness, and temptation. If "idle hands are the devil's tools," then working hands are the Lord's instruments.

In the same vein, Cassian reflects on Paul's instructions to the Thessalonians: Christians should imitate his apostolic model, work quietly, eat their own bread, and not leech off others (2 Thess 3:6–12). Cassian, highlighting the significance of work, writes:

> The holy fathers of Egypt, who were brought up on the basis of the apostolic commandments, do not allow monks to be without work at any time, especially while they are young. They know that by persevering in work monks dispel listlessness, provide for their own sustenance and help those who are in need. They not only work for their own requirements, but from their labor they also minister to their guests, to the poor and to those in prison, believing such charity is a holy sacrifice acceptable to God.[29]

Desert monks, based on apostolic injunctions, knew that work coupled with prayer drives away spiritual opposition. It also provides for basic needs: "Anyone unwilling to work should not eat" (2 Thess 3:10).[30]

---

28. *Philokalia* 1:35 (Proverbs 13:4 is quoted from the LXX, the Septuagint, a Greek version of the Hebrew Bible).

29. *Philokalia* 1:90.

30. Work develops perseverance and other character traits. Work was also viewed as ministry, enabling them to show love and hospitality to guests, the poor, and prisoners. Work was a labor of love, an act of worship to God and kindness to others. Evagrius, Cassian, and other Desert Fathers hold a high view of work. It is not an activity to evade,

Spirituality and Theology

Along with clarifying that the desert is a normal part of spiritual life, and providing spiritual practices for the desert, there is a third reason to study the *Philokalia*. In its writings, there is a close link between spirituality and dogmatic theology (or the authoritative teaching of the church). In other words, as the *Philokalia* provides practical desert wisdom and transformative spiritual practices, it does so in a rich theological environment. As Ware notes, in the *Philokalia*, "The life of prayer is set firmly in the context of Trinitarian theology and Christology."[31] Theological reflection and spiritual practice go hand in hand. Accordingly, the doctrines of the Trinity and Christ are shown to be relevant and practical for spiritual training, not abstruse and inconsequential. Knowing more about trinitarian theology and Christology can help us in desert seasons.

Thus, the *Philokalia* teaches that each of us is made in the image of the Trinity. We are created for intimate friendship with the triune God. In the triune God we live and move and have our being (Acts 17:28). As we pray and put into practice the teachings of Scripture, we receive mystically the Holy Trinity, in the words of Maximus.[32] That is, the Living Word comes to us through the written Word. Because the Word, the Father, and the Spirit are united without division, in the language of trinitarian doctrine, we receive the Holy Trinity as we practice the commands of Scripture (John 13:20; 14:21, 26; 15:10; 16:13–15). We also receive insight into life in communion with the Holy Trinity through the wise counsel of spiritual fathers and mothers, which we consider in the next chapter.

---

so we can "focus on more spiritual and meaningful tasks." With the right frame of mind, work *is* prayer, worship, ministry, hospitality, and love. As Paul urges: "And whatever you do, in word or deed, do everything in the name of the Lord Jesus, giving thanks to God the Father through him" (Col 3:17). "Whatever you do, work at it with all your heart, as working for the Lord . . ." (Col 3:23, NIV).

31. Ware, "The Hesychast Renaissance," in Jones et al., eds., *The Study of Spirituality*, 256.

32. *Philokalia* 4:140–141, 183, 184, 218; 2:154–55.

CHAPTER 11.

Spiritual Mothers and Fathers: Spiritual Guides, Spiritual Direction

"In Christ Jesus I became your father through the gospel."
—1 Cor 4:15

"My little children, for whom I am again in the pain of childbirth until Christ is formed in you."
—Gal 4:19

"In the company of saints we will become saints."
—Teresa of Avila, *The Interior Castle*

"I tell you, therefore, it is far better to walk by the spiritual counsel of a humble and unschooled person with a holy and upright conscience than by that of a well-read but proud scholar with great knowledge. *For one cannot share what one does not have in oneself . . .*"
—Catherine of Siena, *The Dialogue*

"He thinks it easy to be a spiritual guide, not realizing that the care of other men's souls is of all things the most difficult . . . To master any art requires time and much instruction; can the art of arts alone be mastered without being learnt?"
—St. Neilos the Ascetic, *Philokalia* 1:215

A LUMINOUS LIFE, ONE that radiates the presence and glory of God, is a life rooted in Christian community. Relationships characterized by love, trust, and transparency with Christian sisters and brothers are essential to spiritual health and growth. But in addition to spiritual sisters and brothers, we need spiritual mothers and fathers. This is not necessarily age-related, though sometimes it might be. Both Jesus and Timothy, for example, served as spiritual fathers to plenty of people older than themselves. A spiritual mother or father may be young or old.

We have barely ventured into the theme of this chapter, and already questions begin to arise. What is a spiritual mother or father? What is a spiritual director? What is the difference between these roles and that of discipleship? In this chapter, we will address facets of these questions, along with others. However, the aim here is not provide a detailed exposition of what it means to be a spiritual mother, father, or director. The goal is to reflect on some of the characteristics and functions of spiritual mothers, fathers, and directors. We will see that various Christian traditions use different language to describe the roles of spiritual mothers, fathers, and directors. Nonetheless, at the root is a shared reality: the person of Jesus, how he related to his first followers and helped them commune with the Father through the Spirit, and how his future followers help others deepen their relationship with God.

Spiritual Direction and Jesus' Approach to Discipleship

Be With Him

Spiritual direction is intrinsically connected to the way Jesus equipped his disciples to live and share "life with God," in the power of the Holy Spirit. First and foremost, the earliest followers of Jesus were called *to be with him*. The twelve were appointed "to be with Jesus," then to be sent out to proclaim the message of the kingdom (Mark 3:14). This is the heart of Christian spiritual life: to walk with Jesus in intimate friendship, to commune with him through the indwelling Holy Spirit. The order is crucial. It should always be our bedrock priority: first, to be with Jesus, and second, to be sent out to do his work.

Become Like Him

Along with the call to be with Jesus is a second facet of Jesus' approach to disciple making. His disciples are called to *become like him*. Jesus said: "A disciple is not above the teacher, but everyone who is fully trained will be like the teacher" (Luke 6:40).[1] Being with Jesus is transformative. To be with him leads to becoming like him. It is a kind of "spiritual osmosis." For the original disciples, and for us, becoming like Jesus is both "caught and taught." The early disciples were trained for life in the kingdom of God by spending time daily with Jesus, watching how he related to the Father, how he depended on the Holy Spirit, and how he interacted with others.

In a word, to become like Jesus centers on loving God and loving our neighbor (Mark 12:28–31). Becoming like Jesus—growing in love for God and others—entails servanthood. Jesus called his disciples "friends" (John 15:15). He modeled what love and friendship look like. "If I then, the Lord and the Teacher, washed your feet, you also ought to wash one another's feet. For I gave you an example that you also should do as I did to you" (John 13:14–15). To be with him leads to becoming like him. When we are like him, love for God and others compels us, and we serve others in humility.

Follow Him

Third, Jesus called his disciples to *follow him*. The disciples followed their rabbi, the Lord Jesus. They followed his example of love for God and neighbor, of being the servant of all, and his compassion for the marginalized. Jesus followed the guidance of the Father, doing only what he saw the Father doing (John 5:19). The disciples followed this model of dependence, learning to do the will of God, as Jesus did, in the power of the Holy Spirit. They also followed him in the way of the cross. As we considered earlier, to be a follower of Jesus, to live life in the Spirit, involves taking up the cross and pursuing Jesus.

Thus, from the original twelve to all contemporary disciples, Jesus continues to shape his followers in the context of deep relationship. We are his apprentices. Our aim is to be with him, become like him, and follow him. He fills us with his Spirit, to help us accomplish these things. We are filled with the mighty Holy Spirit, our great Helper, clothed with power from on high as Jesus was, and energized by the grace of God as Christ is formed in us. These are the basic contours and promises of discipleship, according to the model of Jesus.

---

1. Translation mine.

A Luminous Life

Facets of Spiritual Direction

The way Jesus relates to his first disciples becomes the paradigm for subsequent discipleship, spiritual direction, and other approaches to Christian spiritual life.[2]

"Spiritual direction," like other theological ideas and practices, has many facets and can be defined in various ways. It is a burgeoning field in contemporary studies of theology and spirituality. There are excellent resources on spiritual direction within Catholic, Orthodox, and Protestant traditions. One recent book by Orthodox scholar, George Demacopoulos, *Five Models of Spiritual Direction in the Early Church*, is a fascinating study of spiritual direction according to Athanasius of Alexandria, Gregory of Nazianzus, Augustine of Hippo, John Cassian, and Pope Gregory I. Demacopoulos proposes a basic, helpful definition of spiritual direction: "By *spiritual direction*, I mean the modus operandi by which religious authorities (in both lay and monastic communities) sought to advance the spiritual condition of those under their care."[3] This definition suggests that spiritual direction includes particular methods, employed by directors in lay and monastic communities, that seek to engender spiritual growth in those they are directing.

Kim Olstad, an evangelical author, adds that spiritual direction entails a process of discernment. It involves a directee and director who listen together to the voice of the Lord in pursuit of a deeper relationship with God and reliance on Jesus in ongoing life choices. Spiritual direction may be a one-on-one relationship, but it can also occur within a group. Spiritual direction is a process of growth, guidance, and transformation. The director serves as a spiritual companion in the spiritual journey of ever increasing intimacy with Jesus, learning to discern and obey his guidance, and discover how to use one's spiritual gifts for the glory of God and the good of others. In the spirit of Galatians 4:19, where Paul speaks about Christ being formed in the lives of Christians, spiritual direction has been referred to as "the midwifery of the soul." The aim of the director is to come alongside the

---

2. There are key differences between discipleship and spiritual direction, spiritual mentoring, and spiritual friendship. "Spiritual mentoring is more focused on the life of the soul in relationship to God than is discipleship." Discipleship "ought to include such mentoring but denotes a more comprehensive process of shaping people into Christians —one that includes, for example, basic introduction to doctrine, ethics, and daily practices." Buschart, "Spiritual Mentoring," 610.

3. Demacopoulos, *Five Models of Spiritual Direction in the Early Church*, 1.

directee as they learn to discern the voice of God, follow the leadership of Jesus, and walk with the Holy Spirit in truth and spiritual freedom. As this occurs, the character of Christ and fruits of the Spirit are formed in the life of the directee.[4]

Though today the term *spiritual director* is used to speak of a person who has been trained, formally or informally, to help others grow spiritually, the concept is broader. For example, in the Christian East, there is a rich tradition of spiritual fathers and mothers who serve as companions and guides on the spiritual journey.[5] In the Greek tradition these elders are called *Geron*, and in the Russian tradition they are known as *Starets*. In the *Philokalia*, we read that a spiritual father or mother teaches others by their own conduct: "It is not words but actions that inspire people to follow a leader ... [T]he Lord Himself first acted and then taught ... It is more convincing to teach through actions than through words."[6] As Jesus provided direction to his disciples through actions then words, so spiritual fathers and mothers guide their followers as they observe the way they relate to God, others, and the world.[7]

Furthermore, evangelical theologian Bruce Demarest discusses spiritual direction in the broader context of other "soul-care ministries." He views spiritual direction on a spectrum of other ministries focused on "spiritual help," from the informal, unstructured, reciprocal side: spiritual friendship and spiritual guidance; to the more formal, structured, one-directional side: spiritual mentoring and spiritual direction.[8] These are but a few of the nuances in the rich conversation about spiritual direction. But in very basic terms, we can say that spiritual direction involves helping others grow in their relationship with God, which brings us to another point.

---

4. Olstad, "Spiritual Direction," 402–3.

5. Simon Chan suggests, "Perhaps we need to go back to the model of the desert father whose 'directorship' was recognized by those who came to him rather than conferred through formal training ... In spiritual direction the learning process is quite different from academic learning; it is more 'caught' than taught." *Spiritual Theology*, 237.

6. *Philokalia* 1:217.

7. The spiritual father is described as doctor, counselor, intercessor, mediator, and sponsor, in the classic study by Hausherr, *Spiritual Direction in the Early Christian East*, xiiff.

8. Demarest, *Satisfy Your Soul*, 195.

The Holy Spirit Is the Ultimate Spiritual Director

In addition to the organic link between Jesus' approach to discipleship and spiritual direction, is a second crucial point: the Holy Spirit is the ultimate spiritual director. Kallistos Ware writes: "The only true 'spiritual director,' in the fullest sense of the word, is the Holy Spirit."[9] This reiterates what Jesus said: "I will ask the Father, and he will give you another Advocate, to be with you forever. This is the Spirit of truth . . . The Holy Spirit, whom the Father will send in my name, will teach you everything . . ." (John 14:16, 17, 26). John explains further in his epistle that the Holy Spirit, the anointing given by Christ, indwells and instructs all Christians: "As for you, the anointing that you received from him abides in you, and so you do not need anyone to teach you. But as his anointing teaches you about all things, and is true and is not a lie, and just as it has taught you, abide in him" (1 John 2:27). This is the fruit of Pentecost. After the death and resurrection of Jesus, the Spirit was poured out on all flesh, empowering all Christians to prophesy and declare the great works of God (Acts 2:1–11). The Spirit also guides all Christians in the way of Christ. There is no better Teacher, no gentler Guide, no wiser Director than the Spirit of God.

This is wonderful news for all believers. Receiving spiritual direction is not reserved for a "privileged few." The outpouring of the Holy Spirit on all flesh democratizes spiritual direction. It is accessible to everyone, in all walks of life. For the nursing mother taking care of her children, who is unable to leave her home and meet with a spiritual director: the Holy Spirit will direct her as she reads her Bible, prays, and follows Jesus. For the disabled veteran unable to walk or leave his home: the Holy Spirit will be his spiritual director. For the young woman in Turkey who recently became a follower of Jesus and does not have access to a spiritual mother or father: the Holy Spirit will be her spiritual guide.

Such good news does not preclude seeking out a spiritual director, when it is a viable option. "Although the Holy Spirit is our ultimate Guide, God has chosen to use fellow believers as instruments of growth . . . His customary way of working good is through other believers."[10] As we have noted at several points, Christian spirituality is a communal venture. Life

---

9. Ware, "The Spiritual Guide in Orthodox Christianity," in *The Inner Kingdom*, 144. Olstad adds: "Since the ultimate director in the process of spiritual direction is the Holy Spirit, the task of the human director is to be attentive to the Spirit, the directee's heart, and his or her own heart as well." *The Dictionary of Christian Spirituality*, 402.

10. Demarest, *Satisfy Your Soul*, 199.

Spiritual Mothers and Fathers

in the Holy Spirit takes place in the body of Christ. Christian spirituality, originating with Jesus and his twelve disciples and expanding to the one hundred twenty women and men in the upper room, is a social endeavor. From the early church to the present day, younger women receive direction from older women, and younger "Timothys" receive direction from older "Pauls" (Titus 2:2–8). Some may prefer a spiritual director of the same gender, so they can address areas of sexuality and the like without reservation, while others may be comfortable with either option. The key is to find a spiritual director who is experienced, wise, discerning, and trustworthy.

Overall Aim: To Help Others Grow

A third point is that the overall aim of spiritual direction is to help others grow in their relationship with God. A spiritual director helps someone connect with God in practical and meaningful ways. The spiritual director understands that spiritual transformation occurs through relationship with the triune God. If the Father is the gardener who cares for the vines, and Jesus is the vine in which we are to abide (John 15), then a spiritual director cooperates with the Father in tending the vine, with tender care and diligence, in the grace and power of the Spirit. Offering personal and practical instruction on how to develop friendship with God is fundamental to spiritual direction. If the Holy Spirit is the ultimate spiritual director, then those who direct others should be known for sensitivity to the work of the Spirit. "For the true guide of the soul is the Holy Spirit, and the function of the human director is to help individuals to recognize where the Spirit is leading."[11] Spiritual directors depend, moment by moment, day by day, on the presence, power, and leadership of the Holy Spirit.

In his brief yet insightful work, *Spiritual Direction and Meditation*, Thomas Merton cites Dom Augustine Baker (1575–1641), a Benedictine mystic: "The director is not to teach his own way, nor indeed any determinate way of prayer, but to instruct his disciples how they may themselves find out the way proper for them . . . In a word, he is only God's usher, and must lead souls in God's way, and not his own."[12] The goal of the spiritual director is to connect others to the love of God, to guide them into deeper experiences of the grace of the Lord Jesus, and to help them commune with the indwelling Holy Spirit (2 Cor 13:14). The usher brings his or her fellow

---

11. Bryant, "The Nature of Spiritual Direction," 568.
12. Merton, *Spiritual Direction and Meditation*, 20–21.

Christian into the presence of the King, who sits on a throne of grace. Better yet, the usher helps them delve into their hearts, where the King dwells in the innermost chambers. This makes the work of the director more feasible. It is not up to him or her to come up with ingenious plans or muster up unrealistic strength. A spiritual director offers practical ways to experience God's transformative presence, love, grace, and mercy. The goal is to help their spiritual sister or brother learn to relate to Jesus for themselves, to prayerfully read and meditate on Scripture, to talk with him, listen to him, discern his plans, and follow his lead.

Spiritual direction involves helping someone become, do, and fulfill what God has intended. There is no "one-size-fits-all" method of spiritual direction. Spiritual direction happens in the context of personal relationship, where there is mutual knowledge and trust: "What the spiritual mother or father gives to the disciple is not a code of written or oral regulations, not a set of techniques for meditation, but a personal relationship." Within this personal relationship, the mother or father "grows and changes as well as the disciple, for God is constantly directing them both."[13] The "art" of spiritual direction requires sensitivity to what the Artist of souls is crafting in each person. Each of us has a unique personality, a unique calling, and a unique way of reflecting the glory of God as creatures made in the *imago Dei*.

Yet there are certain themes and practices that recur in spiritual direction, ways of connecting someone to the love and life-giving Spirit of God: "The director's task may be roughly summarized under four headings: prayer, self-knowledge, vocation, and the ordering of daily life."[14] Helping someone learn how to more consistently talk and listen to God, to better understand who they are (and who they are not!), to discern the call and purposes of God for their life, and how to organize and balance everyday life—this is the job of a spiritual director. Sometimes we have a tendency to complicate things. Even though spiritual direction may require sophisticated wisdom and insights at times—because we are dealing with amazing, complex human beings—it is profoundly simple. Help someone turn to Jesus, usher someone into the way of Christ, listen to them describe what hinders their progress, and suggest a few practical steps to grow in prayer and depend on the Holy Spirit. As they do this, the Spirit will speak to them

---

13. Ware, "The Spiritual Guide in Orthodox Christianity," in *The Inner Kingdom*, 147.
14. Bryant, "The Nature of Spiritual Direction," 568.

Spiritual Mothers and Fathers

about who they are, what they are called to be and do, and enable them to structure their lives accordingly.

Directors Lead Others Where They Have Traveled

Fourth, spiritual directors serve others from their own spiritual history, drawing from their life in God, their growth in the grace and knowledge of the Lord Jesus, and their fellowship with the Holy Spirit. Therefore, a director cultivates and protects his or her own prayer life. "Acquire a peaceful spirit, and thousands around you will be saved," said St. Seraphim (1754-1833). Establish yourself in God, then you can bring others into God's presence.[15] For one must first receive from Jesus in order to give to another. The director learns to sit at the feet of Jesus, practicing "the most necessary thing," then brings others into that place of love and listening, at the feet of the Lord (Luke 10:39-42).

As Merton says: "His first duty, if he wants to be an effective director, is to see his own interior life and take time for prayer and meditation, since he will never be able to give to others what he does not possess himself."[16] Directors, like all Christians, are called first to be lovers of God. Learning to receive and respond to the love of God in prayer is first priority. When the love of God is poured out into the heart through the Holy Spirit (Rom 5:5), through meditation on Scripture, silence, and contemplation of the glory of God in the face of Jesus, the director has love to pour out into the hearts of others. Spiritual directors learn to be alone with God, "and so in the stillness of their own heart they will begin to hear the wordless speech of the Spirit, thus discovering the truth about themselves and about God. Then their word to others will be a word of power, because it is a word out of silence."[17]

A spiritual director is like a travel guide through the diverse terrain of God and the peaks and valleys of the spiritual life. The most effective guides are those who have explored the vastness of God over many years, weathered various and difficult seasons of life, and learned to endure pain, suffering, and slow growth. Like the spiritual mothers and fathers of old, effective directors are "eyewitnesses concerning a country they have been to." Spiritual guides "are not simply right or eloquent and moving, they speak

---

15. Ware, "The Spiritual Guide in Orthodox Christianity," in *The Inner Kingdom*, 133.
16. Merton, *Spiritual Direction and Meditation*, 28.
17. Ware, "The Spiritual Guide in Orthodox Christianity," in *The Inner Kingdom*, 133.

of what they know, they speak from experience of a country where they have been."[18] This does not mean that a director must be "perfect" or "have it all together." Who does?! The fruitful director is acutely aware of his or her own brokenness and weakness, and is clothed in humility. They have a reputation of experience in God, a track record of life in the Spirit. Simon Chan says that a spiritual director "is not merely a resource person who provides information for others." They "must be a fellow traveler along the way." The director is "a fellow mountain climber" who helps others ascend "an ascetical stairway of small steps." The guide provides instruction on the practices of prayer, reading and meditating on Scripture, practicing the presence of God and obeying the voice of God, befriending others, being with God in nature, and sharing with others.[19]

Therapy, Counseling, and Direction

We have noted from the onset that Christian spirituality is holistic. The practice of Christian spirituality is also therapeutic. The presence of the Lord brings healing to the body and soul, to the material and immaterial aspects of human nature. Spiritual direction seeks to connect Christians to *Jehovah Rapha*, the Lord who heals (Exod 15:26). Spiritual direction helps disciples reach out to touch Jesus, whose presence and power heal body and soul (Luke 8:46–48). Direction shares some of the values and objectives of psychiatry, psychology, counseling, and other forms of therapy: healing, wholeness, and integration.[20] Some directors have formal education, training, and experience in these disciplines. This might enhance their understanding of human nature, patterns of behavior, or assessing areas of brokenness that need healing. Yet spiritual directors do not have to undergo formal training in these fields in order to be fruitful. As we have noted from Chan, "Perhaps we need to go back to the model of the desert father whose 'directorship' was recognized by those who came to him rather than conferred through formal training . . . In spiritual direction the learning

---

18. I. V. Kireevsky, in Louth, "The Theology of the *Philokalia*," 355.
19. Chan, *Spiritual Theology*, 237.
20. This is a developing field, with fascinating and informative studies appearing. For example, the work of Cook, "Healing, Psychotherapy, and the *Philokalia*," and *The Philokalia and the Inner Life*; Tympas, *Carl Jung and Maximus Confessor on Psychic Development*; and Miller, ed., *The Oxford Handbook of Psychology and Spirituality*.

process is quite different from academic learning; it is more 'caught' than taught." [21]

While spiritual direction may at times overlap with certain ideas and practices in these disciplines, it is a distinct approach. Direction is a calling, vocation, and "method" that is taught and energized by the Spirit of God. It may include the director drawing from his or her background in psychology or therapy, but it is not necessary.

Merton explains that a spiritual director is not a psychoanalyst, and that they should stick to their divinely given mission. He warns against becoming an amateur in psychotherapy. The director can learn enough to respect someone's unconscious, instinctual nature, and recognize unconscious drives and emotional problems. But the director should understand that psychological problems are beyond the range of their competency. Appreciating the value of psychiatry, the director knows when to refer someone to a psychiatrist for suitable treatment.[22]

Spiritual directors rely on common sense, follow the leading of the Holy Spirit, and utilize connections with others who might help a directee address certain psychological issues and experience healing. Directors know that the Lord brings healing and wholeness in many ways. The way to healing includes contemplation and action, to which we now turn.

---

21. Chan, *Spiritual Theology*, 237.
22. Merton, *Spiritual Direction and Meditation*, 49, 50.

CHAPTER 12.

Service: Contemplatives in Action

> While they were worshiping the Lord and fasting, the Holy Spirit said, "Set apart for me Barnabas and Saul for the work to which I have called them." Then after fasting and praying they laid their hands on them and sent them off.
> —Acts 13:2–3

> "The great need of our age, as far as the spiritual life is concerned, is to put contemplation on the roads."
> —Jacques Maritain, *The Peasant of the Garonne*

> "Just as theology and spirituality ought not to be separated, and are not in the Fathers, nor should contemplation and action . . ."
> —Andrew Louth, *Origins of the Christian Mystical Tradition*

> "Without contemplation and interior prayer the Church cannot fulfill her mission . . ."
> —Thomas Merton, *Contemplative Prayer*

> "Seeking the face of God in everything, everyone, all the time, and his hand in every happening; This is what it means to be contemplative in the heart of the world."
> —Mother Teresa

> "Everything is prayer."
> —Ignatius Loyola

Service

CLASSIC CHRISTIAN SPIRITUALITY, AS we have seen throughout these chapters, involves connection with God *and* transformation of life.[1] In the spiritual journey, the practices of prayer, biblical meditation, fasting (and other ascetic exercises), utilizing desert wisdom, and spiritual direction, are intended to help us cultivate "life with God," a life rooted in love for God and people. The Scriptures and spiritual classics illustrate that ongoing *contact with God* leads to *changed lives*. Life with and in God involves prayer and service. Experiencing the love of God transforms us, empowering us to love and serve others.

Contemplation and Action: Historical Context

Over nearly two thousand years, the Christian spiritual tradition has talked about these two "ways" of life with God under the headings of the *contemplative life* and the *active life*. In this chapter, we will briefly explore the historical development of these two ways or approaches, with illustrations from Eastern and Western Christians. Similar to themes we have considered previously—such as solitude and community, or the cataphatic and apophatic—we will recognize a healthy tension between the contemplative and active ways. Tracing the historical development and discussion of the contemplative and active ways will deepen our understanding of what it means to be people of prayer who serve others.

Classic Greek Philosophy

To address these approaches to life, early Christians appropriated ideas and terminology from classic Greek philosophy. Greek philosophers discussed the life of citizens and their political duties in terms of *bios praktikos*, "the active life," and the life of philosophers and their speculative pursuit of truth as *bios theoretikos*, "the contemplative life." Christians adopted and modified these ideas, utilizing the term *theoria contemplatio* to describe the biblical promise of seeing, knowing, and being united to God through the contemplation of Scripture.

The contemplative and active ways of living were no longer viewed as distinctive methods, but as "related modalities of the life of every believer."

---

1. McGinn's treatment of contemplation and action has informed this section. See McGinn, ed., *The Essential Writings of Christian Mysticism*, 519–20.

The *active life* is "that part of existence in which the Christian is called upon to serve [their] neighbor in love ... ," while the *contemplative life* "is that aspect devoted to love of God and desire for the vision of God." Adjusting these approaches, all Christians "are called upon to make use of both modalities, though in differing degrees depending on their station in the church."[2] Thus, the Christian appropriation of these classic Greek concepts paved the way for the future development of the contemplative and active ways of life in Christ.

Patristic Period

While Christians viewed both of these approaches to life as necessary, there have been various ways of understanding how they relate to one another. The conventional model, established in the patristic period or era of the church fathers (roughly 100–787),[3] viewed the contemplative life as superior and more desirable, while the active life was more pressing because of the Christian commitment to love of neighbor. One example is found in Gregory the Great (c. 540–604), also known as Pope Gregory I. Reflecting on examples in Scripture, Gregory teaches that Christians, especially church leaders, are to alternate between contemplation and action. Interpreting the story of Jacob's ladder allegorically, and finding in it a model for ministry, Gregory says:

> Thus Jacob, as the Lord leaned on the ladder above and the anointed stone was below, saw angels ascending and descending (Gen. 28:11–18), which was a sign that true preachers do not only aspire by contemplation to the Holy Head of the Church above, namely, the Lord, but also descend to its members in pity for them.[4]

Gregory also finds the model of contemplation and action in the life of Moses. Moses always returns to the ark of the covenant to consult and contemplate the Lord, but he oscillates between contemplation and action at other times: "Thus Moses frequently goes in and out of the Tabernacle; and while within he is caught up in contemplation, outside he devotes himself

---

2. McGinn, ed., *The Essential Writings of Christian Mysticism*, 520.

3. The patristic period extends from the end of the New Testament era (c. 100) to either the Council of Chalcedon (451) or the Second Council of Nicaea (787).

4. McGinn, ed., *The Essential Writings of Christian Mysticism*, 523.

to the affairs of the weak. Inwardly he considers the hidden things of God, outwardly he bears the burdens of carnal men."

Further, Gregory discerns the same pattern in Paul. Though Paul was taken into paradise and contemplated "secrets of the third heaven" (2 Cor 12:2-4), he returned in faithful service to attend to the "secrets of those who are weak," who needed his pastoral instruction. A contemplator of mysteries, and active servant of the church, he was willing to become weak to those who are weak (2 Cor 11:29).

Finally, Gregory points to Jesus, who "engaged in prayer on the mountain and worked miracles in the towns (Luke 6:12). He thus showed the way to be followed by good rulers [in the church], who, though they strive after the highest things by contemplation, should nevertheless by their compassion share in the needs of the weak."[5] Nevertheless, according to Gregory and the basic paradigm established in the patristic era, the contemplative life is still superior to the active life.

Late Middle Ages

Meister Eckhart

In the late Middle Ages, some began to question the conventional model, arguing that the highest form of the spiritual life was not solely contemplation, but an integration of contemplation and action. One example is found in Meister Eckhart (c. 1260-1328), the German theologian, philosopher, and mystic. Eckhart wrote a sermon on Luke 10:38-42, commenting on Jesus' interactions with Mary and Martha. As previously mentioned, dating back to Origen, this story had been interpreted spiritually, with Mary representing the contemplative life and Martha signifying the active life. But Eckhart reverses the model, commending Martha over Mary, and suggesting a new perspective on the relationship between the active life and the contemplative life.[6]

In short, Eckhart proposes that Martha had already learned "the better part" that Mary was only beginning to discover and experience: sitting at the feet of Jesus, listening to him (Luke 10:42). Martha, however, was able to engage in a new kind of action "based on a mature ground of being." Martha was concerned that her sister would stay in the place of contemplative

---

5. McGinn, ed., *The Essential Writings of Christian Mysticism*, 522, 523.
6. McGinn, ed., *The Essential Writings of Christian Mysticism*, 529.

joy and sweetness and never proceed to the next stage of maturity, where love for Jesus energizes good works. Eckhart explains:

> Again, some people hope to reach a point where they are free of works. I say this cannot be. After the disciples had received the Holy Spirit they began to do good works. And so, when Mary sat at the feet of our Lord, she was learning, for she had just gone to school to learn how to live. But later on, when Christ had gone to heaven and she received the Holy Spirit, she began to serve: she traveled overseas and preached and taught, acting as servant and washerwoman to the disciples.[7]

This was a fresh, bold interpretation of the well-known story. Eckhart claimed that the starting point was learning to sit at the feet of Jesus, to listen and take delight in what he says, and to contemplate his beauty and glory. Once a person is grounded in this inner practice of contemplation, they are set ablaze with love and sent into the world to do good works. Other mystics shared this conviction, that contemplation is not the highest expression of the spiritual life, but a union of contemplation and action.

Ignatius of Loyola

Ignatius of Loyola (1491–1556), the founder of the Jesuits and author of *The Spiritual Exercises*, was known for his synthesis of the contemplative and active ways. In *The Exercises*, Ignatius taught fellow Jesuits and others how to "find God in all things" and "to love God in all things." This contemplative outlook informed all that Ignatius was and did. Ignatius claimed that Jesuits in training, who were devoting themselves to prayer, studies, and learning, were serving God in a certain way that requires the whole person, and were not less but rather "more pleasing to God" during the season of preparation.[8]

These interrelated themes encapsulate Ignatius' concept of "apostolic spirituality." A Christian serves and pleases God "at some times by focusing attention on him in prayer and at other times by working for him and one's neighbor in love. One should find God in all things and in all one's activities . . ." The practice of "finding God in all things" is what led Jerónimo Nadal, Ignatius's collaborator, to call him a "contemplative while in action."

---

7. McGinn, ed., *The Essential Writings of Christian Mysticism*, 534.
8. Ignatius of Loyola, *Ignatius of Loyola*, 293–94.

Nadal speaks of the grace of contemplation of the Trinity in all Ignatius' activities:

> We know that Father Ignatius received from God the singular grace to enjoy freely the contemplation of the Trinity and to repose in it ... Father Ignatius enjoyed this kind of prayer by reason of a great privilege and in most singular manner, and this besides, that in all things, actions, and conversations he perceived and contemplated the presence of God and an attraction to spiritual things, being a contemplative person even while in the midst of action.[9]

Some think that Ignatius may have learned some of this perspective on contemplation in action from Thomas Aquinas, who addressed the relationship between the two modalities over two hundred years earlier. Their ideas are analogous. Aquinas writes: "As long as a man is acting in his heart, speech, or work in such a manner that he is tending toward God, he is praying; and thus one who is directing his whole life toward God is praying always." Ignatius similarly states: "In the midst of actions and studies, the mind can be lifted to God; and by means of this directing everything to the divine service, everything is prayer."[10]

Further, Aquinas explains that sometimes the necessity of works in the active life impedes contemplation. However, one who is in the unitive stage of spiritual growth, whose chief inclination is toward God and union with God, can remain a contemplative person even while engaged in apostolic activities. Such a person may "merit more by the works of the active life than another by works of the contemplative life, e.g., if through divine love he or she consents to be withdrawn from the sweetness of divine contemplation for a time" to aid a neighbor in need.[11] Ignatius writes in a similar fashion, suggesting that acts of love may surpass continual contemplation:

> The distracting occupations undertaken for his greater service, in conformity with his divine will can be, not only the equivalent of the union and recollection of uninterrupted contemplation, but even more acceptable, proceeding they do from a more active and vigorous charity.[12]

---

9. Ignatius of Loyola, *Ignatius of Loyola*, 44.
10. Aquinas, *Commentary on Romans*, cited in Ignatius of Loyola, *Ignatius of Loyola*,, 459.
11. Cited in Ignatius of Loyola, *Ignatius of Loyola*, 459.
12. Ignatius of Loyola, *Ignatius of Loyola*, 459.

Therefore, according to Ignatius and Thomas, it is possible to direct one's whole attention and life toward God while simultaneously serving others. In other words, the contemplative and active ways can be united. No longer is it either contemplation *or* action, but a third possibility exists: being *a contemplative while in action*. This may in fact be more satisfactory. Action grounded in contemplation, as expounded by Eckhart in the story of Martha and Mary, and the apostolic spirituality of Ignatius lead us to a more compelling and more realistic mode of spiritual life.

Maximus the Confessor

One particularly helpful guide in the study and practice of contemplation is Maximus the Confessor. Among other reasons, Maximus wrote at the culmination of the patristic era, so his perspective draws together various strands from those before him. Further, Maximus served as a bridge between the churches of the Orthodox East and the Catholic West. He is able, therefore, to utilize ideas from Eastern and Western traditions, and provide a helpful synthesis to all Christians.[13] Linking his insights to those of Eckhart, Aquinas, and Ignatius sheds further light on the relationship between contemplation and action.

Three Phases

For Maximus, to contemplate is to search for and see God. It entails a hunger and thirst for God. The Christian who contemplates seeks the presence of God in all things.[14] The goal of contemplation is to experience union with God. Contemplation is an integral part of the spiritual journey. With diligent work, energized by divine grace, one grows in the ability to contemplate.

If you recall, Evagrius spoke of the spiritual journey in three phases: *praktike*, *physike*, and *theologia*. Maximus appropriates this schema in which contemplation plays an important role. Since the goal of contemplation, and the whole spiritual life is to see God with increasing clarity and to experience union with God, *praktike* involves certain "practices" (like

---

13. See Balthasar, *Cosmic Liturgy*, 25, 29, 44–48, 55–57, 152–53, 190–2.

14. See the discussion of the *logoi* and *Logos*, the ideas of God that permeate all things and their relation to Christ, the Word, by Balthasar, *Cosmic Liturgy*, 115–36; and McIntosh, *Mystical Theology*, 56–62.

Service

biblical meditation, prayer, and fasting) that purify the mind and heart and prepare one to better discern the presence of God internally and externally. This is the process of wiping clean the lenses of your spiritual glasses, so that you can more clearly behold the beauty of God within and around you. *Physike* is the contemplation of created things, when the purified mind can discern and encounter the Creator through "physical" creation (Rom 1:20). *Theologia* is the ultimate goal, the culmination of practical exercises and contemplation of God in the physical or natural world, when contemplation ushers one into an experiential knowledge of and unity with God.

Three Arenas

Moreover, Maximus speaks of contemplation in three arenas: the world, Scripture, and self. For Maximus, contemplation of the *world* leads one to discern the presence and fingerprints of God within nature and the created universe. As we just noted in *physike*, this is the grace-empowered contemplation of what God has made so that one is led to the intimate knowledge of the One who made it. Maximus says: "When the mind is completely freed from the passions, it journeys straight ahead to the contemplation of created things and makes its way to the knowledge of the Holy Trinity."[15] In other words, the purified mind sees, through contemplation, the Maker within the created world, and moves toward a more intimate knowledge of the triune God.

The aim of contemplating the world is to see and experience God through it. Likewise, the aim of contemplating *Scripture* is to behold and encounter Christ within it. Maximus suggests that Scripture is like the human body, consisting of body, soul, and spirit. The goal of contemplating Scripture is to move past the external flesh and bones in order to delve deeper into the soul and spirit of its meaning and message. Contemplation takes us beneath the surface of the words, where we encounter the living Word. As the contemplation of the created world brings us into living contact with the Creator, so the contemplation of Scripture draws us into direct encounter with the Word hidden within the words. Maximus says that we can contemplate these "two books," the book of nature and the book of Scripture, and be transformed through the encounter. The book of nature and the book of Scripture, therefore, mediate to us the presence of God

---

15. Maximus, *The Four Hundred Chapters on Love*, in *Selected Writings*, 86, 45.

the Father and God the Son. They are like icons, or windows to heaven, through which we can behold the glory of God.

Finally, Maximus says that we can contemplate the presence of Christ within *ourselves*, the great mystery of which Paul speaks: Christ in you, the hope of glory (Col 1:27). Through ascetic exercises that purify the heart and clarify spiritual vision, and by means of steady contemplation, believers excavate the indwelling presence of Christ, the great treasure of the King and kingdom within:

> The one who through asceticism and contemplation has known how to dig in himself the wells of virtue and knowledge as did the patriarchs will find Christ within as the spring of life. Wisdom bids us to drink from it, saying, "Drink waters from your own vessels and from your own springs." If we do this we shall discover that his treasures are present within us.[16]

Based on his exegesis of Scripture, in the spirit of Origen and the broader Alexandrian tradition, Maximus claims that Christ the Logos indwells the three arenas or spheres of the world of nature, the world of Scripture, and the inner world of human beings. The incarnation of Christ was such a profound and pivotal moment in history that it affected every aspect of creation. Maximus understands that Christ the Logos in some sense incarnates himself, remains hidden, and waits to be discovered in each of these spheres. Contemplation is the way we learn to "see" the presence of Christ, the agent of creation (Prov 8:30–31; Col 1:16), in everything that exists. The perspective Maximus proposes encourages Christians to live contemplatively, to look for the presence of God within and without, to find Christ, the incarnate Logos, indwelling the world, Scripture, and self. In other words, the presence of God in Christ, *in all of the created order*, beckons us to contemplate, behold, encounter, and be transformed.

Contemplation and Action

Maximus also speaks of the relationship between contemplation and action. As Mary and Martha signify this relationship for many classic writers, Maximus suggests that the two apostles, John and Peter, symbolize contemplative knowledge and action. Maximus reflects on the account of John and Peter rushing to the grave of Jesus. They run *together*, overtake one another,

---

16. Maximus, *Chapters on Knowledge* 2, 40, in *Selected Writings*, 156.

are both mutually indispensable, and "neither one has an advantage or disadvantage with respect to the other."[17] They are both equally important modes of seeking and encountering the presence of the resurrected Christ, the Logos who indwells all things. Contemplation and action are united modes of spiritual being, like the relationship between faith and love. They cannot be separated. Maximus claims: "If one seeks for the Lord in contemplation without praxis [practice or action], one does not find him."[18]

Contemplation and action push each other toward the Lord Jesus, and a fuller degree of integration.[19] Contemplation and action mutually strengthen one another. They move the Christian ever closer to the presence of the Word, who indwells the world, Scripture, and the human person. Contemplation and action are conduits through which the love of God enters our hearts. They are human responses to divine love. Contemplation and action are rooted in love, fueled by love, and united in love.

In light of the historical conversation about contemplation and action, including concepts from classic Greek philosophy, Gregory, Eckhart, Aquinas and Loyola, and Maximus, it might be helpful to synthesize our discoveries as we conclude this chapter.

Integral Relationship

First, *there is an integral relationship between contemplation and action*. It is not an "either or" relationship, but "both and." Theophan the Recluse (1814-1894) underlines the essential link between the contemplative and active ways, and their common goal to unite Christians to God:

> We should invariably link contemplation to action and action to contemplation. When the two are so joined they quickly enable the soul to advance, cleansing it from evil and strengthening it in good . . . There are two ways to become one with God: the active way and the contemplative way. The first is for Christians who live

---

17. Maximus, *Ambigua*, cited in Balthasar, *Cosmic Liturgy*, 332.

18. Maximus, *Quaestiones ad Thalassium*, cited in Balthasar, *Cosmic Liturgy*, 333.

19. Balthasar comments on Maximus's view: "Action and knowledge, then, penetrate each other inseparable and push each other toward a constantly fuller degree of integration. Action, in the end, is only the 'revelation' (φανέρωσις) of knowledge, just as knowledge is the bright interior of action. But are not *actives and contemplatives* in the Church, seculars and monks, still in contrast with each other? Surely, their ideals are not the same; yet both are simply predominant emphases within a single overarching ideal, and to that degree—at least in a certain sense—both are of equal value." *Cosmic Liturgy*, 334.

in the world, the second for those who have abandoned all worldly things. But in practice neither way can exist in total isolation from the other. Those who live in the world must also keep to the contemplative way in some measure.[20]

Contemplation and action share a symbiotic connection. When the two ways are operational alongside one another, they swiftly move the soul toward God, purifying and fortifying it. Whether one follows Jesus as a layperson, minister, or monk, contemplation and action are an integral part of the spiritual life. Like the twin commands Jesus highlights, contemplation and action are inseparable:

> The first is, "Hear, O Israel: the Lord our God, the Lord is one; you shall love the Lord your God with all your heart, and with all your soul, and with all your mind, and with all your strength." The second is this, "You shall love your neighbor as yourself." There is no other commandment greater than these (Mark 12:29–31).

Love for God and neighbor are a unity. Those who love God love their neighbor and their sisters and brothers (1 John 4:20–21). Love is demonstrated by action, not simply words (1 John 3:18). Teresa of Avila reiterates the teaching of Jesus and the apostle: "The surest way to determine whether one possesses the love of God is to see whether he or she loves his or her neighbor. These two loves are never separated. Rest assured, the more you progress in love of neighbor the more your love of God will increase."[21] Therefore, the two ways and the two commandments center on love and are united in love.

While there may be seasons in which contemplation or action seem to be the focal point, we understand that they are ultimately united, they cannot be divided, and they fuel each other. Seasons of intense prayer, meditation, and contemplation set the heart on fire. When we contemplate the Lord, who is a consuming fire, we are set ablaze and sent into the world to serve, to carry the fire of love, to be the body of Christ. Teresa of Avila says:

> Christ has no body but yours, no hands, no feet on earth but yours, yours are the eyes with which he looks with compassion on this world, yours are the feet with which he walks to do good, yours are the hands, with which he blesses all the world. Yours are the hands, yours are the feet, yours are the eyes, you are his body. Christ has

---

20. Theophan the Recluse, in Chariton, ed., *The Art of Prayer*, 235.
21. In Bruss, *Carrying the Presence*, 28.

no body now but yours, no hands, no feet on earth but yours, yours are the eyes with which he looks compassion on this world. Christ has no body now on earth but yours.[22]

The Lord Jesus works through us, as we contemplate him, and remain in vital contact with him through prayer.

Contemplatives in Action

Second, my hope is that these reflections on contemplation and action stoke the flame within you and encourage you to be *a contemplative in action*. In some circles, we hear leaders calling Christians to activism in a variety of causes. For example, Christians are called to go to the mission field, serve the poor, or address problems like human trafficking. These are crucial, biblically mandated causes. However, throwing ourselves into causes without lives based on prayer, worship, and friendship with God can lead to activism that results in burnout. Mission is fueled by intimacy with God. Only as Christians freely receive from Christ do they have something to give to the world.

In other circles, we hear leaders calling Christians, especially young adults, to invest time in the "prayer room," growing in worship and prayer. The prayer room movement is expanding in certain Protestant charismatic churches. This movement illustrates an important point. The call to prayer, contemplation, and worship is worthwhile, a correction to a distorted Christian activism that lacks the spirit of worship, prayer, and devotion.

Nevertheless, investing time in the prayer room should be coupled with regular times of serving others outside the prayer room. In prayer we contemplate the glory of God, we rest in the presence of God, we receive the love of God, we enjoy God. In this we catch glimpses of the age to come, when we will gaze upon the glory of God in the face of Christ, forever. We will see him as he really is (1 John 3:1–3). But contemplation of the glory and beauty of God in this age leads not only to rest and enjoyment in God, but to mission. Again, Teresa's insights on this are bracing:

> When I see people very diligently trying to discover what kind of prayer they are experiencing and so completely wrapped up in their prayers that they seem afraid to stir, or to indulge in a moment's thought, lest they should lose the slightest degree of the

---

22. In Moynahan, *Once Upon a Mystery*, 43.

> tenderness and devotion which they had been feeling, I realize how little they understand of the road to the attainment of union. They think that the whole thing consists in this. But no, sisters, no; what the Lord desires is works.[23]

Getting stuck on figuring out what kind of prayer we are experiencing, being wrapped up in prayer, fearfulness of losing that feeling of devotion or of prayer being interrupted—these are indicators that we have some maturing to do. The road to union with God joins contemplation *and* action. "We should desire and engage in prayer, not for our enjoyment, but for the sake of acquiring this strength which fits us for service."[24]

The prayer room can be the operating room where the Lord performs surgery that heals hearts, or the spiritual war room where the Lord's strategies and directives are received. In prayer rooms as we pray with others, and in our personal times and places of prayer, the Spirit of the Lord speaks, reveals, heals, and empowers. This activity of the Spirit, however, inculcates a mind-set for mission and engenders a passion for service. Clark Pinnock writes:

> A longing to enter a more conscious relationship with the Spirit is not a selfish desire, because euphoria is not the goal. The goal is vocation and mission. We need the power of the Spirit to be disciples of Jesus Christ. We are chosen not to privilege but to service, to be God's partners in the mending of creation . . . The goal is not experience as such, but power for mission and fruit-bearing.[25]

A desire for intimate communion with the Holy Spirit is a good thing; for the Spirit is not an ambiguous force, but a Person, the third Person of the Holy Trinity. There may be times of ecstasy in worship and prayer. If only more Christians lived in the fullness of the reality that the church is the vehicle of an ongoing Pentecost![26] For the whole aim of the Christian life is "to be a Spirit-bearer, to live in the Spirit of God."[27]

We observe in the early church that the upper room, Pentecost, and mission are intrinsically connected. Jesus reminded his followers of the promise of the Father, that the Spirit would be poured out on them, that they would receive power from on high, that they would be clothed with

---

23. Teresa of Avila, *The Interior Castle*, 5:3, 12.
24. Teresa of Avila, *The Interior Castle*, 7:4.
25. Pinnock, *Flame of Love*, 171–72.
26. Ware, *The Orthodox Church*, 242–43.
27. Ware, *The Orthodox Way*, 90.

Service

the power of the Spirit *to be his witnesses* (Acts 1:8). Their time in the prayer room prepared them for Pentecost and mission. Prayer, the empowerment of the Spirit, and mission—these are interrelated dynamics for the life of a contemplative in action, a contemplative reformer who is partnering with God in the mending of human lives and all of creation.

A luminous life, informed and formed by Scripture and the spiritual classics, entails *missional spirituality*. We are members of the mystical body of Christ. Christ dwells in us through the Holy Spirit. We are in Christ and on mission with Christ. The mystical and the missional are one. Like the early Egyptian Christians of the fourth century, we seek to be "people who bear the name of Christ, the only-begotten Son of God, and do all good to all men."[28]

---

28. Chitty, *The Desert a City*, 7.

Conclusion: Go in the Strength of God's Love

Moses said, "Show me your glory, I pray." And he said, "I will make all my goodness pass before you, and will proclaim before you the name, 'The Lord'; and I will be gracious to whom I will be gracious, and will show mercy on whom I will show mercy."
—Exod 33:18–19

"One thing I have asked from the Lord, that I shall seek: That I may dwell in the house of the Lord all the days of my life, To behold the beauty of the Lord and to meditate in His temple."
—Ps 27:4, NASB

"I want to know Christ and the power of his resurrection and the sharing of his sufferings by becoming like him in his death."
—Phil 3:10

"And the true vision of God consists in this, in never reaching satiety of the desire. We ought always to look through the things that we can see and still be on fire with the desire to see more."
—Gregory of Nyssa, *Life of Moses*

Seek the Presence

As we conclude, I leave you with a few parting reflections. First, the overall aim of this book has been to encourage you to seek the presence of God. Thankfully, the Lord is not far from each of us. Jesus tells his followers that he sends his Spirit to indwell us. The Spirit guides, empowers, transforms, and never leaves us. Still, there is a journey on which to embark, an inward journey of union with Jesus as the Spirit establishes the kingdom of God within our hearts. It is a journey of prayer and descent into the heart. Orthodox monk Theophan the Recluse writes, "To pray is to descend with the mind into the heart, and there to stand before the face of the Lord, ever-present, all seeing, within you." The goal of this inward journey is the face of the Lord Jesus, to contemplate him, to know him, to be loved by him.

Further, the spiritual journey is one of ascent. Martin Luther (1483–1546) said, "Prayer is climbing up into the heart of God." Through prayer, we call out to God as Abba, as beloved children of the Father. Through prayer, God draws us into deeper friendship. Prayer, as we see in Scripture and the spiritual classics, is the pathway to intimacy with the Father, through the Son, by the Holy Spirit. It is the means by which God draws us to himself. Through prayer, we pour out our hearts to God, and God pours out his love into our hearts through the Holy Spirit (Rom 5:5). This two-way communication transforms us, developing in us the mind of Christ, and empowering us to participate in the mission of Christ.

Wisdom of Spiritual Classics

Second, we have considered the wisdom of the Christian spiritual classics. The writings of ancient, medieval, and modern followers of Jesus have spoken to us, just as they have to countless Christians before us. Today we are living in the midst of a renaissance of Christian spirituality, a rebirth, a return to the great classics. Christians return to these classics because the Lord continues to speak through them. These classics are permeated with the Word of God. They are rooted in and suffused with Scripture. Reading them is like sitting alongside the author during their prayer time. We get to listen in as they interact with God and encounter the living Word within the pages of Scripture and in the depths of their hearts. Their insights into the spiritual life, what the Lord graciously revealed to them about himself and his ways, are there for us to ponder and practice.

In our own quest for God, the spiritual classics provide wisdom, perspective, and sustainable practices. The classics were written by real people who faced real struggles in their pursuit of God. The insights and instructions found in their writings encourage us to endure the various seasons of the spiritual life, to keep going, to not give up.

CONCLUSION

On Fire for More

The luminous life is a journey of ever increasing friendship with God and intimacy with Jesus. The quote above from Gregory of Nyssa suggests that on our journey toward the true vision of God, we never reach the point of being sated, of completely satisfying the Godward desire that leads us. In a mysterious fashion, God is the only satisfying Goal we humans can pursue, yet we are always left wanting more of God. We are, as Gregory says, eternally on fire with desire to see and experience more of God, who stretches out before us like an expansive ocean of love and goodness.

Third, we have been reminded that a luminous life is a journey of ever increasing friendship with God and intimacy with Jesus. Because we journey into the boundless mystery of God and the love of God in Christ, the journey ultimately never ends. Though one day we will see the Lord Jesus as he really is, and be transformed into his likeness (1 John 3:2), there will always be more to explore and learn of him. The epigraph above by Gregory of Nyssa speaks to this. Our goal is the true vision of God, the God of love who saves us in Christ through the power of the Holy Spirit. In this life, we catch glimpses of this vision. We see the glory of God in the face of Jesus, but as if we are looking at the reflection of a mirror or through smoky glass (1 Cor 13:12). We are created to behold this glory. It is the only thing that truly satisfies the desire that burns and aches within us. Our hearts are restless . . . until they rest in the Lord. Yet, as Gregory says, we are never fully satisfied. We are satisfied, but left wanting more. We look through the things that we can see, beholding the glory of God through creation, through Scripture, through one another, through the body of Christ. We see the beauty of God in Christ, through the Holy Spirit, and we are still on fire with the desire to see more.

Go . . . in the Strength of God's Love

In your pursuit of God, I hope that you will further explore some of the things you encountered in the Scriptures and spiritual classics. What theological ideas, insights, or practices stood out to you or piqued your interest? What did the Lord reveal to you about your spiritual life, your relationship with him, his people, or the world around you? Consider reviewing some of the portions you marked or highlighted, the footnotes that provide further reading, or the suggested reading in the appendix.

A Luminous Life

Finally, the wonderful thing about a luminous life is that the Father desires it for you more than you ever could. The Father longs to be gracious to you (Isa 30:18), to give you the Holy Spirit (Luke 11:13), and to give you life in the Holy Spirit (Rom 8:1–13). It is up to you to receive and walk in the grace of the Lord Jesus Christ, the love of God, and the fellowship of the Holy Spirit (2 Cor 13:14). The Lord is at work in you, and will complete the work he started (Phil 1:6). Go now in the power he provides, in the strength of his love, as his face shines on you.

Appendix. Fasting: Practical Suggestions

Practical Suggestions

IN ADDITION TO THE discussion on fasting in chapter 5, I want to offer a few practical suggestions.

Pray Often

First, pray as much as possible during your fast. Ask God to help you learn to pray without ceasing (1 Thess 5:17). During your fast—whether you are a mother or dad at home, a teacher, a student, or a business owner or employee—turn to the Lord who dwells within your heart. Express your love for God throughout the day. Set an alarm or reminder on the hour, so you can turn your attention to the Lord. Develop what I call specific "fasting prayers." One of my favorites is based on John 4:34, where Jesus says that his food is to do the will of God who sent him and to complete God's work. During your fast, you could ask God to make this a reality in your life: "Father, my food is to do your will; help me complete the work you have for me." Another fasting prayer, based on Matthew 5:6, could be: "Lord Jesus, help me hunger and thirst for righteousness. Fill me with your Spirit. Empower me to work with you as you bring your kingdom." A further example, from Psalm 63:1, is: "God, I seek you earnestly. My soul thirsts for you; my body longs for you. Your presence is my food and drink in a dry and weary land where there is no water." Also consider linking these and other prayers to normal activities throughout your day. Routine, mundane activities such as going to the bathroom, washing your hands, cleaning up the house or office, or getting in and out of your car, can become moments to turn to the Lord in prayer. For example, while washing your hands, give thanks to God for giving you clean hands and a pure heart so you can ascend the hill of the Lord (Ps 24:3–4). Over time, the mundane activities of our day serve as reminders to turn to Jesus. A transformation takes place. The mundane is transformed into space for worship, prayer, and practicing his presence; and we are transformed into fiery lovers of God and people.

Be Prepared

A second suggestion is to be prepared for what may rise up in your heart and mind during your fast. Sometimes fasting draws things to the surface of your heart. Physiologically, fasting can help detoxify our bodies. This may also be the case spiritually. "Toxins" in our heart and mind are drawn up; through prayer, confession, counseling, and the transformative power of God's love, we can be set free and healed.

Drink, Link, and Hygiene

A third recommendation is to drink plenty of fluids during your fast. Fasting from fluids is not advisable. It may be inconvenient as you have to visit the restroom more frequently, but your body needs the fluid. Plus, as I just mentioned, you can link prayer to each visit to the restroom. Pray a "fasting prayer" on your way to the restroom. As you push open the door, ask Jesus to open doors in your life only he can open. Look for other ways to infuse the mundane with spiritual exercise and meaning. Further, water with a bit of lemon juice stirred in helps with the metallic taste and mucous that might form in your mouth. Tea or coffee might work for some, though be careful about beverages that can trigger excessive stomach acid. For some, antacids might be helpful. Be aware that your breath will probably smell during a fast. Some chew peppermint gum or use mints to help. Brushing your teeth and tongue three times or more a day helps, too. There is nothing "unspiritual" about good hygiene! As a matter of fact, good breath is important as we interact with others. I can recall receiving prayer from others who needed some practical advice on fresh breath.[1]

---

1. While Paul was not talking about fasting and hygiene in 2 Corinthians 2:16—"To the one we are an aroma that brings death; to the other, an aroma that brings life"—we want to carry the aroma of life, not the "breath of death"!

APPENDIX

Break Wisely

Fourth, be wise when breaking a fast. Ease yourself back into eating and drinking in healthy ways. Eat a small portion of more easily digested food. Avoid heavy, rich, fried, or spicy food. Work with your stomach, not against it. You may be tempted to consume an unusual serving (a whole pizza!), but it is better to eat smaller servings more frequently. Wisdom on breaking a fast can be found in books and articles by seasoned authors.[2]

Ease into It

Finally, ease into the practice of fasting. In light of the reflections in chapter 6, be a wise spiritual athlete. Start small. Skip one meal if you can. Fast from dessert, your soda of choice, an app on your phone. As you develop some fasting experience and history, you can venture into other arenas. Remind yourself at every turn: God does not need me to fast. I am fasting in order to focus more on the presence of God within me. Meditate on Isaiah 58 and other passages that deal with fasting. Ask Jesus to teach you how to engage in the kind of fasting God "chooses." Pray during your fasts, that God will develop you as a spiritual athlete who finishes the course, who loves the Lord with all your heart, soul, mind, and strength, and loves your neighbor as yourself. Our aim is to grow in love. Fasting, along with all our spiritual activities, means nothing without love (1 Cor 13:1–3).

---

2. For example, see Wallis, *God's Chosen Fast*.

Acknowledgements

A LUMINOUS LIFE IS one of reflected light. The Lord's face shines like the noonday sun (Rev 1:16). Like mirrors, our lives reflect the light and glory of his countenance. In a similar way, this book is reflected light. I joyfully admit that everything in these pages is light derived from others, those who have looked to his shining face. As Thomas Oden writes: "Some may think it mildly amusing that the only claim I make is that there is nothing whatever original in these pages."[1] Upon completing this book, I find myself thinking yet again: *What do I have that I have not received?* (1 Cor 4:7)

I am grateful to the many people from whom I have received. When the Lord ambushed my life in 1987, my parents were incredibly supportive and accommodating, particularly in what they called my "monk" season. Some of the seeds of this book were sown back in those early days. Attending the Anaheim Vineyard in the late 1980s was a time of deep learning from John Wimber, Jack Deere, and others. Friendship with God, "doing the stuff" (proclaiming and demonstrating the gospel of the kingdom), "everyone gets to play" (to do the works of Jesus in the power of the Holy Spirit), remembering the poor and marginalized, church planting, being people of the Word and Spirit, acquiring passion for Jesus and power to serve him: these Vineyard values and practices shaped my theological perspective from the beginning. They course through the pages of *A Luminous Life*.

While studying at Trinity Evangelical Divinity School in the 1990s, Wayne Grudem became a mentor, friend, and model for sound, biblical theology and life in the Holy Spirit. Wayne invited me to his church, the Evanston Vineyard, where I met Steve Nicholson. Steve became a mentor and lifelong friend. The influence of Wayne, Steve, and the kingdom

---

1. *Systematic Theology* I, xiii.

Acknowledgements

theology of Wimber and the Vineyard movement reverberates throughout this book.

After a decade of pastoral ministry and running a business, doctoral studies at Loyola University Chicago proved to be another time of receiving from seasoned Christian scholars, including Mark McIntosh (my dissertation supervisor and teaching mentor), Dennis Martin, John McCarthy, and Susan Ross. I am grateful to each of them for investing in my training as a constructive theologian. During this season, Bradley Nassif became a dear friend and helpful guide in the study of Orthodox theology and spirituality.

A season of teaching at Wesleyan College also informed the research behind this book. Interaction with colleagues, especially Michael Muth, reinforced the importance of theology that bridges the academy and church. Years in the classroom with the outstanding students of Wesleyan, reading and discussing theological and spiritual classics, informs *A Luminous Life*. Their curiosity, questions, and passion for learning demonstrated how important and fun theological formation is.

Reentering pastoral ministry at Our Lord's Community Church has influenced the latter stages of this book. Working with the leaders of Our Lord's—particularly Brad Kilman, Mike Milner, and Wallace Walcher—has been deeply rewarding, as we serve Jesus and his church together. Establishing All Saints Center for Theology, Spirituality, and Leadership at Our Lord's, with the invaluable assistance of Connie Willems, has provided a context for applying much of what *A Luminous Life* entails. I am grateful to be part of this community of worship and formation on mission with Jesus.

Working with Rodney Clapp, Zecheriah Mickel, Heather Carraher, and others at Wipf and Stock has been a delight. The Wipf and Stock team helped bring this project to fruition. For all their expertise and work, I am thankful.

Finally, I would like to thank my children, Mia and Jake, for their love, encouragement, and laughter they share around the house and table; and my wife, Amanda, my beloved, friend, and wise counselor.

Bibliography

Arbesmann, Rudolph. "Fasting and Prophecy in Pagan and Christian Antiquity." *Traditio* 7 (1949) 1–71.
Athanasius. *On the Incarnation of the Word*. In *Christology of the Later Fathers*, edited by Edward R. Hardy, 55–110. Library of the Christian Classics. Louisville: Westminster John Knox, 1977.
Augustine of Hippo. *Augustine: Earlier Writings*. Edited by John H. S. Burleigh. Library of Christian Classics. Louisville: Westminster John Knox, 2006.
———. *Teaching Christianity. The Works of St. Augustine: A Translation for the 21st Century* vols. I and II, translated by Edmund Hill. Hyde Park, NY: New City, 1996.
von Balthasar, Hans Urs. *Cosmic Liturgy: The Universe According to Maximus the Confessor*. A Communio Book. 3rd ed. San Francisco: Ignatius, 2003.
———. *Prayer*. San Francisco: Ignatius, 1986.
———. *Prolegomena*. Vol. 1 of *Theo-Drama: Theological Dramatic Theory*. San Francisco: Ignatius, 1988.
———. "Theology and Sanctity." In *Explorations in Theology: The Word Made Flesh*, translated by A. V. Littledale and Alexander Dru, 1:181–209. San Francisco: Ignatius, 1989.
———. *The World Made Flesh*. Vol. 1 of *Explorations in Theology*. San Francisco: Ignatius, 1964.
Barton, John, and John Muddiman, eds. *The Oxford Bible Commentary*. New York: Oxford University Press, 2001.
Bauckham, Richard, and Benjamin Drewery, eds. *Scripture, Tradition, and Reason: A Study in the Criteria and Christian Doctrine*. Edinburgh: T. & T. Clark, 2004.
Behr, John, et al., eds. *Abba: The Tradition of Orthodoxy in the West: Festschrift for Bishop Kallistos (Ware) of Diokleia*. Crestwood, NY: St. Vladimir's Seminary Press, 2003.
Bingaman, Brock. *All Things New: The Trinitarian Nature of the Human Calling in Maximus the Confessor and Jürgen Moltmann*. Princeton Theological Monograph Series. Eugene, OR: Pickwick, 2014.
———. "A Common Vision: John Cassian and al-Ghazali's Correlative Visions of the Spiritual Life." *Islam and Christian-Muslim Relations* 20.2 (2009) 171–82.
———. "Orthodox Spirituality and Contemporary Ecology: John Cassian, Maximus the Confessor, and Jürgen Moltmann in Conversation." In *Spirit and Nature: Christian Spirituality in a Time of Ecological Urgency*, edited by Timothy Hessel Robinson and Ray Maria McNamara, 98–124. Princeton Theological Monograph Series. Eugene, OR: Pickwick, 2011.

Bibliography

———. "Scripture as Divine Mystery: The Bible in the *Philokalia*." In *What Is the Bible? The Patristic Doctrine of Scripture*, edited by Matthew Baker and Mark Mourachian, 103–19. Minneapolis: Fortress, 2016.

Bingaman, Brock, and Bradley Nassif, eds. *The Philokalia: A Classic Text of Orthodox Spirituality*. Oxford: Oxford University Press, 2012.

Blowers, Paul M., ed. *The Bible in Greek Christian Antiquity*. Notre Dame, IN: University of Notre Dame Press, 1997.

Bonaventure, Saint. *Breviloquium*. Vol. 9 of *The Works of St. Bonaventure*. Bonaventure Texts in Translation Series. Edited by Dominic V. Monti. Saint Bonaventure, NY: The Franciscan Institute, 2005.

Bonhoeffer, Dietrich. *Life Together*. London: SCM, 2015.

Boyd, Gregory A., et al. *The Nature of the Atonement: Four Views*. Downers Grove, IL: IVP Academic, 2006.

Bruce, F. F. "Scripture in Relation to Tradition and Reason." In *Scripture, Tradition, and Reason: A Study in the Criteria and Christian Doctrine*, edited by Richard Bauckham and Benjamin Drewery, 35–64. Edinburgh: T. & T. Clark, 2004.

Bruss, Ryan. *Carrying the Presence: How to Bring the Kingdom of God to Anyone, Anywhere*. Shippensburg, PA: Destiny Image, 2019.

Bryant, Christopher. "The Nature of Spiritual Direction: Sacramental Confession." In *The Study of Spirituality*, edited by Cheslyn Jones et al., 568–70. London: SPCK, 1992.

Burton-Christie, Douglas. *The Blue Sapphire of the Mind: Notes for a Contemplative Ecology*. New York: Oxford University Press, 2012.

———. "The Luminous Word: Scripture in the *Philokalia*." In *The Philokalia: A Classic Text of Orthodox Spirituality*, edited by Brock Bingaman and Bradley Nassif, 73–86. Oxford: Oxford University Press, 2012.

———. *The Word in the Desert: Scripture and the Quest for Holiness in Early Christian Monasticism*. New York: Oxford University Press, 1993.

Buschart, Nancy R. "Spiritual Mentoring." In *The Dictionary of Christian Spirituality*, edited by Glen G. Scorgie et al., 609–10. Grand Rapids: Zondervan, 2011.

Calvin, John. *Institutes of the Christian Religion*. Library of Christian Classics. Louisville: Westminster, 1970.

Carter, J. Kameron. *Race: A Theological Account*. New York: Oxford University Press, 2008.

Casey, Michael. *Sacred Reading: The Ancient Art of Lectio Divina*. Liguori, MO: Triumph, 1996.

Cassian, John. *The Conferences*. New York: Newman, 1997.

———. *The Institutes*. Translated by Boniface Ramsey. Mahwah, NJ: Newman/Paulist, 2000.

Catherine of Sienna, Saint. *The Dialogue*. Classics of Western Spirituality. New York: Paulist, 1980.

Chalmers, Thomas. *The Expulsive Power of a New Affection*. Minneapolis: Curiosmith, 2012.

Chan, Simon. *Spiritual Theology: A Systematic Study of Christian Life*. Downers Grove, IL: InterVarsity, 1998.

Chariton, Igumen, ed. *The Art of Prayer: An Orthodox Anthology*. London: Faber and Faber, 1997.

Chia, Roland. "Salvation as Justification and Deification." *Scottish Journal of Theology* 64.2 (May 2011) 125–39.

Bibliography

Chitty, Derwas James. *The Desert a City: An Introduction to the Study of Egyptian and Palestinian Monasticism Under the Christian Empire*. Yonkers, NY: St. Vladimir's Seminary Press, 1977.

Chryssavgis, John, and Bruce V. Foltz, eds. *Toward an Ecology of Transfiguration: Orthodox Christian Perspectives on Environment, Nature, and Creation*. New York: Fordham University Press, 2013.

Colless, Brian E. "Syriac Mysticism." In *The Wiley-Blackwell Companion to Christian Mysticism*, edited by Julia A. Lamm, 177–89. Oxford: Wiley-Blackwell, 2013.

Cone, James. *The Cross and the Lynching Tree*. Maryknoll, NY: Orbis, 1997.

———. *Theology of the Oppressed*. Maryknoll, NY: Orbis, 2017.

Cook, Christopher C. H. "Healing, Psychotherapy, and the *Philokalia*." In *The Philokalia: A Classic Text of Orthodox Spirituality*, edited by Brock Bingaman and Bradley Nassif, 230–39. Oxford: Oxford University Press, 2012.

———. *The* Philokalia *and the Inner Life: On Passions and Prayer*. Eugene, OR: Pickwick, 2012.

Cross, F. L., ed. *The Early Christian Fathers*. Studies in Theology 1. London: Duckworth, 1960.

Cunningham, Mary. "The Place of the Jesus Prayer in the *Philokalia*." In *The* Philokalia: *A Classic Text of Orthodox Spirituality*, edited by Brock Bingaman and Bradley Nassif, 195–202. Oxford: Oxford University Press, 2012.

Demacopoulos, George E. *Five Models of Spiritual Direction in the Early Church*. Notre Dame, IN: University of Notre Dame Press, 2011.

Demarest, Bruce. *Satisfy Your Soul: Restoring the Heart of Christian Spirituality*. Colorado Springs: NavPress, 1999.

Demarest, Bruce, ed. *Four Views on Christian Spirituality*. Grand Rapids: Zondervan, 2012.

"Desert in the Bible." http://www.newadvent.org/cathen/04749a.htm.

Dreher, Rod. *The Benedict Option: A Strategy for Christians in a Post-Christian Nation*. New York: Sentinel, 2017.

Eiesland, Nancy L. *The Disabled God: Toward a Liberation Theology of Disability*. Nashville: Abingdon, 1994.

Eliade, Mircea. *The Sacred and the Profane: The Nature of Religion*. San Diego: Harvest, 2004.

Florovsky, George. *Bible, Church, Tradition: An Eastern Orthodox View*. Vol. 1 of *The Collected Works of George Florovsky*. Belmont: Nordland, 1987.

———. *Christianity and Culture*. Vol. 2 of *The Collected Works of George Florovsky*. Belmont, MA: Nordland, 1974.

Flynn, Gabriel, and Paul D. Murray, eds. *Ressourcement: A Movement for Renewal in Twentieth-Century Catholic Theology*. New York: Oxford University Press, 2014.

Forest, Jim. *Praying with Icons*. Maryknoll, NY: Orbis, 2008.

Foster, Richard J. *Celebration of Discipline: The Path to Spiritual Growth*. 10th Anniversary Edition. San Francisco: HarperCollins, 2002.

———. *Streams of Living Water*. New York: HarperCollins, 2001.

Foster, Richard J., and Emilie Griffin, eds. *Spiritual Classics: Selected Readings on the Twelve Spiritual Disciplines*. New York: HarperCollins, 2007.

Gillet, Lev. *On the Invocation of the Name of Jesus*. Springfield, IL: Templegate, 1985.

Gregory of Nyssa, Saint. *The Life of Moses*. Translated by Abraham J. Malherbe and Everett Ferguson. Mahwah, NJ: Paulist, 1978.

Bibliography

———. "Preface." In *The Life of Moses*, translated by Abraham Malherbe and Everett Ferguson, xi–xvi. Classics of Western Spirituality. Mahwah, NJ: Paulist, 1978.

Grudem, Wayne A. *Systematic Theology: An Introduction to Biblical Doctrine*. Grand Rapids: Zondervan, 2009.

Gundry, Stanley N., and Bruce Demarest, eds. *Four Views on Christian Spirituality*. Grand Rapids: Zondervan, 2012.

Gunter, W. Stephen, et. al. *Wesley and the Quadrilateral: Renewing the Conversation*. Nashville: Abingdon, 1997.

Guyon, Jeanne. *Experiencing the Depths of Jesus Christ: One of the Grandest Christian Writings of All Time*. Auburn, ME: Christian, 1975.

Hafeman, Scott J. "Suffering." In *The Dictionary of Paul and His Letters: A Compendium of Contemporary Biblical Scholarship*, edited by Gerald F. Hawthorne et al., 919–21. Downers Grove, IL: IVP Academic, 1993.

Hall, Thelma. *Too Deep for Words: Rediscovering Lectio Divina*. Mahwah, NJ: Paulist, 1988.

Harrison, Nonna. *God's Many-Splendored Image: Theological Anthropology for Christian Formation*. Grand Rapids: Baker Academic, 2010.

Harvey, Susan Ashbrook, and David Hunter, eds. *The Oxford Handbook of Early Christian Studies*. New York: Oxford, 2008.

Hauerwas, Stanley, and William H. Willimon. *Resident Aliens: Life in the Christian Colony*. Expanded 25th Anniversary Edition. Nashville: Abingdon, 2014.

Hausherr, Irénée. *The Name of Jesus. The Names of Jesus Used by Early Christians. The Development of the Jesus Prayer*. Translated by Charles Cummings. Kalamazoo, MI: Cistercian, 1978.

———. "Pour comprendre l'orient chrétien: La primauté du spirituel." *Orientala Christiana Periodica* 33 (1967) 351–69.

———. *Spiritual Direction in the Early Christian East*. Kalamazoo, MI: Cistercian, 1990.

Holder, Arthur G., ed. *The Blackwell Companion to Christian Spirituality*. Oxford: Blackwell, 2005.

———, ed. *Christian Spirituality: The Classics*. London: Routledge, 2010.

Hume, David. *Dialogues Concerning Natural Religion*. Edited by N. K. Smith. Oxford: Oxford University Press, 1935.

Hunt, Anne. *The Trinity: Insights from the Mystics*. Collegeville, MN: Liturgical, 2010.

Ignatius of Loyola. *Ignatius of Loyola: The Spiritual Exercises and Selected Works*. Edited by George E. Ganss et al. Classics of Western Spirituality. New York: Paulist, 1991.

Irenaeus. *Against Heresies*. In *The Ante-Nicene Fathers* vol. 1., edited by Arthur Cleveland Coxe, Alexander Roberts, James Donaldson, Philip Schaff, and Henry Wace, 309–567. Peabody, MA: Hendrickson, 1994.

Jansons, Linards. "What is the Second Naiveté? Engaging with Paul Ricoeur, Post-Critical Theology, and Progressive Christianity." Presentation given by Linards Jansons to the teaching faculty of Australian Lutheran College, October 30, 2014. https://www.academia.edu/14690650/What_is_the_Second_Naivet%C3%A9_Engaging_with_Paul_Ricoeur_Post-Critical_Theology_and_Progressive_Christianity.

Johnson, Elizabeth A. *She Who Is: The Mystery of God in Feminist Theological Discourse*. 10th Anniversary Edition. New York: Crossroad, 2002.

Jones, Cheslyn, et al., eds. *The Study of Spirituality*. London, SPCK, 1992.

Kallistos of Diokleia. *The Power of the Name*. Oxford: SLG, 2014.

Bibliography

Kardaras, Nicholas. "It's 'Digital Heroin': How Screens Turn Kids into Psychotic Junkies." *New York Post*, August 27, 2016. http://nypost.com/2016/08/27/its-digital-heroin-how-screens-turn-kids-into-psychotic-junkies/.

Kärkkäinen, Veli-Matti. *An Introduction to Ecclesiology: Ecumenical, Historical, and Global Perspectives*. Downers Grove, IL: IVP Academic, 2002.

———. *Pneumatology: The Holy Spirit in Ecumenical, International, and Contextual Perspective*. Grand Rapids: Baker Academic, 2002.

Keener, Craig S. *Acts: An Exegetical Commentary: Introduction and 1:1–2:47*. Grand Rapids: Baker Academic, 2012.

Kidwell, Clara Sue, Homer Noley, and Tink Tinker. *A Native American Theology*. Maryknoll, NY: Orbis, 2001.

Konstantinovsky, Julia. *Evagrius Ponticus: The Making of a Gnostic*. Farnham: Ashgate, 2009.

Krawiec, Rebecca. "Asceticism." In *The Oxford Handbook of Early Christian Studies*, edited by Susan Ashbrook Harvey and David Hunter, 764–85. New York: Oxford, 2008.

Lane, A. N. S. "Scripture, Tradition, and Church: An Historical Survey." *Vox Evangelica* 9 (1975) 37–55.

Lewis, C. S. *Mere Christianity*. New York: HarperCollins, 2001.

Livingston, James C. *The Anatomy of the Sacred: An Introduction to Religion*. Upper Saddle River, NJ: Pearson, 2009.

Lockyer, Herbert. *All the Prayers of the Bible*. Grand Rapids: Zondervan, 1977.

Lovat, Terence J. "Bonhoeffer: Interfaith Theologian and Practical Mystic." *Pacifica: Australasian Theological Studies* 25.2 (2012) 176–88.

Lossky, Vladimir. *The Mystical Theology of the Eastern Church*. Crestwood, NY: St. Vladimir's Seminary Press, 1976.

Louth, Andrew. "The Desert Fathers." In *The Wilderness of God*, 53–70. London: Darton, Longman & Todd, 2003.

———. *The Origins of the Christian Mystical Tradition: From Plato to Denys*. 2nd ed. Oxford: Oxford University Press, 2007.

———. "The Theology of the *Philokalia*." In *Abba: The Tradition of Orthodoxy in the West: Festschrift for Bishop Kallistos (Ware) of Diokleia*, edited by John Behr et al., 351–61. Crestwood, NY: St. Vladimir's Seminary Press, 2003.

———. *The Wilderness of God*. London: Darton, Longman & Todd, 2003.

Maddox, Randy. "John Wesley and Eastern Orthodoxy: Influences, Convergences, and Differences." *Asbury Theological Journal* 45.2 (1990) 29–53.

Mairs, Nancy. *Carnal Acts: Essays*. Boston: Beacon, 1996.

———. *Ordinary Time*. Boston: Beacon, 1993.

Marjanen, Antti. "Gnosticism." In *The Oxford Handbook of Early Christian Studies*, edited by Susan Ashbrook Harvey and David Hunter, 203–20. New York: Oxford, 2008.

Mattson, Mark. "Are There Any Proven Benefits to Fasting?" *Johns Hopkins Health Review* 3.1, Spring/Summer 2016. http://www.johnshopkinshealthreview.com/issues/spring-summer-2016.

Maximus the Confessor. "The Church's Mystagogy." In *Maximus Confessor: Selected Writings*, translated by George C. Berthold, 181–226. Classics of Western Spirituality. Mahwah, NJ: Paulist, 1985.

———. *Maximus Confessor: Selected Writings*. Translated by George C. Berthold. Classics of Western Spirituality. Mahwah: Paulist, 1985.

Bibliography

———. *Questions to Thalassius*. In *The Essential Writings of Christian Mysticism*, edited by Bernard McGinn, 408–11. New York: Modern Library, 2006.

McGinn, Bernard, ed. *The Essential Writings of Christian Mysticism*. New York: Modern Library, 2006.

———. *The Presence of God: A History of Western Christian Mysticism*. 7 vols. New York: Crossroad, 1991–2013.

McGrath, Alister E. *Christian Spirituality: An Introduction*. Oxford: Blackwell, 2013.

McGuckin, John A. "The Making of the *Philokalia*: A Tale of Monks and Manuscripts." In *The* Philokalia: *A Classic Text of Orthodox Spirituality*, edited by Brock Bingaman and Bradley Nassif, 36–49. Oxford: Oxford University Press, 2012.

———. *The Orthodox Church: An Introduction to Its History, Doctrine and Spiritual Culture*. Oxford: Wiley-Blackwell, 2011.

McIntosh, Mark A. *Discernment and Truth: The Spirituality and Theology of Knowledge*. New York: Crossroad, 2004.

———. *Mystical Theology: The Integrity of Spirituality and Theology*. Challenges in Contemporary Theology. Oxford: Wiley-Blackwell, 1998.

Merton, Thomas. *Contemplative Prayer*. New York: Image, 1989.

———. *Spiritual Direction and Meditation*. Mansfield Centre, CT: Martino, 2013.

Miles, Rebekah L. "The Instrumental Role of Reason." In *Wesleyan and the Quadrilateral: Renewing the Conversation*, edited by W. Stephen Gunter et al., 77–106. Nashville: Abingdon, 1997.

Miller, Lisa J., ed. *The Oxford Handbook of Psychology and Spirituality*. Oxford Library of Psychology. Oxford: Oxford University Press, 2014.

Moltmann, Jürgen. *A Broad Place: An Autobiography*. Minneapolis: Fortress, 2008.

———. *The Coming of God: Christian Eschatology*. London: SCM, 2005.

———. *The Crucified God*. Minneapolis: Fortress, 2015.

———. *Experiences in Theology: Ways and Forms of Christian Theology*. Minneapolis: Fortress, 2000.

———. *God in Creation: A New Theology of Creation and the Spirit of God*. Minneapolis: Fortress, 1993.

———. *The Trinity and the Kingdom: The Doctrine of God*. Minneapolis: Fortress, 1993.

Moynahan, Michael E. *Once Upon a Mystery: What Happens Next?* Mahwah, NJ: Paulist, 1998.

Nassif, Bradley. "Concerning Those Who Think That They Are Justified by Works: The Gospel According to St. Mark—the Monk." In *The* Philokalia: *A Classic Text of Orthodox Spirituality*, edited by Brock Bingaman and Bradley Nassif, 87–101. Oxford: Oxford University Press, 2012.

Nassif, Bradley, and Bruce Demarest, eds. *Four Views on Christian Spirituality*. Grand Rapids: Zondervan, 2012.

Nicholas of Cusa. *Selected Spiritual Writings*. Classics of Western Spirituality 89. Mahwah, NJ: Paulist, 2005.

Nouwen, Henri J. M. *Behold the Beauty of the Lord: Praying With Icons*. Notre Dame, IN: Ave Maria, 2007.

Oden, Thomas C. *Classic Christianity: A Systematic Theology*. 3 vols. San Francisco: HarperOne, 2009.

———. *The Living God*. Systematic Theology 1. Peabody, MA: Prince, 1998.

Bibliography

Oden, Thomas C., ed. *Ancient Christian Commentary on Scripture*. 29 vols. Ancient Christian Commentary on Scripture Series. Downers Grove, IL: InterVarsity, 2000–2010.

Olstad, Kim. "Spiritual Direction." In *The Dictionary of Christian Spirituality*, edited by Glen G. Scorgie, 402–3. Grand Rapids: Zondervan, 2011.

Origen. *Commentary on the Song of Songs*. In *The Essential Writings of Christian Mysticism*, edited by Bernard McGinn, 6–12. New York: Modern Library, 2006.

Otto, Rudolf. *The Idea of the Holy: An Inquiry into the Non-rational Factor in the Idea of the Divine and Its Relation to the Rational*. London: Oxford University Press, 2007.

Pennington, Basil. *Lectio Divina: Renewing the Ancient Practice of Praying the Scriptures*. New York: Crossroad, 1998.

The *Philokalia: The Complete Text*. 4 vols. Compiled by St. Nikodimos and St. Makarios of Corinth. Translated and edited by G. E. H. Palmer, Philip Sherrard, and Kallistos Ware. London: Faber and Faber, 1990.

Pinnock, Clark. *Flame of Love: A Theology of the Holy Spirit*. Downers Grove, IL: InterVarsity, 2015.

Piper, John. *A Hunger for God: Desiring God Through Fasting and Prayer*. Wheaton, IL: Crossway, 1997.

Plato. *Phaedrus*. In *Complete Works*, edited by John M. Cooper, 524–31. Indianapolis: Hackett, 1997.

Poteat, William H. *Polanyian Meditations: In Search of a Post-Critical Logic*. Durham, NC: Duke University Press, 1985.

Pseudo-Dionysis. *Pseudo-Dionysius: The Complete Works*. Classics of Western Spirituality. Translated by Paul Rorem. Mahwah, NJ: Paulist, 1998.

Rahner, Karl. *Concern for the Church*. Vol. 20 of *Theological Investigations*. Freiburg im Breisgau: Herder and Herder, 1981.

———. *Foundations of Christian Faith*. London: Darton, Longman & Todd, 1976.

Ricoeur, Paul. "Conclusion: The Symbol Gives Rise to Thought." In *The Symbolism of Evil*, 347–57. Boston: Beacon, 1969.

———. *The Symbolism of Evil*. Boston: Beacon, 1969.

Roberts, Alexander, et al., eds. *The Apostolic Fathers with Justin Martyr and Irenaeus*. Vol. 1 of *Ante-Nicene Fathers: The Writings of the Fathers Down to A.D. 325*. Peabody, MA: Hendrickson, 2004.

Rousseau, Philip. "The Desert Fathers, Antony and Pachomius." In *The Study of Spirituality*, edited by Cheslyn Jones et al., 119–30. London: SPCK, 1992.

Schaff, Philip, et al. *Sulpitius Severus, Vincent of Lerins, John Cassian*. Vol. 11 of *The Nicene and Post-Nicene Fathers: Series II*. Edinburgh: T. & T. Clark, 1994.

Schneiders, Sandra Marie. "Scripture and Spirituality." In *Christian Spirituality: Origins to the Twelfth Century*, 1:1–20. New York: Crossroad, 1985.

———. "Theology and Spirituality: Strangers, Rivals, or Partners?" *Horizons* 13.2 (1986) 253–74.

Scorgie, Glen G., ed. *Dictionary of Christian Spirituality*. Grand Rapids: Zondervan, 2011.

Sertillanges, A. G. *The Intellectual Life: Its Spirit, Conditions, Methods*. Washington, DC: The Catholic University of America Press, 1998.

Snyder, Howard A. *Yes in Christ: Wesleyan Reflections on Gospel, Mission and Culture*. Tyndale Studies in Wesleyan History and Theology 2. Toronto: Clements, 2011.

Sölle, Dorothee. *Suffering*. Minneapolis: Fortress, 1984.

Špidlík, Tomáš. "The Bible in Use among the Greek Church Fathers." In *The Bible in Greek Christian Antiquity*, edited by Paul M. Blowers, 105–93. Notre Dame, IN: University of Notre Dame Press, 1997.

———. "Meditative Reading." In *Prayer: The Spirituality of the Christian East*, 2:130–51. Kalamazoo, MI: Cistercian, 2005.

Staniloae, D. *Orthodox Dogmatik. Ökumenische Theologie*. Zürich: Benziger, 1985.

———. *Revelation and Knowledge of the Triune God*. Vol. 1 of *Orthodox Dogmatic Theology: The Experience of God*. Brookline: Holy Cross Orthodox Press, 1998.

Stevens, Sufjan. "The Fourth of July." *Carrie & Lowell*. New Jerusalem Music, 2015.

Stewart, Columba. *Cassian the Monk*. Oxford Studies in Historical Theology. New York: Oxford University Press, 1999.

Stgileschurchoxford. "The Desert Fathers and Mothers." YouTube, February 12, 2015. https://www.youtube.com/watch?v=noVX9lRQkDA.

Sugarman, John. "Are There Any Proven Benefits to Fasting?" *Johns Hopkins Health Review*, Spring/Summer 2016. https://www.johnshopkinshealthreview.com/issues/spring-summer-2016/articles/are-there-any-proven-benefits-to-fasting.

Szabo, Lynn R. "Spiritual Direction." In *The Dictionary of Christian Spirituality*, edited by Glen G. Scorgie, 402–3. Grand Rapids: Zondervan, 2011.

Taylor, Charles. *A Secular Age*. Cambridge, MA: The Belknap Press of Harvard University Press, 2007.

Teresa of Avila. *The Book of Her Life*. In *The Collected Works of Saint Teresa of Avila*, translated by Kieran Kavanaugh and Otilio Rodriguez, 2:110–18. Washington, DC: ICS, 1980.

———. *The Interior Castle*. In *The Collected Works of Saint Teresa of Avila*, translated by Kieran Kavanaugh and Otilio Rodriguez, 2:263–455. Washington, DC: ICS, 1980.

———. *The Way of Perfection*. In *The Collected Works of Saint Teresa of Avila*, translated by Kieran Kavanaugh and Otilio Rodriguez, 2:1–200. Washington, DC: ICS, 1980.

Tertullian. *Latin Christianity: Its Founder, Tertullian. I. Apologetic; II. Anti-Marcion; III. Ethical*. Vol. 3 of *The Ante-Nicene Fathers*. Edited by A. Cleveland Coxe, et al. Peabody, MA: Hendrickson, 1995.

———. "Against Praxeus." In *The Ante-Nicene Fathers: Latin Christianity: Its Founder, Tertullian. I. Apologetic; II. Anti-Marcion; III. Ethical*, edited by A. Cleveland Coxe et al. Peabody, MA: Hendrickson, 1995.

Thunberg, Lars. *Microcosm and Mediator: The Theological Anthropology of Maximus the Confessor*. Peru, IL: Open Court, 1995.

Tickle, Phyllis. *The Divine Hours*. New York: Image, 2006.

Tracy, David. *The Analogical Imagination: Christian Theology and the Culture of Pluralism*. New York: Crossroad, 1998.

Twombly, Charles. *Perichoresis and Personhood: God, Christ, and Salvation in John of Damascus*. Eugene, OR: Wipf and Stock, 2015.

Tympas, G. C. *Carl Jung and Maximus the Confessor on Psychic Development: The Dynamics Between the "Psychological" and the "Spiritual"* New York: Routledge, 2014.

Vanhoozer, Kevin J. *The Drama of Doctrine: A Canonical-Linguistic Approach to Christian Theology*. Louisville: Westminster John Knox, 2005.

Verdon, Timothy. *Art and Prayer: The Beauty of Turning to God*. Brewster, MA: Paraclete, 2014.

Volf, Miroslav. *After Our Likeness: The Church as the Image of the Trinity*. Grand Rapids: Eerdmans, 1997.

Bibliography

Wallace, Mark I. *The Second Naiveté: Barth, Ricoeur, and the New Yale Theology.* Macon, GA: Mercer University Press, 1995.

Wallis, Arthur. *God's Chosen Fast: A Spiritual and Practical Guide to Fasting.* Fort Washington, PA: CLC, 2016.

Walsh, James, trans. *The Cloud of Unknowing.* Classics of Western Spirituality. Mahwah, NJ: Paulist, 1986.

Ward, Benedicta. *The Desert Fathers: Sayings of the Early Christian Monks.* London: Penguin, 2003.

Ward, Patricia A. *Experimental Theology in America: Madame Guyon, Fénelon, and Their Readers.* Waco, TX: Baylor University Press, 2009.

———. "Madame Guyon (1648–1717)." In *The Pietist Theologians,* edited by Carter Lindberg, 161–74. Malden, NJ: Blackwell, 2005.

Ware, Kallistos. "The Hesychast Renaissance." In *The Study of Spirituality,* edited by Cheslyn Jones et al., 255–59. London, SPCK, 1992.

———. "The Human Person as an Icon of the Trinity." *Sobornost* 8.2 (1986) 1–16.

———. *The Inner Kingdom.* Vol. 1 of *The Collected Works.* Crestwood, NY: St. Vladimir's Seminary Press, 2001.

———. *The Orthodox Church.* London: Penguin, 1997.

———. *The Orthodox Way.* Crestwood, NY: St. Vladimir's Seminary Press, 2002.

———. *The Orthodox Way.* Rev. ed. Crestwood, NY: St. Vladimir's Seminary Press, 1995.

———. "The *Philokalia*: A Book for All Christians." *Sourozh* 100 (2005) 5–21.

———. *The Power of the Name: The Jesus Prayer in Orthodox Spirituality.* Oxford: SLG Press, 2007.

———. "The Spiritual Guide in Orthodox Christianity." In *The Inner Kingdom: The Collected Works,* 1:127–52. Crestwood: St. Vladimir's Seminary Press, 2001.

———. "St. Nikodimos and the *Philokalia*." In *The* Philokalia: *A Classic Text of Orthodox Spirituality,* edited by Brock Bingaman and Bradley Nassif, 19–25. Oxford: Oxford University Press, 2012.

———. "Ways of Prayer and Contemplation: Eastern." In *Christian Spirituality: Origins to the Twelfth Century,* edited by Bernard McGinn et al., 1:395–414. New York: Crossroad, 1987.

Webber, Robert E. *Ancient-Future Faith: Rethinking Evangelicalism for a Postmodern World.* Grand Rapids: Baker, 1999.

Wilken, Robert Louis. *The Spirit of Early Christian Thought: Seeking the Face of God.* New Haven, CT: Yale University Press, 2008.

Williams, D. H. *Evangelicals and Tradition: The Formative Influence of the Early Church.* Grand Rapids: Baker Academic, 2005.

Williams, Garrath. "Kant's Account of Reason." https://plato.stanford.edu/entries/kant-reason/.

Williams, Rowan. "Life, Death, and Neighbours." In *Silence and Honey Cakes: The Wisdom of the Desert,* 22–40. Oxford: Lion, 2003.

Index

Abraham and Sarah, 23
abyss, looking over the bottomless, 136
academy and church, bridging, 10–12
act of prayer, 68, 69, 82
action
    contemplation and, 184, 186–87
    as only the "revelation" of knowledge, 187n19
    teaching through, 171
active life (*praxis* or *praktike*), 37
the active way and the contemplative way, 187–88
acts of love, 183
ad fontes (back to the sources), during the Renaissance, 5
Adam and Eve, 143
affirmation, 129, 132, 135
alertness, fasting heightening, 95
All Things New (Bingaman), 14n35
allegory, desert as, 160–61
alone yet not alone, learning to be, 104
already and the not yet, dwelling between, 141
American Academy of Religion, 15
Ananias, 141
Ancient Christian Commentary on Scripture, 26
angels, covering their faces in the presence of the Lord, 126, 133
Anna, fasting and prayer by, 90
Anselm of Canterbury, 51
Antony the Great, Saint of the Desert, 17n41, 157–61

apophatic approach, 131, 132–36, 147–49
apophatic or "negative way," 38, 122
apophatic spirituality
    biblical foundations of, 125–27
    insights into, 127–32
    inspires us on the edge of the precipice, 136
    sources of, 122n4
apophatic theology, 123, 124
apophatic thread in Scripture, 125–27
apophatic way, 122, 123, 124, 134
apostleship, suffering as a mark of, 141
apostolic Christianity, versus Gnosticism, 86–88
apostolic church, prayer as a mark of, 116
"apostolic spirituality," Ignatius' concept of, 182
apostolic teaching, 59, 114
apprentices, disciples of Jesus as, 169
Aquinas, Thomas, 51, 52, 124–27, 183
"Are There Any Proven Benefits to Fasting?" (Mattson), 95n18
arenas, of contemplation, 185–86
Aristetolianism, gave birth to modern "secularism," 52
Aristotelian philosophy, application to theology, 51
aroma of life, 198n1
asceticism, 19, 85, 85n3, 99, 186
Ash Wednesday, 146
Athanasius, 31n14, 87–88, 157–58

Index

athletes, willing to discipline themselves, 93
Augustine of Hippo
  on a "good will" reaching the highest wisdom, 63
  interpreting the Scriptures, 34
  on needing to turn inward, 72
  on remaining spiritually hungry and thirsty, 22
  on "the spoils of Egypt," 52
  turning point in the conversion of, 156n3
authors of the spiritual classics, 27
autobiographical aspects, of this book, 14–15

"baby steps," in spiritual journeys, 18n43
Baker, Dom Augustine, 173
Balthasar, Hans Urs von, 50, 187n19
baptism, 111
Barnabas, 90, 91
Barth, Karl, 57
Bartimaeus, 76
"Be ye perfect" command, 30n11
becoming like Jesus, 168–69
being with Jesus, 168, 169
Bernard of Clairvaux, 51
Bethlehem, at the edge of the Judean desert, 154
betrothal and union, of Christ and the Christlike soul, 43
beverages, during a fast, 198
Bible
  biblia in Greek meaning "books," 55
  pointing to a greater reality, 48
  reading, 46, 48
  as the record of revelation, 57
  recording 650 prayers, 67
  as the source of ideas, 56
biblical foundations, of apophatic spirituality, 125–27
biblical ideas, keeping in mind before a fast, 87–88
biblical images
  of the desert, 151–54

  example, 22–33
  of the spiritual life, 20–34
biblical inerrancy and infallibility, 46
biblical meditation, 69, 70–74
biblical metaphors, on Christian spiritual life, 110–13
biblical texts, 45, 48, 56
biblical world, distance from the reader's world, 46
biblicism, 57n21
bodies, 78, 98, 139
the body, as the outer wall of the castle, 41
body and soul, Jesus healing, 176
body of Christ, 111–12
Bonaventure, 63
Bonhoeffer, Dietrich, 5, 109
The Book of Common Prayer, 116
bread of life, eating, 161
breaking
  of bread, 115
  a fast with wisdom, 199
breath, caring for during a fast, 198
"breath of death," not carrying, 198n1
breathing, connecting the Jesus Prayer to, 78
Bruce, F. F., 53–54, 58n25
Buddha, on existence as suffering, 138n1
burning bush, Moses seeing God in the light of, 127
butterfly, silkworm emerging as a beautiful, 43

call of God, sensing, 7
Calvin, John, 125, 134
carpe diem ("seize the day"), 98
Cassian, John
  on all extremes as equally harmful, 84, 98, 98n21
  on a day's fast as beneficial, 101
  on moderation in fasting, 85n1
  on overcoming "the eight deadly sins," 25
  on Paul's instructions regarding work, 165
  on solitude, 108

Index

castle metaphor, 40, 41
cataphatic and apophatic spirituality, 121–36
cataphatic or "positive way," 121–22, 124
cataphatic spirituality, 122n2
cataphatic tradition, 123
Catherine of Siena, 138
Cause of all, God as, 131
celebration and rejoicing, of feasts, 22–23
Celebration of Discipline (Foster), 10, 10n22
Centuries on Love (Maximus), 34
Chalmers, Thomas, 78n27
Chan, Simon, 171n5, 176
changed lives, contact with God leading to, 179
chaos, 139
children of God, power to become, 113
Christ. *See* Jesus Christ
Christian East, spiritual traditions of, 10
Christian fellowship. *See* fellowship
Christian life, 12–13, 24, 137
Christian spiritual classics, 4, 11, 55, 194
Christian spirituality
    as cross-centered, 137
    fueled by rigorous theological reflection, 63
    as holistic and therapeutic, 176
    meaning of classic, 4
    renaissance of, 5, 5n8, 194
    rooted in the divine-human drama of Scripture, 55
    sources of, 12n28
Christian Spirituality (McGrath), 22
Christian teaching, 54, 62
Christian thinkers, appropriating knowledge and wisdom, 52
Christians
    destined to be transformed into the likeness of Christ, 32–33
    discerning the revelation of God in three realms, 38
    drawn to seek the face of God in the desert, 154–55
    in Greco-Roman society, 156
    invited to learn to pray without ceasing, 73
    leaders calling to activism in a variety of causes, 189
    in the Middle East opposed by Muslim authorities, 25
    more familiar with the cataphatic way, 122
    showing the love of Christ to others, 117
Christie, Douglas, 155
Christlike love, model of, 142
Christlikeness, growing in, 36
Christology, helping in desert seasons, 166
Chrysostom, John, 123, 125, 134
church
    strengthening of, 161
    as the vehicle of an ongoing Pentecost, 190
church at Antioch, "worshiping the Lord and fasting," 90
church fathers, on rationality, 123
church leadership, fasting linked to appointing, 91
Church of God, as an image of God, 111–12
churches, tending to water down traditions, 10
"the circle," as a multivalent symbol, 118n17
Clare of Assisi, 36
clarity, meditating on death bringing, 147
"classic Christian spirituality," meaning of, 4
Classic Christianity (Oden), 14n33
clean hands and a pure heart, thanking God for, 198
Clement, 37
clothing, reflecting inward states or attitudes, 89
cloud, as a stage for Gregory, 39

Index

"the cloud of unknowing," God encountered in, 130
cognitive limitations, being aware of, 64
Combattimento Spirituale ("Spiritual Combat") (Scupoli), 25
"A Common Vision" (Bingaman), 15n36
communal venture, Christian spirituality as, 172
communion
    between the bride and Bridegroom, 50
    with the Father in the wilderness, 154
    with God, 62, 73n14
    God drawing us into ever deeper, 68
    growing in with the Lord, 83
community
    of creation, 118–20
    of faith, 64
    images of, 110–13
    solitude and, 103–20
concepts, 21, 39
Cone, James, 15n37, 140
conscious life, Antony bent upon reclaiming, 158
consolations, 42, 81
constancy, 78
contemplation
    action and, 179, 186–87, 188
    advancing in the spiritual journey, 37
    arenas of, 185
    encountering the living Word, 185
    experiencing, 40
    of God, 38, 189
contemplative and active ways, uniting, 184
contemplative life (*theoria*), stages of, 37
contemplative lifestyle, fasting to cultivate, 102
contemplative outlook, of Ignatius, 182
contemplative person, engaged in apostolic activities, 183
contemplatives in action, 184, 189–91
corporate celebration, aim of, 62
covenant relationship, between God and Israel, 26
creation, 38, 118n17, 119–20
creation narrative in Genesis, 151
creature, always remaining creature, 83
critical stage, transitioning to a more analytical perspective, 46–48
cross of Christ, 137–38, 143
cross of suffering, embracing, 41
crucified carpenter, following, 140
The Crucified God (Moltmann), 144n10
cruel God, suffering not inflicted on us by a, 143–46
cultivating, moments for solitude and silence, 109–10
cup of salvation, drinking, 161

daily life, ordering of, 174
daily martyr, Antony as, 157–58
Damian, Peter, 51
Daniel, 89, 101, 116
"Daniel fast," 101–2
darkness
    atop Mount Sinai as a stage for Gregory, 39
    as the blazing white light of divine glory, 136
    God causing light to shine out of, 2
    incomprehensibility of God as, 128
    Karl Rahner on understanding grounded in, 64n49
    Moses approaching God in thick, 122, 122n4, 127
    seeking God in, 130
David, 92–93, 116, 146
death, 146–47, 149, 198n1
deconstruction, in the desert, 162
Deere, Jack, 14n34
deification, as a biblical image, 28–33

Index

"delightful" pain, 44
Demacopoulos, George, 170
Demarest, Bruce, 171
demons, fasting's spiritual power to drive out, 95
denominational background, of the author, 9
Denys. *See* Pseudo-Dionysius
dependence, increased by fasting, 92–93
desert, 150–66
    as allegory, 160–61
    as the apocalyptic vision of prophets, 162
    biblical images of, 151–54
    as a quiet place in our heart, 163n21
    reframing the, 150–51
    as the road to Paradise for Antony, 159
    symbolizing life circumstances, 161–62
desert cave, Elijah encountered the Lord in, 152
desert dwellers, 154–60, 162
desert experiences, 160–61, 163
the Desert Fathers, writings from, 163
desert monasticism, 155, 160
desert monks, 157, 165
desert practices, of Antony, 158
desert spirituality, Antony as a model of, 159–60
desert survival manual, the *Philokalia* as, 163–66
desires
    every idle man full of, 165
    other natural as good, 94
    sexual, 143
    worldly, 24
Diadochos of Photiki, 88, 97
dialogue, between different traditions, 15n36
didache (apostles' teaching), 114
digital devices, 103, 109n7
Emperor Diocletian, persecuted Christians, 157

Dionysius the Areopagite. *See* Pseudo-Dionysius
directee, 171
directors. *See* spiritual director(s)
"directorship," desert father model for, 176
The Disabled God: Toward a Liberatory Theology of Disability (Eiesland), 149
discernment, 44n15, 170
disciples
    drawing into the one mystical body of Christ, 111
    on the road to Emmaus, 115
    trained by spending time daily with Jesus, 169
    welcoming and integrate new on Pentecost, 113
discipleship, 140–43, 168–71, 170n2
discipline for Israel's rebellion, 152
disobedience, wilderness symbolizing, 153
distractions, solitude clarifying, 107–8
divine action, silence in response to, 127
divine love, piercing the very depths of the soul, 43–44
divine nature, 28, 33
divine strength, displayed through human weakness, 140
divine truth, understanding by simple cognition, 74n15
divine withdrawal, notion of, 41
divine-human love relationship, metaphor of, 26–27
divinization, beginning in this present life, 33
divisions, washed away in the baptismal waters, 32
Doctor of the Church, women granted the title of, 138
The Doctrine of Deification in the Greek Patristic Tradition (Russell), 28
doubt, act of faith as a constant dialogue with, 64n47

Index

dwelling places, passage through seven interior, 39–40

early Christian desert dwellers, 154–60
early Christians
    called themselves followers of "the way," 24
    portraying the spiritual life in two stages, 37
    prayed in the Jewish temple, 116
    sharing a meal in one another's homes, 115
    sought the Father in solitude and silence, 106
    unified theology and spirituality, 50–51
early church, 113–17
early church fathers, teachings of, 73
earnestness, fasting and, 89, 96
earth, keeping silence before the Lord, 105, 131
Eastern Christian spirituality, growing interest in, 10n22
Eastern Christians, tradition and, 58n25
eating disorders, 99
Eckhart, Meister, 181–82
ecumenical approach, of this book, 8–10
Ecumenical Councils, 8n17, 60
"ecumenism," 8n17
egalitarian vision, of this book, 12–13
Egyptian desert, spiritual wisdom from, 155
Eiesland, Nancy L., 149
Elijah
    encountered the Lord while being alone, 104
    encountering the Lord in silence, 75, 110n8, 126
    fasting and praying before encountering God, 91
    fled to the wilderness, 152
empire, building in the desert, 162
end of your life, remembering, 147n13

energies of God, participating in, 32
engagement with others, solitude preparing for healthier, 108
environment, addressing a threatened, 13–14
essence, of the spiritual life, 33–34
Esther, led fasting among the Jews, 89
eucharistic calling, in the community of creation, 119
"eucharistic" moment, 116
Evagrius
    acting as if [we are] going to die tomorrow, 98
    on fasting preparing you for God's presence, 92
    on fleeing lust but pursuing hospitality, 108
    on inner stillness involving "pure prayer," 75
    of Pontus, 37
    on providing yourself with work, 165
    on remembering the day of death, 146
    on the spiritual journey in three phases: *praktike*, *physike*, and *theologia*, 184
    on theology and prayer as interrelated activities, 51
Eve, natural feelings given to, 143
evil forces, 41, 77
the exodus, as a biblical image of the desert, 151–52
experience, 54, 61–62. See also desert experiences; mystical experiences
Experiencing the Depths of Jesus Christ (Guyon), 71
The Expulsive Power of a New Affection sermon (Chalmers), 78n27
external struggle, 25
extremes, 85, 109
Ezekiel, 26
Ezra, 92

faith

Index

Christian spirituality in a
  community of, 64
  coming to the Lord by, 72
  living core of Christian, 54
  pre-critical, 46
  salvation received by grace
    through, 87
  spiritual journey as growth in,
    160–61
  supreme mystery of, 63
  taking risks and advancing boldly,
    64n47
  training ourselves for a long race
    of, 93
  transcending differences, 111
"fall," from what God intended, 138
"fallen material world," 86–87
family, of God, 112–13
fasting, 84–102
  attainable, balanced, 84–85
  benefits of, 92–97
  creative and healthy approaches
    to, 102
  customary for Jews on the Day of
    Atonement, 92
  extremes regarding, 85
  from fasting, 99
  as a good option or not, 99–100
  immoderate, 85n1
  length of, 100
  other options for, 101–2
  practical suggestions for, 197–99
  reasons for, 88–92
  as spiritual athletes, 85–86
  in the words of Platonic
    philosophy, 87
fasting mentality, cultivating, 100
"fasting prayers," developing specific,
  197
the Father, longing to be gracious to
  you, 196
Father's rewards, fasting opening the
  door to receive, 97
the feast, as a biblical image, 22–23
feasting together, as sacred as fasting,
  116

fellow believers, using as instruments
  of growth, 172
fellowship, 114, 115
Fénelon, Francois, 70
fifth dwelling places, of the interior
  castle, 42–43
first dwelling places, of the interior
  castle, 41
First Water step, described by Teresa
  of Avila, 80
*Five Models of Spiritual Direction
  in the Early Church*
  (Demacopoulos), 170
Florovksy, Georges, 161–62
fluids, drinking during a fast, 198
followers, of "the way," 24
following, Jesus, 169
food, 197, 199
fool for Christ, becoming, 81
"Footsteps" story, of Jesus, 140
Ford, David, 117n16
Foster, Richard, 23
four sources, 54–55, 65
fourth dwelling places, of the interior
  castle, 42
"The Fourth of July" song by Sufjan
  Stevens, 147n14
Fourth Water step, of Teresa of Avila,
  82–83
French mystic, on biblical meditation,
  70–74
friendship, 36, 68, 117–18, 169

Gandhi, Mahatma, 96n19
garden, metaphor of, 79, 80
garden of Eden, recovery of, 154
Germanus, 108
Geron, in the Greek tradition, 171
glory of God, 29, 106, 195
gluttony, 98
Gnosticism, 86–88, 86n4
God. *See also* the Lord
  adapting to our limited capacity
    to understand, 125
  all-encompassing love for, 33–34
  as always more, 123

God (*continued*)
- beyond all human perception, 131
- beyond assertion and denial, 132
- beyond understanding, 126, 131
- bringing about union with Christ, 44
- causing light to shine out of darkness, 2
- coming face to face with, 136
- in the darkness, 130
- developing a secret history of fasting with, 97
- discovering in all the beings he has created, 119
- dwelling within the soul, 43
- family of, 112–13
- finding great joy in us, 18n42
- finding in all things and all activities, 182
- giving the Light of the knowledge of, 2
- human beings never transformed into, 32
- known in the darkness, 122
- leading his people out of spiritual bondage, 24
- looking upon all of creation as "very good," 24
- as loving, good, and quick to forgive, 90
- as a loving Creator, 87
- loving us beyond comprehension, 112
- making us into a god or goddess, 30n11
- maximal union with, 31n14
- as more than Aquinas could imagine, 124
- no human can see and live, 125
- no one has ever seen, 126
- not literally Father, 112n13
- not needing us to fast, 88
- as the only satisfying Goal, 195
- only the Son making known, 126
- partaking of the very nature of, 28
- pouring out his love into our hearts, 194
- providing spiritual nourishment, 161
- remaining an awesome, expansive mystery, 136
- responding to the grace of, 68
- revealing the divine name, "I Am Who I Am," 125
- saved by a loving, 87
- seeing by not seeing, 128
- seeing in and through all that God has made, 38
- seeking the presence of, 193–94
- solitude deepening our relationship with, 107
- struggle with, 25–26
- surpassing the reach of our limited minds, 147
- symbolic nature of language about, 113
- transcending all existence, language, and symbols, 13
- transcending human intellect and words, 123n8
- transforming sinful human beings, 30
- as the ultimate loving parent, 18, 112
- as unknowable, 123
- walking with through life, 46

God in Creation: A New Theology of Creation and the Spirit of God (Moltmann), 119

God of the universe, encountering the uncreated, 16

God-given equilibrium, producing in our intellect, 78

Godhead, possessing neither maleness nor femininity, 112n13

God's love, strength of, 193–96

good, enjoying incomprehensible, 82

gospel of God's grace, 7n14

Gospel of life, "passing on," 61

grace
- empowering us, 83

of God, 68, 88, 108
illuminating human nature, 8
grace-empowered contemplation, 185
grave of Jesus, John and Peter rushing to, 186–87
the Great I Am, encountering in stillness, 105
greatness of God, left Job humbled, 133
Greek Fathers, on the passions, 94
Greek philosophy, 51, 86, 87, 179–80
Pope Gregory I. *See* Gregory the Great
Gregory of Nyssa, 39, 127, 128, 195
Gregory of Sinai, 75, 77n23
Gregory the Great, 180–81
grieving, with those who grieve, 148
growth of love, as a biblical image, 26
Grudem, Wayne, 14n34, 89n10, 93n14, 201
"the guarding of the intellect" (*nepsis*), 74–75
guidance, as a reason for fasting, 90–91
Guyon, Madame Jeanne, 67, 70–74, 75

Hausherr, Irenee, 162
heart, fasting drawing things to the surface of, 198
heart of God, road map into, 6
hearts, becoming fragrant gardens, 83
heavenly water, in the Fourth Water step, 82
Hebrew prophets, 26, 152–54
Hebrews (book of), using the image of a race, 24
Hesychios, 74–75, 76–77, 78, 146, 146n11
heuristic devices, 21
hiding, the desert as the place of, 151
"hierophanies," 48
historical models, of spiritual development, 35–48
historical periods, of spiritual development, 36
Holder, Arthur, 4
holistic salvation, of soul and body, 112

Holy Name, continual invocation of, 76–78
Holy One, living within us, 112
Holy Spirit
 compelling Christians to engage with others, 117n16
 democratizing spiritual direction, 172
 desire for intimate communion with, 190
 empowering the church, 115
 enabling us to gaze upon the glory of the Lord Jesus, 70
 establishing the kingdom of God within our hearts, 194
 helping us weed out that which hinders communion with God, 108
 inculcating a mind-set for mission and engendering a passion for service, 190
 setting your mind on the indwelling, 72
 taught the saints to pray over the centuries, 67
 temple of, 112
 as the ultimate spiritual director, 172–73
Holy Trinity
 apophatic spirituality centering on, 129
 being indwelt by the presence of, 29
 Christians called to participate in the very life of, 30
 each of us made in the image of, 166
 encountering the intellectual vision of, 44
 grace to enjoy freely the contemplation of, 183
 prayer awakening us to communion with, 68
 receiving mystically, 166
 as the ultimate image of partnership, communion, and fellowship, 114

Index

homogeneity, Christian equality as not, 13
Hosea, 26, 153
hospitality, mature spiritual teachers becoming, 108
hostility, against Christians, 25
hours, praying the, 80
human anguish, before God, 145
human beings
    fulfilling our responsibility, 118n17
    God recreating, 29
    looking to the created world for, 24
    as meditating creatures, 69–70
    penetrated by the Spirit of God, 32
    as praying creatures, 67–68
human conception, God transcending all, 132
human intelligence, working to attain knowledge, 65
human life, suffering as part of, 138–40
human nature, metaphors on deification of, 31–32
human reason. *See* reason
human rebellion, as the genesis of suffering, 138
human soul, as a dwelling place for the Lord Jesus, 40
Hume, David, 144
humility, 41, 92–93, 132–33, 169, 176
hunger, 22, 93, 94
hygiene, maintaining during a fast, 198

"I Am Who I Am," as the divine name, 125
iconoclast, God as the great, 135
idolatry, safeguarding against, 134–35
Ignatius of Loyola, 182–84
image of the Lord, transformed by the Spirit into, 29
imageless prayer, 75
images
    cataphatic as the approach with, 122
    common elements shared with models, 21–22
    easier to reflect upon than ideas, 22
    helping explain concepts, 20
    from the natural world describing spiritual realities, 79
imago Dei (the image of God), 8n15, 110
imago Trinitatis (the image of the Trinity), 110
immanent God, as also the transcendent God, 132
Immaterial, approaching in an immaterial manner, 38
incarnation, 31, 131, 186
inclusive language, addressing God in, 13
incomprehensibility, of God, 128
indwelling presence of Christ, excavating, 186
inner and outer self, seasoning and sweetening, 75
inner kingdom, intellect guarding, 74–75
inner life, 2, 40, 75
inner monk, having the mark of, 107n2
"Inner Mountain," of Antony, 159
inner posture, cultivated by Antony, 158
"inner stillness" (*hesychia*), 75, 78
inner world, building and strengthening, 2
"The Instrumental Role of Reason" (Miles), 63n40
integral relationship, between contemplation and action, 187
intellect
    as the highest faculty in human beings, 74n15
    plunging into darkness, 130–31
    producing God-given equilibrium, 78

Index

turning towards the inner self, 76
as unable to fully understand union, 43
watchful over the inner kingdom, 74
intellectual capacities, God exceeding all human, 132
intercessory prayers, intensifying by fasting, 89
interested language, theology as, 15n37
interfaith friendship, 117, 118
Interfaith Youth Core, 117n16
The Interior Castle (Teresa of Avila), 25, 36, 39–45
intermittent fasting, 95
internal struggle, against temptation, 25
interpersonal act, of prayer, 69
interpretation, to answer difficult questions, 47
"interruptions," to solitude as opportunities, 108
intimate relationship, with the Lord Jesus, 83
invitation, 3, 8, 22
inward journey, goal of as the face of Jesus, 194
inward reality, fasting as an outward demonstration of, 89
Irenaeus, 31, 94
iron sword, plunging into fire, 31–32
St. Isaac the Syrian, 74n15
Isaiah, wilderness transfigured for, 153–54
Isaiah 53:10, on God the Father crushing the Son, 144
Isaiah 58, describing fasting, 96–97
Isaiah the Solitary, on passions, 94
Israel, 23–24, 153
Israelites, shared the Passover meal, 115

Jacob, 25–26, 104, 180
Jehovah Rapha, the Lord who heals, 176
Jesuits, founder of, 182
Jesus and his followers, solitude and silence of, 105–6
Jesus and Timothy, served as spiritual fathers, 168
Jesus Christ
abiding in, 71, 71n9
approach to discipleship, 168–71
bearing the name of, 191
becoming like, 168–69
as the bread of life, 23
calls his disciples, "the friends of the bridegroom," 27
communed with God in solitude, 105–6
contemplating the glory of God in the face of, 8
contemplating the presence of within ourselves, 186
counterattacked Satan, 77
deepening your relationship with, 3
discovering spiritual riches in, 6
drawing together desert experiences, 154
embraced the desert and emerged filled with the power of the Spirit, 105
emptied and lowered himself, 31
engaged in prayer on the mountain and worked miracles in the towns, 181
on the essence and foundation of the law and prophets, 33
example in regard to solitude, 109
as the "exegesis" of the Father, 56n17
experience of union with, 42–43
on expert interpreters of Scripture in his day, 57
fasted for forty days and returned filled with the power of the Holy Spirit, 95
fellowshipping with those on the margins of society, 22
felt forsaken by God, 145
finding a solitary place to seek the Father, 105

Jesus Christ (*continued*)
   followed the guidance of the Father, 169
   following, 169
   found at the inmost part of the soul, 44
   as fully divine and fully human, 143
   as the groom and his people as the bride, 92
   as a high priest, 31
   on the Holy Spirit, 172
   indwelling human beings, 29, 132
   interactions with Mary and Martha, 181
   on the kingdom of God as like a great feast, 22
   longing for the return of as a reason for fasting, 92
   as a man of prayer, 106, 116, 154
   never married, 143
   on "The old is good," 5n9
   on the pouring out of the Spirit, 190–91
   praying to the Father on behalf of his followers, 110
   providing salvation to human beings, 87
   retreated in order to re-engage, 105, 113
   Revelation describing as a warrior-king and bridegroom, 27
   on seeking to love the Lord with all our mind, 65
   served as an example to Gandhi, 96n19
   shared meals, 115
   sitting at the feet of as the starting point, 182
   on spiritual leaders bringing out new treasures as well as old, 5
   suffering increases dependence on, 43
   sufferings of, 140, 143
   tempted in the desert, 140, 154
   took on human flesh in order to redeem us, 87
   uprooting weeds and planting good seed, 79
   urging "Take up your cross and follow me," 137
   vision of equality and unity in, 13
   walking with in intimate friendship, 168
   wielded the sword of Scripture to rebuff Satan, 77
   as the Word (*logos* in Greek), 56
   working through us as we contemplate him, 189
Jesus Prayer, 76–78, 77n25
Jews, return to Jerusalem, 24
Jezebel, 91
Job, 132–33, 148
Joel, 90, 96
John, 172
John and Peter, symbolizing contemplative knowledge and action for Maximus, 186
John Klimakos, 94
John of Karpathos, 99
John the Baptist, 26–27, 92, 154
Johnson, Elizabeth, 134
journey, 16, 23–24, 194. *See also* spiritual journey
joy, facing suffering with, 142
Justin Martyr, 63

Kallistos of Diokleia, 163n21
Kant, Immanuel, 65
kenosis of Christ, 31
"the king of the Jews," Jesus known as, 140
kingdom of God, 2, 18, 74, 140–43
knowledge (*gnosis*), 86, 126, 128
knowledge of God, ways or approaches to, 121
koinonia, 114–15

language, 130, 131
"the last supper," 115
last water, Teresa of Avila's, 82n36

Index

laughter, in the midst of suffering, 139
Brother Lawrence, practicing the presence of God in the kitchen, 93
lectio divina ("divine reading"), 16, 71
legal and political theory of John Calvin, legacy of, 132–35
Lewis, C. S., 30n11, 135
life, 64, 161. *See also* inner life; luminous life; prayer life; spiritual life
The Life of Moses (Gregory of Nyssa), 127
The Life of Teresa (Teresa of Avila), 39
light, 2, 39, 126
limits, to what can be known about God, 123
listening ear, as comforting, 148
living sacrifice, presenting our body as, 112
living Word, 55, 56
the Lord. *See also* God
   appearing in this center of the soul, 44
   appearing to Moses out of a flaming bush, 151
   beholding as a kind of prayer, 72–73
   coming to Elijah in a gentle whisper, 91
   confronted Job from the whirlwind, 132–33
   fasting conveying a return to, 96, 100
   meeting you in your spirit, 72
   speaking to Moses face to face, 104
   teaching us to pray in silence, 164
"Lord Jesus Christ, Son of God, have mercy on me," as the Jesus Prayer, 76
Lord's Supper, 23
Lossky, Vladimir, 53
love, 24, 183, 188
love and grace of God, keeping at the center, 17–18
love of Christ, surpassing knowledge, 126
love of God
   cleansing the mind and heart, 108
   expressing throughout a fast, 197
   poured out through the Holy Spirit, 106
   receiving as the essence of the spiritual life, 34
   revealed in the world through *koinonia*, 115
   solitude as a space to focus on the, 107
love relationship, between man and woman as a symbol, 27
loving Creator, God as, 87
loving God and loving our neighbor, 169
loving parent, God as the paradigm of, 112
Loyola University, 14n35
luminous life, 8, 195
Luther, Martin, 194

Maddox, Randy, 29n9
Mairs, Nancy, 149
St. Makarios of Corinth, 73
manna, 161
Mark the Ascetic, 68n3, 88, 109
marriage, as a biblical image, 26–27
Martha, "based on a mature ground of being," 181–82
Martha and Mary, story of, 81n34
martyrs, blood of as the seed of the church, 140–41
Mary, learning as she sat at the feet of Jesus, 182
Mary and Martha, Jesus' interactions with, 181
material body, God not having, 131
material world, as inferior to the spiritual world, 86
Maximus the Confessor
   author's dissertation on, 9
   on being united to God, 111
   on Christ the Logos indwelling the three arenas, 186

Index

Maximus the Confessor (*continued*)
   connecting the three stages to the church community, 37
   on the created world, 24
   on fasting out of love for God, 90
   on God as a "boundless, astonishing sea of goodness," 88n8
   on grace illuminating human nature, 8
   on having power to speak and dissolve demons, 77
   on the human being as microcosm and mediator, 138n2
   on human nature never being changed into divine, 31
   on the inner monk, 107n2
   linking justification and deification, 29–30
   on our creaturely existence not being evil, 87
   on our inner life, 2
   on the radical love of God for human beings, 34
   on reading the Bible, 56–57
   on receiving the Holy Trinity, 166
   on the study and practice of contemplation, 184–87
   on transcending differences through faith, 111

McGrath, Alister, 22, 26, 122–23
McGuckin, John A., 60
McIntosh, Mark A., 9
medical doctor, advice on fasting, 99
medieval theologians, on the unity of theology and spirituality, 51
meditating creatures, human beings as, 69–70
meditation
   on the Bible, 69
   on death, 147
   on suffering, 138–49
   transformation through, 70
   upon biblical text, 22
meditation (*hagah*), Old Testament word for, 70n5

Merton, Thomas, 6n10, 173, 175, 177
Methodist family heritage, of the author, 14
methods and features, of this book, 8
Middle Ages, spiritual life in the late, 181–84
"the midwifery of the soul," spiritual direction as, 170
Miles, Rebekah L., 63n40
mind
   bringing under control, 72–73
   conceiving of God, 134
   as a gift from God, 65
   learning to conquer sin and demons, 37–38
   pumping thoughts through our inner life, 69–70
   sharpness and clarity of occurring during fasting, 95
   transformed by the renewing work of the Spirit, 112
mind and heart, as a blank canvas in prayer, 75
minister to the poor, fasting providing the opportunity to, 96
ministry, work viewed as, 165n30
mirror, as a common image in Christian spirituality, 8n15
mission, 189
missional spirituality, a luminous life entailing, 191
missionary activity, fasting as part of seeking guidance for, 90
models, of spiritual growth, 36–48
moderation, valuing, 19
moderation and balance, as requisite for solitude, 109
Moltmann, Jürgen
   on developing a "theology for the people," 11
   drawing from "the ecological wisdom," 119
   on giving greatest honour to "the flesh," 87n5
   on his future as ecumenical, 9

Index

influential book *God in Creation: A New Theology of Creation and the Spirit of God*, 118–19
interpretation of the cross, 144n10
monastic traditions, 107
monasticism, 106, 107n1, 155
monk (*monachos*), meaning "solitary" or "alone," 107n2
monks, 37, 106–8, 165
Mordecai, 89
Moses
    approaching God in "thick darkness," 122n4
    fasting on Mount Sinai, 91
    Gregory's exposition of the story of, 127
    killed an Egyptian, 151
    manifestations of God to, 39
    as a model for apophatic journey, 130
    model of contemplation and action, 180–81
    pitched the tent of meeting outside the camp where he would meet with the Lord, 104
    questioning that he is the right person for the job, 152
    told the Israelites to keep still as the Egyptians advanced on them, 105
Mother, symbols portraying God as, 113
mother of the virtues, prayer as, 68n3
mother-in-law of the author, suffering of, 148–49
multiple sclerosis (MS), suffering caused by, 148
mundane activities of the day, as reminders to turn to Jesus, 198
mutual knowledge and trust, spiritual direction requiring, 174
mysterium tremendum (tremendous mystery), 133
mystery of God, 127, 135, 147
mystical experiences, 44n15
mystical prayer, transition to, 42
mystical theology, of Pseudo-Dionysius, 128–32
The Mystical Theology of the Eastern Church (Lossky), 6n12
The Mystical Theology (Pseudo-Dionysius), 128–29

Nadal, Jeronimo, 182–83
Nassif, Bradley, 123
Native American traditions, learning from, 118n17
natural contemplation, of God, 38
natural feelings, given to Adam and Eve, 143
natures of Christ as divine and human, 111
negation, 129, 131
negative spiritual forces, overcoming, 37–38
negativity, fasting from, 102
Nehemiah, 89
neighbor, progressing in love of, 188
neighbors and coworkers, sensitizing us to, 117
new covenant, God entering into with believers, 115
New Testament, desert images, 154
Cardinal Newman, 135
Nicene-Constantinopolitan Creed, 60
Nicholas of Cusa, 83n37
Nicholson, Steve, 14n34
Nicodemus of the Holy Mountain, 11–12, 73, 76
Nineveh, 89
nonsensical ways, attributing God's involvement in, 46n20
norming norm, Word of God as, 55–56

obedience and victory, desert as a place of, 154
Ochs, Peter, 117n16
Oden, Thomas, 4, 54, 58–59
Old Testament, solitude and silence in, 104–5

Index

Olstad, Kim, 170, 172n9
one-day fast, 101
oral tradition, 58–59
Origen of Alexandria, 27, 37, 160–61
"orthodox," meaning "right worship or opinion," 32n17
Orthodox Church, 32n17
Orthodox East and the Catholic West, Maximus as a bridge between, 184
"Outer Mountain," of Antony, 157

"pagan philosophers," Antony dialogued with, 159
pain, living with chronic, 145
pain and suffering, Jesus rescuing from, 139
panentheistic view, contrasted to pantheistic, 119
pantheism, 32
parables, Jesus using bride, groom, and wedding imagery in, 27
passion, fueling to explore Christian spirituality, 6
passion (*pathos*), meaning of, 94
passions, 37–38, 185
passive or infused contemplation, transition to, 42
Passover, Jesus as the full realization of, 115
Patel, Eboo, 117n16
patristic period, 180–81, 180n3, 184–87
Patristic theologians, on the relationship of Jesus with his church, 27
Paul
    appealed to the Lord to take away his "thorn in the flesh," 142
    on being crucified with Christ and no longer living, 82
    on Christ being formed in the lives of Christians, 170
    on dying every day, 146
    encouraged Christians to endure suffering with joy, 142
    encouraging churches to be patient in the midst of adversity, 142
    faithful service to the "secrets of those who are weak," 181
    on honor and eternal dominion to the Lord, 133
    on the image of a spiritual journey, 24
    on the Lord's Supper looking backward and forward, 23
    on the love relationship between the Lord Jesus and his people, 27
    on many individual parts, but one body, 13
    mystical experience with Christ on the Road to Damascus, 44
    on spiritual training enabling Christians to run, 24
    urged disciples to endure suffering, 141
    urging the church to run the race to win, 86
    on whatever you do being in the name of the Lord Jesus, 166n30
    on work, 165
Paul and Barnabas, 90, 91
peace, of God, 126
Pentecost, 62, 113, 172
"people of the book," Jesus and the apostles as, 55–56
"perfect contemplation," 40
perichoresis, 110
persistence, of prayer, 78
personal act, of prayer, 68–69
personal experience, corporate tradition and, 61
personal relationship, spiritual mother or father giving, 174
personal transformation, in relationships with other people, 17
personally experienced word, 55, 61
Peter, 113
Pharisees, 92

Index

Philo of Alexandria, 26
Philokalia
    as a desert survival manual, 163–66
    on harnessing the threat of suffering and death, 146
    offering rich instruction on prayer, 73–74
    the Orthodox compendium of classics on prayer and the spiritual life, 67
    preface to, 11
    universal appeal of, 11n26–12n26
philosophy
    emerged as a discipline alongside theology, 52
    Greek, 51, 86, 87, 179–80
physical appetites, learning to control, 93–94
"physical" creation, discerning the Creator through, 185
physical practices, linking the Jesus Prayer to, 78
physike, as the contemplation of created things, 185
physike stage, of the threefold way, 38
pillar of cloud and fire, God revealed in, 127
Pinnock, Clark, 33n18, 190
Plato, 36n1, 94n17
the poor, fasting providing the opportunity to minister to, 96–97
post-critical, signifying responses to critical approaches to knowledge, 45n17
post-critical stage, of reading the Bible, 47–48
power, 76–77, 141, 142
practices, helping us clear the mind and heart, 42
praktike, involving certain "practices," 184–85
praktike stage, of the threefold way, 37–38
"pray without ceasing," addressed to everyone, 12n27

prayer(s)
    act of, 68, 69, 82
    ascending the mountain of with Jesus, 106
    beginners in, 80
    benefits of, 189
    commentary on all biblical, 67n1
    communion with God through, 67, 164
    cultivating intimate friendship with Jesus, 79
    deepening our friendship with the Lord, 83
    delivering from the enemy, 100
    devising creative ways to turn to the Lord, 116
    devoting ourselves to, 116
    fasting allowing more attention to, 93
    helping someone learn, 174
    holding nothing back before God, 145
    as informative and transformative, 16–17
    involving ongoing remembrance of Jesus, 164
    as the lifeblood and power source for the early church, 116
    linking to each visit to the restroom, 198
    meaning the shedding of thoughts, 38
    as the mother of spiritual virtues, 66–83
    as our response to God, 68
    as the pathway to intimacy with Holy Trinity, 194
    suggesting practical steps to grow in, 174
    taking refuge in with thanksgiving, 99
    in times of suffering as a source of strength, 145
    together as a vital part of fellowship, 116
    types of, 67
prayer life, 135–36, 175

Index

"the prayer of the quiet," experienced in the Second Water step, 80
prayer of union, 42
prayer room, 190, 191
prayer room movement, 189
prayerful activities, suggested in the *Philokalia*, 74–78
praying
    during fasts, 197–98, 199
    the hours, 80
    the Scripture, 71
    without ceasing intended for everyone, 73
praying creatures, human beings as, 67–68
pre-critical faith, as by no means fundamentalism, 46
pre-critical stage, naïve realism of, 45–46
preparation, for a fast, 198
presence of God
    becoming aware of, 72
    drawing strength from, 139
    experiencing when no one is around, 104
    as food and drink in a dry and weary land, 197
    seeking, 6–7, 193–94
profound paradox, of understanding by not understanding, 83
prophetic place, desert as, 162
Psalm 119, meditating on, 70n6
psalmody, silence and stillness practiced with, 164
Psalms, illustrating the beauty and power of meditation, 70
Pseudo-Dionysius, 128–32, 128n16–29n16
psychic wall, built by Antony, 158
psychological problems, as beyond of spiritual directors, 177
"pure prayer," in which the intellect is "naked," 75
purified mind, seeing the Maker within the created world, 185
Puritans, 25

the quadrilateral, 53–55
"quiet cave," each of us finding our own, 110n8
quietism, Guyon swept into, 71n7

radiant glory, Lord dwelling in, 133
Rahner, Karl, 5, 5n10–6n10, 64, 64n49
reading with prayer, 71
reason, 41, 62–65, 74n15
redemption, 138
Brother Reginald, friend and secretary of Aquinas, 124
regular prayer, throughout the day, 116
relationships, 17, 69, 117
relativism, not suggested, 47n22
religious persecution, as one source of suffering, 143
remembered Word, tradition as, 58, 61
renaissance, of Christian spirituality, 5, 5n8, 194
repentance, 89–90, 96
resident aliens, Christians as, 156
resources, on spiritual direction within different traditions, 170
respect, according to American Indian culture, 118n17
ressourcement, theological and spiritual, 12n29
revealed word, Christ as, 55
revelation, 15n37, 63, 91
Revelation (book of), 27
rich young man, Antony heard the story of, 157
Ricoeur, Paul, 36, 45–48
righteousness, hungering and thirsting for, 197
Road to Damascus, Saul met the resurrected Jesus on, 141
road to Paradise, desert as, 159
Romans 8:28, on the Lord causing all things to work together for good, 148
Rome, 25, 140

Index

rooted and relevant, goal of being, 12
roots, rediscovering ancient through prayerful reflection, 7–8
"ruling," over all creation as license to exploit nature, 118n17
Rupert of Deutz, 161
Russian Orthodox believers, persecuted under Stalin, 25

sackcloth, symbolized mourning and humbling oneself before God, 89
salvation, 87, 88, 105
Samuel, 89
Sarah, 23
Satan, 77
Saul of Tarsus, 141
Schneiders, Sandra M., 3, 50
Scriptural Reasoning movement, 117n16
Scripture. *See also* written Word
　aim of, 57
　always fresh ancient wisdom of, 60
　contemplating to delve deeper into the soul and spirit, 185
　doctrine of *theosis* rooted in, 28–30
　as first in the quadrilateral, 55–58
　on God as both Father and Mother, 112
　God descending to us in the written words of, 125
　inviting us into a corporately remembered experience, 62
　like manna falling from heaven, 161
　as a manifestation of tradition, 60
　as a means to encounter the living God, 48n25
　meditation on, 41, 69, 158
　occupying a leading place in tradition, 58n25
　praying, 71
　as preeminent tradition, 59–60
　role in the life of a Christian, 21
　as a source of spiritual wisdom and power, 58
　teaching radical ideas on deification, 30
　urging to not despise small beginnings, 18
　validated through personal experience, 62
second dwelling places, of the interior castle, 41
second naiveté, 36, 45–48
Second Water step, of Teresa of Avila, 80–81
"seeing God," only after wrestling with God, 26
self-discipline, fasting exercising, 93–94
self-knowledge, better understanding, 174
sense of presence, beyond all words and symbols, 39
senses, accustomed to distractions, 80
sentinels, keeping watch at the gate of our hearts, 74
separate spheres, separation of theology and spirituality into, 52–53
St. Seraphim, on acquiring a peaceful spirit, 175
seraphs, covered their faces in the presence of the Lord, 126, 133
servanthood, becoming like Jesus entailing, 169
seventh dwelling places, of the interior castle, 44–45
sexual desires, Jesus tempted with, 143
sexuality, no such thing in God, 112n13
shared meals, 115, 116
Shema, in the Jewish tradition, 33
shorter fasts, 100, 101
Shuttlesworth, Fred, 140
silence
　as a crucial part of intimacy with God, 105

silence (*continued*)
    Elijah encountering the Lord in, 126
    generating and protecting prayer, 164
    interrelated with stillness in the Old Testament, 104–5
    intimidating to some Christians, 103
    linked to fruitful prayer, 164
    as one of the purest expressions of worship, 105
    preparing Christians to receive the Holy Spirit, 164
    in response to divine action, 127
    in response to the holy presence of God, 131
    sharing before an icon of Christ, 116
silkworm, metamorphosis of, 43
sin, 41, 138
sinful habits, 78n27
sixth dwelling places, of the interior castle, 43–44
social endeavor, Christian spirituality as, 173
social practice, breaking of bread as, 115
social process, deification as, 33
Socrates, 128
soil of our heart, becoming a prayerful garden, 79
solitude, 103–20
    deepening our experience of divine and human community, 110
    as intimidating to some Christians, 103
    opportunities to practice, 109–10
solitude and silence, 104–6, 109–10
Sölle, Dorothee, 144n10
the Son, as the image of the Father, 132
Song of Solomon, 27
soul
    aflame with love for God, 44
    coming to fully rest in the Lord, 81
    dwelling in God, 43
    experiencing suffering in, 139
    leaving in God's hands, 42
    as like a castle, 40
    made blind and deaf in the sixth dwelling places, 44
    uniting Mary and Martha in the Third Water step, 81–82
"soul-care ministries," spiritual direction in, 171
sources, of suffering, 143
sources and guidelines, for Christian theology and spirituality, 53
sovereignty of God, balanced perspective on, 46n20
Spirit. *See* Holy Spirit
spirit of contemplation, recovering, 6n10
Spirit of God, conceives and births Christlike character, 68
Spirit of God (*Ruach Elohim*), brooding over all of creation, 119
spiritual activities, prayer as the highest of all, 164
spiritual and mental alertness, fasting heightening, 95
spiritual athletes, 19, 85–86, 158, 159–60
spiritual battle, Jesus prepared himself for, 95
spiritual being, modes of, 187
spiritual classics, 4, 194
spiritual delights, as "supernatural," 42
spiritual desert, 150, 163
spiritual development, historical models of, 35–48
spiritual direction
    connected to the way Jesus equipped his disciples to live, 168
    connecting Christians to *Jehovah Rapha*, 176

Index

energized by the Spirit of God, 177
facets of, 170–71
helping others grow in their relationship with God, 171, 173–75
Holy Spirit democratizing, 172
Spiritual Direction and Meditation (Merton), 173
spiritual director(s)
  having in your life, 99
  Holy Spirit as the ultimate, 172–73
  leading others where they have traveled, 175–76
  learning to be alone with God, 175
  offering ways to experience God's presence, 174
  providing therapy, counseling, and direction, 176–77
  seeking out, 172, 173
  serving as a spiritual companion, 170
  usage of the term, 171
spiritual discipline, 99
The Spiritual Exercises (Ignatius), 182
spiritual exercises or disciplines, 7
spiritual father or mother, 171, 171n7
spiritual fitness, fasting increasing, 85
spiritual glasses, wiping clean the lenses of, 185
spiritual goals, of spiritual athletes, 19
spiritual growth, 36–48, 65
spiritual guides, speaking of what they know, 175–76
"spiritual help," ministries focused on, 171
spiritual hunger and thirst, God satisfying, 22
spiritual instinct, prayer as, 68
spiritual journey. *See also* journey
  characterized by painful progression, 48
  including time in the desert, 160–61
  as never ending, 195
  as one of ascent, 194
  phases of for Evagrius and Maximus, 184–87
  proceeding from light to darkness, 128
spiritual judo, Jesus Prayer like, 77
spiritual knowledge, 128
spiritual leaders, great Catholic, 9
spiritual life
  biblical images of, 20–34
  essence of, 33–34
  following the example of Jesus, 113
  image of the feast and, 22
  journey of, 7
  meaning of, 3–4
  universal or perennial theology of, 15
"spiritual marriage," in the seventh dwelling places, 45
spiritual mentoring, 170n2
spiritual mothers and fathers, as spiritual guides, 167–77
spiritual practices, 98, 164
spiritual reality, 21
spiritual renewal, 162
spiritual riches, 6n11
spiritual strength, fasting increasing, 95–96
spiritual traditions, 10, 15n36
spiritual training, models on the necessity of, 21
spiritual transformation, through relationship with the triune God, 173
spiritual warfare, 25, 158
spiritual wisdom, 155, 158
spirituality, 49–65. *See also* apophatic spirituality; Christian spirituality; spiritual life
  born in the desert, 155–56
  as a division of moral theology, 53
  as life in, with, and by the Holy Spirit, 63
  linking with theology, 166
  theology entailed for early Christians, 50–51

Index

"spirituality for the people,"
  developing, 11
"the spoils of Egypt," belonging to the
  people of God, 52
stages, of the threefold way, 37
Staniloae, Dumitru, 31n14
Starets, in the Russian tradition, 171
Stephen, Saul watched and approved
  the martyrdom of, 141
Stevens, Sufjan, 147n14
Stewart, Columba, 107–8
still intellect, hearing marvelous
  things from God, 78
Stithatos, Nikitas, 74n17
Streams of Living Water (Foster),
  10n22
struggle, 24–26, 41
suffering
  of Christ as unique and sufficient,
    142
  as difficult, 145
  embracing the path and role of,
    43
  engendering a more generous
    spirit, 149
  in the face of a good and loving
    God, 144
  following Jesus involving, 137
  humbled before the mystery of,
    147
  meditations on, 138–49
  not inflicted on us by a sadistic
    God, 143–46
  as part of human life, 138–40
  of Paul, 142
  reminding that all paths lead to
    the grave, 146
Summa Theologica (Aquinas), 124
supernatural power of grace, in the
  Second Water step, 80
"supernatural prayer," experiencing,
  40
sustainable practices, building a
  spiritual life based on, 98
symbiotic connection, of
  contemplation and action,
  188

symbiotic relationship, between body
  and soul, 94
symbolic marriage relationship,
  between God and the people
  of God, 26–27
symbols, 48, 134
Symeon the New Theologian, 11,
  11n24, 132

"table fellowship," sharing meals as,
  115
tears, of God watering the garden, 80
technology, 109, 109n7
tectonic shifts, massive, 2
temple, of the Holy Spirit, 112
temptation, 25, 96
tempted or tested (*pepeirasmenon*),
  143
Teresa of Avila
  on Christ having no body but
    yours, 188–89
  on determining whether one
    possesses the love of God, 188
  insightful teaching on prayer, 79
  on people wrapped up in their
    prayers, 189–90
  prayer after receiving the
    Eucharist, 82
  on seeking Christ in the depths of
    the heart and fighting against
    sin, 25
  on the spiritual life as like
    cultivating a garden, 18n43
  teaching on the four waters in the
    life of prayer, 67
Tertullian, 63, 141
texts, understanding difficult like the
  utter destruction of Jericho,
  47
thanksgiving, delivering from the
  enemy, 100
"theodicy," 144, 144n9
theo-drama, overall story of the Bible
  as, 55
theologia, ultimate goal of, 185
theologia stage, of the threefold way,
  38–39

Index

theological environment, of the *Philokalia*, 166
theologically grounded spiritually, 49–65
theologies, contextual nature of all, 15
theologizing, 135
theology
    divisions of established by Thomas Aquinas, 52
    increasingly took on a scholastic form, 51
    philosophical tools and insights engendered changes for, 52
    as reflection on God in the presence of God, 50, 63
    study of without the practice of spirituality, 53
"Theology and Sanctity" (Balthasar), 51n2
theology and spirituality, as divided or united, 50–53
"theology at prayer," superseded by "theology at the desk," 53
Theophan the Recluse, 187, 194
theophanies (manifestations), of God, 127, 127n13
theosis or deification, as a biblical image, 28–33
thick darkness, Moses meeting God in, 127
third dwelling places, of the interior castle, 41
Third Water step, described by Teresa of Avila, 81–82
Thomas Aquinas. *See* Aquinas, Thomas
"thorn in the flesh," kept Paul from boasting, 142
thoughts, Jesus Prayer counterattacking, 77
the threefold way, 36, 37–39
Tickle, Phyllis, 116
Tikhon of Zadonsk, 57
Timothy, served as a spiritual father, 168
"toxins," in our heart and mind, 198
tradition (*traditio*)
    "handed down" from generation to generation, 58
    as living and creative, 60–61
    openness to other, 10
    as reexperiencing of the Christian message, 60n33
    rooted in a particular as a good thing, 9
    as a second source and guideline for Christian theology and spirituality, 58–61
    validated through personal experience, 62
tranquility, attaining a state of inner, 38
transcendent mystery, 38, 39, 83, 123
transfiguration, 106
transformation, through meditation, 70
travel guide, spiritual director as, 175
trinitarian doctrine, of the Word, the Father, and the Spirit, 166
trinitarian prayer, Jesus Prayer as, 77
trinitarian theology, helping in desert seasons, 166
Trinity. *See* Holy Trinity
Trinity Evangelical Divinity School, 14n34
triune God, as the supreme mystery, 63
twelve to sixteen hour fast, 100
"two books," contemplating the book of nature and the book of Scripture, 185–86

union, 42, 43
union with Christ, 45
union with God
    as a common goal of classic teachers, 7n13
    goal of contemplation as experiencing, 184
    joining contemplation and action, 190
    as the ultimate purpose, 11
    as union with the divine energies but not the divine essence, 32

INDEX

unity and equality, among those in Christ, 32
unity of theology and spirituality, shift from, 51–52
unwillingness, of Antony to recoil from the world, 159
urgency, fasting expressing, 96
usher, spiritual director as God's, 173–74

victories, celebrating small, 18
Vineyard Church, 14n34
Vineyard movement, 14
the visible, moving beyond, 130
vision of Christ and the Trinity, as delightful in the extreme interior, 44
visions, fasting as preparation to receive, 91
vocation, discerning, 174
void, describing the desert or wilderness, 151

"waiting on the Lord," as a kind of prayer, 72
Wallace, Mark I., 47–48
Ward, Benedicta, 156n3
Ware, Kallistos
  on deification, 32
  on the desert within each of us, 163
  on faith coexisting with doubt, 64
  on God as the cause of our wonder, 128
  on the Godhead possessing neither maleness nor femininity, 112n13
  on higher levels of contemplation, 39
  on the Holy Spirit as the only true "spiritual director," 172
  on the life of prayer, 166
  on man's encounter with God as being on the edge of a precipice, 136
  on needing to use negative as well as affirmative statements, 135
  on pre-eminence belonging to the Bible, 59–60
  on the real purpose of Bible study, 57
  on the spiritual journey from light to darkness, 128
  on *theosis* as a calling for all Christians, 33
watchfulness, seasoning and sweetening our life, 75
water, with a bit of lemon juice during a fast, 198
water of the Spirit, ways the garden obtains, 80–83
waters, breaking forth in the wilderness and streams in the desert, 153
waterwheel and buckets, using to draw water, 80
"way of affirmation." See cataphatic or "positive way"
way of being, encouraging, 7–8
Way of Perfection (Teresa of Avila), 40
way of the cross, 142, 169
"ways" of life, with God, 179
the weak, sharing in the needs of, 181
weakness, of Paul making him strong, 142
Wesley, John, 54, 70
"Wesleyan Quadrilateral," 12
Western world, current cultural context of as challenging, 1–2
What About Bob? 1991 film, 18n43
"the whole armor of God," Christians putting on, 24–25
wilderness, 95, 152, 153
Wilken, Robert Louis, 56
Wimber, John, 14, 14n34
wisdom, 98, 99, 194
withdrawal, to return in the Orthodox Church, 17n41
"without images," apophatic as the approach, 122
women and men, created equally in the image of God, 13
Word, 28, 57

Index

The Word in the Desert: Scripture and the Quest for Holiness in Early Christian Monasticism (Christie), 155
Word made intelligible, reason as, 55, 62–65
Word of God, 55, 70n5, 136
word pictures, insights into life with God, 21
work, 165, 165n30
works, 88, 190
world
    contemplation of, 185
    not homeland for Christians, 156
    as a sacrament of God's hidden presence, 119

worldly desires, 24
worship, 62, 90, 105, 133–34
"wounds of love," mystical suffering of, 43–44
written tradition, 59
written Word, 48, 55, 56. *See also* Scripture

Zinzendorf, Nicolaus, 9

www.ingramcontent.com/pod-product-compliance
Lightning Source LLC
Chambersburg PA
CBHW031355230426
43670CB00006B/547